PEARL HARBOR

H.P. WILLMOTT

with Tohmatsu Haruo and W. Spencer Johnson

HARBOR

H.P. WILLMOTT with Tohmatsu Haruo and W. Spencer Johnson

CASSELL&CO

CON

Cassell & Co
Wellington House, 125 Strand
London WC2R 0BB

First published 2001

British Library Cataloguing-in-Publication Data
A catalogue record for this book is available
from the British Library

ISBN 0-304-35884-3

Designed by Harry Green

Distributed in the USA by
Sterling Publishing Co. Inc.,
387 Park Avenue South
New York, NY 10016-8810

Printed and bound in Spain
by Graficas Estella

TENTS

Chromius and Aretus went also with them,

And their hearts beat high with hope

That they might kill the men and capture the horses –

Fools that they were, for they were not to return

Unscathed from their meeting with Automedon . . .

Homer, *The Iliad*,

BOOK XVII, LINES 494–498

FOREWORD

Very occasionally there is an event when, to use the description that has come down to us through the centuries, 'the world turns'. One thinks instinctively of the assassination of President Kennedy on 22 November 1963 and the fact that virtually everyone can remember where they were and what they were doing when they heard the news. Equally, one can remember the tearing down of the Berlin Wall on 11 November 1989 and knowing, as one watched the images on television, that one was seeing something of utmost significance, although exactly what the future would bring remained unknown. Turning back the centuries, one can pick other events of similar pedigree. The return of the *Vittoria* to Spain on 8 September 1522 after the first circumnavigation of the world, the trial of Galileo on 22 June 1633 and the fall of the Bastille on 14 July 1789 are just three occasions which the individual of the day, without understanding the detail of what these things entailed, might instinctively, and correctly, have recognised as evidence of profound change, a passing of an old order.

The Japanese attack on the US Pacific Fleet at its base at Pearl Harbor on the morning of Sunday, 7 December 1941, was such an event. It was the moment when, in the midst of what seemed a disastrous defeat, the United States of America was forced to assume the responsibilities of power and began to tread the road that, very shortly, was to lead her into her inheritance as the greatest power in the world. Here, in this one moment, were to be combined two very separate wars, one that had been fought in eastern Asia since July 1937 and another that had begun within Europe in September 1939. The result was one world war, the most terrible and costly war in history. It was a war in which the United States, through a process that included both defeats and victories, emerged as the world's greatest naval and air power, possessed of an unrivalled atomic capacity, and vested with something like three-quarters of the world's industrial output by 1945. With such power, she was to be the architect of the United Nations, and she was to underwrite the Bretton Woods arrangements and Marshall plan which provided an international credit and trading system that were to last almost two generations. At the end of this war the United States was not alone in being possessed of global presence, but she was alone, unchallenged and unchallengeable, as a global power.

And if this war was to transform the world and its international order, the Japanese attack on Pearl Harbor was to ensure something else, that the Pacific dimension of this war transformed the United States. In 1941 the United States was primarily an eastern seaboard state with a hinterland which reached across a continent. Admittedly in this hinterland were major cities and sources of production, but it was the commitment of a Pacific war which saw the United States transformed by the redistribution of population and industry throughout the whole of central and western United States, and which marked the United States' emergence as a continental power as opposed to a power that occupied a continent. And just as American society was profoundly changed by this event and the conflict it initiated, so the very organisation of the American state itself was altered.

The United States, confronted by a war of unprecedented violence and scope, could only fight it by a gathering of power with the executive and at the expense of the legislature which was without parallel in American history. The Pearl Harbor attack began a process which saw power gather itself in the Oval Office, and later the Pentagon, at the expense of the Congress and State Departments respectively. Indeed, as far as the Congress was concerned, there was really to be no redress until 7 November 1973 when, over-riding presidential veto, it passed legislation that required it be informed and consulted in any matter involving the use of American armed force. It was to take the Vietnam war, and specifically the Laos debacle, to reverse arrangements which had been crafted in the wake of America's entry into the Second World War, and which had been intended to enable America's fighting of that war and the first part of the Cold War that followed in its wake.

All this together in one moment of time, one single event? (And no mention has been made of the virulent hatreds unleashed by this conflict or the great wrongs done to those Americans who were made scapegoats for Pearl Harbor.) To the purist, whether of historical or philosophical persuasion, the answer has to be negative: no single event or time can ever fully encapsulate all this and claim it for its own. Yet Pearl Harbor symbolises the Pacific war in a way which perhaps no other single episode does, at least for Americans. Certainly there is no single episode in the European war that by its name or image embodies that conflict in the way that the burning battleships of Battleship Row do for the Pacific war.

The only possible rival is the raising of the flag on Mount Suribachi, Iwo Jima, in 1945, and even that event, despite its having been enshrined in Washington, lacks the power and force of the photographs taken on the morning of 7 December 1941 or the wholeness of the *Arizona* memorial – that great battleship still lying where she was destroyed by the Japanese attack – which since 1962 has been the token of national remembrance for all of those who died on this day.

Since 1941, the world has grown familiar with the reality of American power. There was no such reality 60 years ago, but in the 44 months that followed the attack on the Pacific Fleet the United States Navy grew into a strength and acquired a technique that was unmatched in terms of carrier and amphibious operations. If in the years that followed the role of other American services was more obvious, the US Navy remained the basis of the *pax Americana*, and it did so after having prosecuted one of the most successful and quickest naval victories in recorded history, one which reached across the whole of the Pacific. Few nations and services have ever recovered from such a defeat at the outset of hostilities to win so comprehensive a victory in the course of a single war as did the United States and the US Navy between December 1941 and August 1945. This is the story of the start of this process, and of the Date That Will Live In Infamy.

Key to maps and diagrams

General military symbols

Japanese advances/attacks

American movement/deployment

■ Japanese base

■ British base

■ American base

■ Dutch base

Japanese Aircraft

Nakajima B5N2 (torpedo bomber)
Allied identification code name: KATE

Nakajima B5N2 (level bomber)
Allied identification code name: KATE

Mitsubishi A6M2 Reisen, Zero (fighter)
Allied identification code name: ZEKE

Aichi D3A (dive bomber)
Allied identification code name: VAL

Political

■ Japan, colonial possessions and occupied territories

Other possessions c.1941

British

United States

Dutch

French

Portuguese

Geographical symbols

 urban area

river

seasonal river

canal

internal border

international border

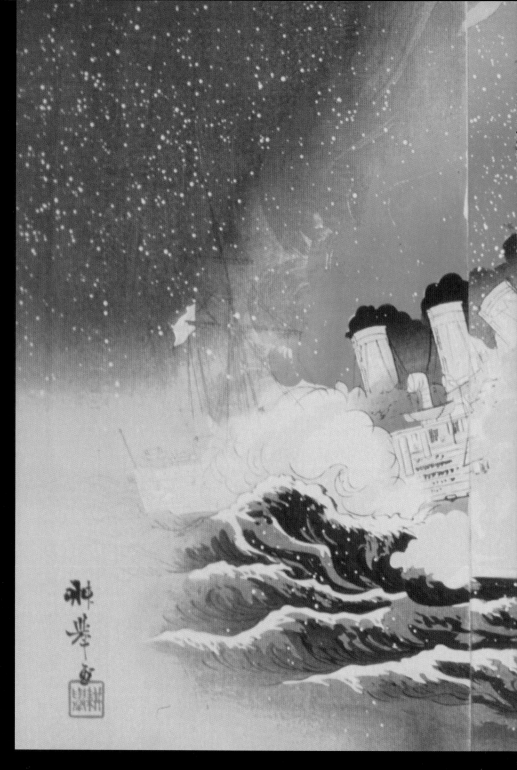

RIGHT A Japanese woodcut purporting to show the torpedoing of the Russian battleship *Petropavlovsk* in February 1904. An intricate, heroic representation, in the Japanese style, of an incident that did not, in fact, take place.

Wherein lie the origins of the Japanese attack on the US Pacific Fleet at its base at Pearl Harbor, in the Hawaiian Islands, on the morning of Sunday 7 December 1941? The answer resides amid the reasons why Japan and the United States found themselves on a path to war. But here there are genuine problems. Wars generally have easily identifiable dates, and normally, with the advantage of hindsight and a sense of inevitability, the road to war is well marked and can be discerned without undue difficulty. The Second World War in Europe provides an obvious example on all counts. It is given dates of September 1939 and May 1945, and its immediate origins lie in the period 1933–1939 and are synonymous with the person and policies of Hitler. The Second World War in the Far East, however, is very different.

To westerners the dates of this conflict are simple enough. It began on 8 December 1941 with the Japanese landings in southern Siam and northern Malaya, these by a matter of minutes taking place before the attack, on the other side of the international date line, on Pearl Harbor on 7 December, and it ended either on 15 August 1945, when Japan announced her willingness to accept the terms of the Potsdam Declaration that demanded her unconditional surrender, or on 2 September 1945, when the instrument of her surrender to her various enemies was signed in the US battleship *Missouri* in Tokyo Bay. But such chronological exactitude ignores the obvious.

THE ROAD TO WAR

我驅逐艦速鳥朝霧買大風雪
旅順野沈敵艦之圖

The Second World War in the Far East was not one war but two, and the war that is identifiable in terms of the 1941–1945 time frame – a war fought primarily in the Pacific and south-east Asia and between Japan and western powers – may have been the most important single

But the Japanese official histories of the Second World War begin not in 1941 and not even in 1937 but in September 1931, with the invasion and occupation of three of Manchuria's four provinces, and if the path between 1931 and 1937 is both difficult and indirect, no

BELOW Japanese representation of the naval action at Wei-hai-wei that followed the capture of the base, 30-31 January 1895.

part of this conflict, at least in terms of outcome, but it was not the first part of this war. What Japan had dubbed a 'special undeclared war' had been in existence since July 1937 in the form of 'The China Incident'. The major fighting in this conflict had taken place between July 1937 and November 1938 and had brought under Japanese control much of northern China and the Yangtze valley as far as the Wuhan cities. But Japan's subsequent inability to bring an end to this war, whether by feat of arms or by political means, bestowed on her a lingering legacy of open-ended commitment and of alienation from the major powers in the Far East, and it was this legacy which lay at the heart of the crisis of July–November 1941 that was resolved by Japan's offensive operations against Britain and the United States.

one should doubt its existence. The link between 1931 and 1937 cannot be gainsaid, and it is as real as the link between 1937 and 1941. But to suggest that the situation of 1941 stemmed directly from 1931 would be contentious, and would bestow upon events a determinism that contains paradox: few would deny such a link, but few would accept a linear cause-and-effect relationship between the two sets of events – although interestingly on 7 November 1941 the Chief of the Japanese Naval General Staff, Admiral Nagano Osami, in discussions with the chief of staff of the Combined Fleet, Vice Admiral Ugaki Matome, expressed the view that the origins of 'the present situation' could be traced back to 1931 and the Manchurian Incident. Be that as it may, most people would see the 1931–1937–1941 or

ABOVE Hirohito as Crown Prince. Born in 1901 and Regent after 1921, he became Emperor in 1926 and reigned until January 1989.

Manchuria–China–Pacific relationship as only one of many factors that were at work in the making of a conflict between 1941 and 1945 which was fought on land over 60° of latitude and which saw the sinking of Japanese warships over 218° of longitude.

ABOVE Soldiers of a Japanese unit undergoing an inspection in Manchuria in September 1931 in the aftermath of the Mukden Incident. The photograph illustrates the importance of manpower in the Imperial Army: very little of the service was mechanised or motorised, and it was not until the aftermath of the 1939 defeat at Soviet hands that these aspects of organisation commanded *Rikugun* attention.

A number of events or dates present themselves as the starting point of any examination of the process which led to the Japanese attack on Pearl Harbor and the start of the Pacific war. In July 1853 an American squadron of ships under Commodore Matthew Perry had arrived in Yedo Bay with a demand that Japan open trade relations, and it was the concessions extracted from the Japanese in 1853–1854 which initiated Japan's slow emergence from some 250 years of self-exclusion from the outside world. By 1868 this emergence had led to the abolition of the shogunate and the establishment of the Meiji system. And then in 1898 the United States acquired the Philippines, purchasing the islands from Spain after her war with that country. This acquisition, more than any other single event, brought about a physical propinquity that both contributed to the process of confrontation and made war between Japan and the United States possible, even though against this unavoidable fact of life must be ranged another: in 1934 the United States ceded the principle of Philippine independence.

Quite clearly, to suggest that the origins of this war are to be found in any of these events would indicate a determinism spread over many decades that would be very difficult to justify, although it is undeniable that by 1914 both Japan and the United States thought directly in terms future enmity. The two countries committed themselves to naval construction programmes in no small measure shaped and determined by the other's provisions, and in terms of strategic planning regarded one another as more than budgetary enemies. The First World War saw this rivalry come to centre stage. In 1916 the United States committed herself to securing a navy 'second-to-none', and the Japanese responded by adopting a capital ship programme specifically aimed at ensuring some degree of national security in the face of this American commitment. But by 1921 financial circumstances were everywhere straitened, and such naval programmes threatened to bankrupt all involved in a 'beggar-my-neighbour' race. Accordingly, the major powers met at Washington to limit naval armaments and to craft arrangements to ensure order and security in the western Pacific and eastern Asia. In the process, the US Navy attained parity with the Royal Navy, but if the Depression and empty treasuries ensured that limitation continued into the Thirties, the attempt to ensure security through controls and limitation miscarried: arms races were the symptom, not the cause, of national rivalries, and these re-asserted themselves with unprecedented virulence in the Thirties.

Between them, the First World War and the Great Depression of the Thirties provide the basis for an understanding the origins of the Second World War in the Far East. The consequences of both were profound. The First World War removed from the Far East powers and influences critical in shaping the affairs of the area over the previous 70 or 80 years. Russia, in effect, was eliminated as a power in the Far East for at least a decade, and when she re-appeared she did so in an ideological garb that ensured

Japanese enmity. The various European powers were eliminated entirely or their positions, specifically their military positions, were gravely compromised. In effect, the First World War brought Japan a local supremacy in the Far East which could only be challenged by full-scale war. Peace after 1919 confirmed this as Japan took control of German concessions in China and colonial possessions in the Pacific north of the Equator. No less importantly, the First World War strengthened Japan immeasurably in terms of trade and industry. Other than various operations in 1914 which resulted in the elimination of Germany's holdings in the Far East and the Pacific, and the deployment in 1917 of light naval forces to the eastern Mediterranean, Japan was spared the cost of war.

At the same time the First World War, by distracting the great powers, provided Japan with opportunity. The weakening or disappearance of the European powers in the Far East, the absence of restraints after 1914, left Japan in a position of potentially overwhelming advantage in Far Eastern matters, specifically in her dealings with a China that in 1911–1912 divested herself of her imperial identity and, after 1916, set about the process of collapse, disintegration and civil war with single-minded determination. The fact that Japan overplayed her hand in 1915 with the infamous 'Twenty-One Demands' by which she sought to establish herself as China's overlord did not affect the situation one way or another. Japan's main demands were deflected by the efforts of her allies and a neutral United States, but the concessions which she nonetheless obtained were very substantial and provided her with considerable privilege and power. Moreover, as China's divisions deepened, so the Japanese position was further strengthened, though at a price. China's difficulties presented a Japan intent on establishing her leadership of eastern Asia and carving out for herself a position of pre-eminence within China with the dilemmas of choice.

With the onset of China's civil wars and fragmentation came a basic need for Japan to define one thing: whether or not her interests in China were best served by Chinese weakness and division. To this was attached a second and more immediate problem: which, if any, of the various warring parties in China should be supported, and for

RIGHT A Russian artillery battery overlooking the Liao plain and the approaches to Port Arthur during the early stages of the war of 1904-1905. Defeat in this and the First World War, plus revolution at home, ensured that Russia, and then the Soviet Union, played no major role in the Far East until 1938-1939.

what purpose? The position of Japan in China – indeed, the position of privilege of all the powers in China – was dependent on Chinese weakness, yet a certain stability and order had to be maintained as a guarantee of that privilege. For Japan, there was the basic choice of whether to seek to preserve central government as the basis of future co-operation or to seek to encourage fragmentation, and to rely upon local influences, and immediately available Japanese force, to sustain Japan's interests and investments. But underlying this was an inescapable reality: that the position of leadership which Japan assigned for herself in eastern Asia precluded genuine co-operation on an equal basis with any authority within China. And there was another problem: Japan sought physical control of resources as the best means of ensuring their availability. There was no question for the Japanese of allowing a relatively backward China, racked by corruption and inefficiency and lacking the advanced skills of a sophisticated capitalist economy, to share control of resources – Japanese ideas of leadership and co-operation were very clear in terms of leader and the led.

But this was not the sum of Japan's difficulties. At the heart of her dilemma was a force of nationalism which produced an inconsistency: Japan recognised the force of nationalism, her own nationalism, but not the force of nationalism of any of her Asian neighbours. And just as in Korea she had ruthlessly suppressed Korean nationalist aspiration, so in China she could not accept Chinese nationalist resurgence as the basis of future co-operation lest it became directed against herself. Thus in China's civil wars an irresolute Japan was caught between conflicting choices. At the same time, Japanese military forces in Manchuria and various parts of northern and central China learned that they could undertake unauthorised local initiatives which the nominal authorities in Tokyo found impossible to repudiate, and this was to have disastrous consequences in the Thirties.

The two world wars have been described as the mountain ranges of twentieth century history, but mountain ridges are separated by low ground and the Great Depression, which followed in the wake of the Wall Street crash of 28 October 1929, was arguably as important in shaping the history of the twentieth century as the two world wars. Certainly the rise of Hitler, and the general emergence of totalitarian tendencies in Europe in the course of the Thirties, were the direct products of the Depression, as was, at least in part, the enfeeblement of the western democracies in the face of the challenge pre-

sented by the new malignancies. As far as Japan was concerned, the economic devastation caused by the Depression struck early: the hardships imposed bore heavily upon both the countryside and an army very conscious of rural distress in the home islands. Simultaneously, as elsewhere, the obvious failure of economic liberalism served to discredit its political counterpart: under the impact of the Depression, representative

ABOVE Japanese troops massed behind breastworks outside Tieling, a small town astride the railway line to Changchun which the Russians chose to make a centre of resistance as they sought to disengage after the defeat at Mukden in March 1905. There was no protracted fighting in this area.

ABOVE Intervention and the Siberian war. Japanese forces occupied Vladivostok on 20 December 1917, and proved the most persistent of the anti-Bolshevik interventionist forces during the Russian civil war, not finally evacuating Russian territory until 1925.

and responsible government, somewhat delicate growths in even the most benevolent times in Japan, were reduced to a status akin to that of a condemned man under sentence.

In September 1931, Japan embarked upon the Manchurian campaign, which was to continue until March 1932. The initiative for the campaign came from the Kwantung Army, the Japanese army of occupation in southern Manchuria, and was a direct response to the desperation which gripped the home islands in the wake of the Depression. The inability of government to control the Kwantung Army, and the widespread and fanatical support within Japan that the conquest of Manchuria created, amounted to a death sentence for political liberalism in Japan, and over the next five years what was essentially a system of government by assassination established itself.

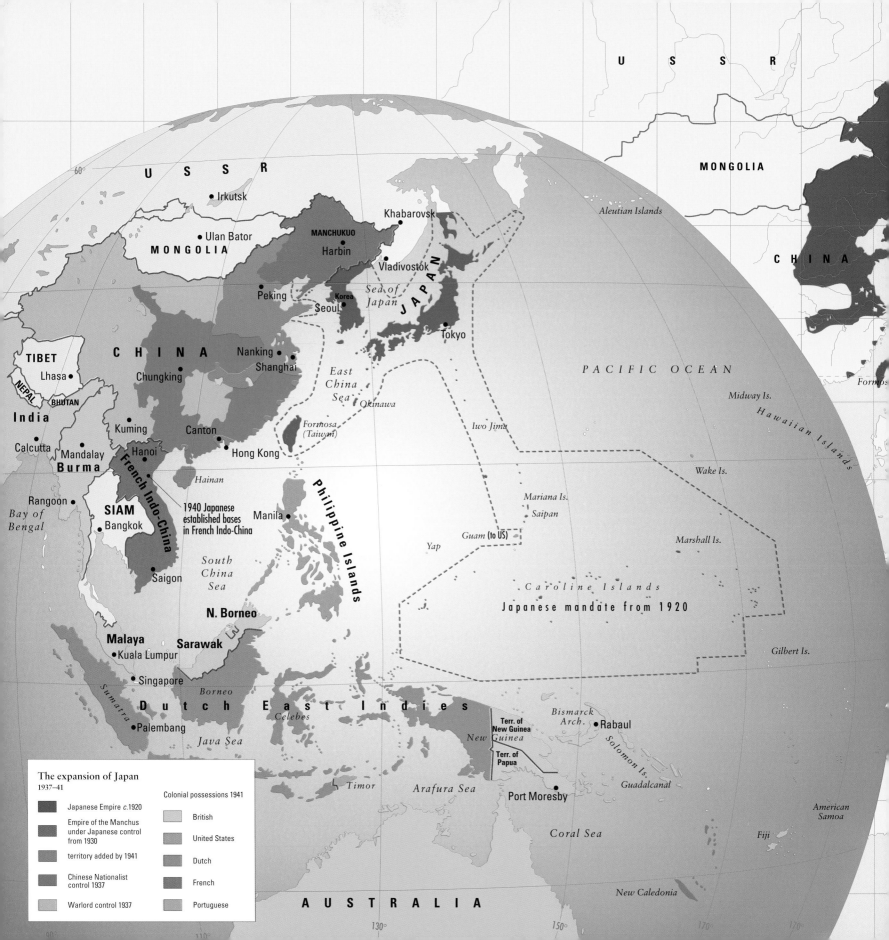

U S S R

MONGOLIA

CHINA

Formosa

U S S R

• Irkutsk

MONGOLIA

• Ulan Bator

MANCHUKUO

Harbin

Khabarovsk

Vladivostok

Peking

Korea

Seoul

Sea of Japan

JAPAN

Tokyo

Aleutian Islands

TIBET

Lhasa •

NEPAL

BHUTAN

India

CHINA

Nanking

Shanghai

Chungking

East China Sea

Okinawa

Formosa (Taiwan)

P A C I F I C   O C E A N

Midway Is.

Hawaiian Islands

Calcutta •

Mandalay •

Burma

Kuming •

Canton •

Hong Kong

Hainan

Iwo Jima

Wake Is.

Rangoon •

French Indo-China

Hanoi •

1940 Japanese
established bases
in French Indo-China

Manila •

Philippine Islands

Yap

Mariana Is.
Saipan

Guam (to US)

Marshall Is.

Bay of Bengal

SIAM

Bangkok •

South China Sea

Saigon •

Malaya

• Kuala Lumpur

Sarawak

N. Borneo

Borneo

Celebes

Caroline Islands

Japanese mandate from 1920

Gilbert Is.

• Singapore

Dutch East Indies

Java Sea

Palembang •

Sumatra

**Terr. of
New Guinea**

Bismarck Arch.

• Rabaul

Solomon Is.

New Guinea

**Terr. of
Papua**

Guadalcanal

Timor

Arafura Sea

Port Moresby

American Samoa

Coral Sea

Fiji

New Caledonia

AUSTRALIA

The expansion of Japan
1937–41

Japanese Empire *c.*1920

**Empire of the Manchus
under Japanese control
from 1930**

territory added by 1941

**Chinese Nationalist
control 1937**

Warlord control 1937

Colonial possessions 1941

British

United States

Dutch

French

Portuguese

In part this process was both personal and physical but, more importantly, in part it was institutional as a result of the structure of the state as arranged in the Meiji era. In the Japan which had emerged from centuries of self-exclusion, the principle of civilian primacy and the subordination of the military to the political had been observed not because these were institutionalised or incorporated into the body politic but because they were both understood and observed by the closely knit associates who ruled Japanese society. But by the Thirties these men had passed from the scene and so had the principles they espoused, as government was reduced to a position of *minor inter pares* relative to the Army and the Navy.

The two armed services, however, worked to very different agendas and pursued aims which were as often as not diametrically opposed to one another. At work within both the Army and the Navy in the Thirties, but also to a lesser extent in the Twenties, was what can only be described as a culture of insubordination, and this insubordination was directed towards both government and

service hierarchies. Equally, under the impact of the march of events, factions within the services increasingly identified their aims and intentions with those of their service and the state: in effect, they set their own interests above those of state and society. In the Imperial Navy, the *Kaigun*, this culture was built around resistance to naval limitation. The principle established at Washington in 1922 and restated at London in 1930 was bitterly resisted for both professional and nationalist reasons: there was deep anger at Japan's apparently being afforded second-class status relative to Britain and the United States. Indeed, such was the resentment within the *Kaigun* of the London treaty that this agreement was only accepted on the condition that future limitation treaties would be repudiated. The Navy's attitude therefore ensured that when in due course Japan elected to turn her back on limitation, she was also casting aside the security afforded by restrictions placed upon American naval construction, with all that this entailed for relations between the two countries. But there was an additional dimension to the

LEFT A photograph supposedly of fighting inside Shanghai on 25 November 1937. If the date is correct the fighting probably took place in either Wuhsing or Wusin as Japanese forces, having forced the Chinese nationalist army's evacuation of Shanghai after 11 November, moved on Nanking. The attempt to deny the Japanese control of Shanghai over a three-month period left the Chinese army unable to respond to a Japanese broadening of the war by amphibious landings that isolated Shanghai. Nanking fell on 13 December, after minimal resistance.

A light tank and infantry of the Fujimoto armoured formation during the advance on Nanchang, Kiangsi province, which was taken by the Japanese on 27 March 1939. Various coastal enclaves excepted, Nanchang, along with Shangcheng in Hunan province, formed the southern limit of Japanese conquests in China prior to the general Japanese offensive in southern China in 1944.

of the Miyazaki Plan of 1936–1937 which involved the expansion of heavy industry with a view to enabling Japan to wage total war for three years, and the start of Japan's 'special undeclared war' with China.

Japan's ever-closer identification with Germany and Italy in the course of the Thirties possessed symbolic rather than practical value: Japan's hope that the Treaty would serve to check the Soviet Union was to prove stillborn. The significance of Japan's association with Germany and Italy was not missed by the western democracies, but in the event this association need not have been significant. What was far more significant, however, was the outbreak of war in China following a clash between Chinese and Japanese forces outside Peking on 7 July 1937. At first this clash did not seem unduly important: there was every possibility that it could be resolved by the Japanese in exactly the same way that numerous incidents in northern China had been resolved over the four previous years. After their overrunning of Manchuria in 1931–1932 the Japanese had set about a deliberate encroachment on Chinese territory, Jehol being invaded and occupied in January–February 1933 and the Chinese squeezed from Hopei in June 1935 and from Charar in the following month. In the aftermath of the clash of July 1937, the Japanese, by their standards, were restrained, confining themselves to the occupation of Tientsin and Peking. There was good and obvious reason for such restraint, not least the paucity of Japanese forces in northern China, but in the event the determination of the Kwantung Army in Manchuria to force the issue of Inner Mongolia and the outbreak of fighting in Shanghai on 13 August pushed Japan toward general war. By the end of September the Japanese Army had despatched ten divisions to northern China and five divisions to Shanghai, primarily to rescue the naval formations which had provoked the August clash in an attempt to ensure that the Army did not steal a march on its sister service in matters Chinese.

In reality, deeper forces were at work in producing Japan's 'special undeclared war' with China, specifically China's attempts after December 1936 to resolve her civil wars so as to present a united front against future Japanese aggression. Within the Japanese high command, therefore,

Kaigun's waywardness. As the junior service, the Navy was very conscious of its weakness relative to the Army and it was also very well aware of its institutional and budgetary vulnerability should the Army secure unchallenged control of the political process.

Within the Army, divisions ran deeper and were even more bitterly fought than in the *Kaigun*, but in one sense this was predictable: the issues between factions within the Army centred upon the state itself, the control of society and the direction of the nation's foreign policy. The period of fratricidal strife within the Army and simultaneously increasing military encroachment on the policy-making process was notable for three developments that first placed Japan on the road to war and then led her to war. These were the Army's negotiation of the Anti-Comintern Pact with Germany and Italy in November 1936, the institution there were elements that sought to forestall such a development, and with the spread of war, and the inability of Tokyo either to contain the conflict or to end it by negotiations, Japanese operations quickly assumed their own momentum. Within four months of the outbreak of general war, the Kwantung Army had secured Inner Mongolia and installed a puppet regime at Kueisui, while by the end of 1937 much of China north of the Yellow River – considered by some of the Japanese military to be the minimum sphere of influence that was acceptable – had been overrun. It was in central China, however, that the main story unfolded, specifically with the Japanese capture of Shanghai in November and the capture of Nanking, amid scenes of mass murder, rape, torture and pillage, in December.

In the course of 1938, Japanese forces in northern China cleared Shansi and Shantung and advanced to the Pinglu–Kaifeng–Suchow–Taierhchaung line, while from their positions on the lower Yangtze the Japanese were able to develop offensives which cleared Anhwei north of the river and moved into the Wuhan cities, the Chinese having ceded the middle Yangtze in order to withdraw into the fastness of Kweichow and Hunan. With the simultaneous seizure of Canton, Japanese success in the course of 1938 was impressive, yet it represented failure and for obvious reasons. The basic dilemmas which had proved so intractable during the Chinese civil wars of the Twenties presented themselves anew. The Japanese were confronted by the basic question of whether to seek to destroy the Nationalist regime of Chiang Kai-shek or to preserve it as the only authority that might deliver a negotiated settlement: they also faced the related question of whether to sponsor rival regimes in an attempt to put pressure on the Nationalists to come to a settlement or to consider these regimes as genuine alternatives to the Nationalist government in Chungking.

Success in the field merely confirmed the truth of the Clausewitzian observation that it is easy to conquer but hard to occupy. In the vastness of China it was impossible to force a military victory; by the beginning of 1938 guerrilla warfare had taken hold in many areas nominally under Japanese control while banditry had revived inside

Manchuria as a result of the reduction of Japan's garrisons in order to provide for operations in China. With the Nationalists having opted for 'a sustained strategy of attrition' which in the end the Japanese could never counter, 1938 also saw clashes with the Soviets, which in turn presented another conundrum: whether operations in China were to be curtailed in order to ensure the security of Manchuria or developed without reference to the distinct possibility of further, serious clashes with the Soviet Union.

No less seriously, the China war in effect wrecked the Miyazaki Plan of industrial expansion: Japan could have her plan or her war, but not both. But by 1938 Japanese industrial ambitions were beginning to fall apart in any case. The idea of developing heavy industry and the resources of Manchuria and northern China in order to ensure self-sufficiency had twin results. It restricted the development of the merchant fleet by ensuring its concentration on short-haul trade and it increased Japanese dependence on foreign finished products and credits without which major development of industrial plant was not possible. By 1939, given Europe's movement toward war, such credit was increasingly scarce and expensive, as was the foreign shipping needed to carry the raw materials which Japan needed for her very existence. What made Japan's position even worse was the fact that while the China war cost a prohibitive $5,000,000 a day, her holdings on the mainland and resultant pattern of trade had the effect of wrecking her trade balances. By 1939 something like 75–80 per cent of all Japanese trade was directed to her so-called partners within her newly created Yen Bloc, but the credits that she earned therein by a ruthless manipulation of exchange rates could not provide the hard cash she needed in order to pay for her real needs – her purchases of industrial goods and raw materials from the outside world.

In addition, by 1939 yet another problem was emerging in the form of the naval re-armament programme initiated in 1937 with the ending of limitation treaties. It was not that Japan could not fulfil her own programme but that the limitations of her shipyards had a triple consequence: she could not meet the demands of naval and

merchant shipping programmes simultaneously, at least not on a scale sufficient to meet her requirements; the demands of shipbuilding meant that Japan could not maintain the rate of maintenance needed to keep the merchant fleet fully operational; and the congestion of shipyards imposed massive delays on the completion of the most important fleet units. And then, in the summer of 1939 as Japanese forces in Mongolia were being quite literally taken apart by their Soviet opposite numbers in battle at Nomonhan, Germany chose to conclude a non-aggression pact with the Soviets preparatory to her attack on Poland and the start of general war in Europe.

Comprehensive defeat in Mongolia, disillusionment with Germany and a new-found respect for Britain and France, which had at last showed the will to resist Hitler, caused a chastened Japan to make for the sidelines after September 1939, to wait upon events, even though her basic problems remained unresolved. But in the spring of 1940 one set of circumstances was no longer uncertain: Germany's victory in north-west Europe rekindled admiration and support for Germany within Japan, specifically within the Army, and Japan's adherence to a treaty of alliance with Nazi Germany and Fascist Italy, the Tripartite Pact, followed on 27 September 1940. By this action Japan committed herself irreversibly to the new order which was reshaping the international community, and perhaps this was inevitable: the defeat of France in May and June 1940 removed, in the form of French Indo-China, the European colonial empires' first line of defence in south-east Asia, thus providing Japan with maximum temptation at apparently little risk to herself. Within weeks of France's defeat, Japan had forced the French authorities in Indo-China and the British via Burma to close down supply routes to the Nationalist regime in Chungking, and in so doing Japan initiated a process that was to end one year later with the crisis which was to lead to general war throughout the Pacific and south-east Asia.

LEFT *Kaigun* activity provoked a number of incidents, often involving the use of Japanese naval infantry ashore, in towns in coastal China during the Thirties, most notably in Shanghai in 1932 and, much more seriously, in 1937.

Historically, sea power has been the means by which states have attempted to ensure in wartime their retention of maritime rights automatically enjoyed in times of peace. The prime consideration here has been to ensure immunity against physical invasion and raids from the sea, and the secondary consideration has been the maintenance of sea-borne lines of communication and the safety of oceanic trade. These defensive aspects of sea power have their counterparts in the use of the sea to take war to an enemy's territory and his shipping: they can also ensure a degree of choice in the aim, scale and timing of offensive operations. In addition, sea power has been the instrument of deterrence and presence, and outside of war it has been the means of enforcing maritime rights and law. And when occasion has demanded, of course, warships have also been required to assist in humanitarian and relief operations.

One of the major problems which has beset naval history is the fact that in modern times the history of sea power was dominated by the British experience, and that history managed to interpret British naval history erroneously. The basic interpretation of generations of historians was that British naval victories provided supremacy: in reality British victory in battle was largely the product of supremacy. There was clearly a two-way process at work. British victories had to be fought for and won but, for the most part, Britain's superiority in geographical position, numbers of warships, officer quality, manpower and training,

NAVIES, BATTLES

AND CAMPAIGNS

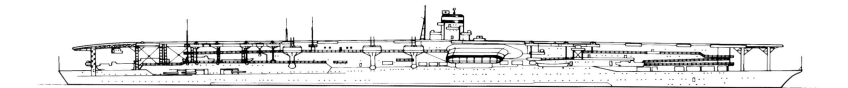

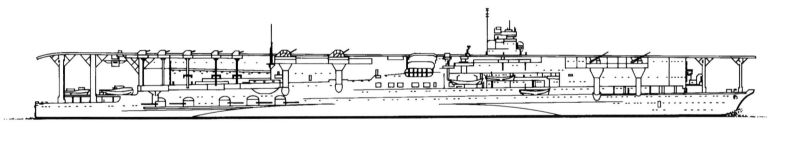

TOP The aircraft carrier *Kaga*. Named after the old name for the country and laid down as a battleship, she was rebuilt with a full-length flight deck between June 1934 and June 1935. She served throughout the China war and was regarded as a lucky ship. She was sunk off Midway Islands in June 1942.

ABOVE RIGHT The aircraft carrier *Hiryu*. Named 'Heaven-bound Dragon' and supposedly sister-ship of the *Soryu*, she represented a heavily revised design with considerable increase of tonnage and island to port as opposed to starboard. She was scuttled off Midway Islands in June 1942.

TOP LEFT The aircraft carrier *Akagi*. Named after a mountain and laid down as a battlecruiser, she was rebuilt with a full-length flight deck between October 1935 and August 1938. She was scuttled off Midway Islands in June 1942.

BOTTOM LEFT The battleship *Nagato* was amongst the most powerful battleships in the world at the time she was laid down in August 1917. She and her sister ship *Mutsu* were the first units of the 8-8-8 programme. Surrendered in August 1945 and destroyed in the Bikini atomic weapons tests in July 1946.

along with her financial advantage over her various enemies, ensured victories which were almost invariably partial. The idea of 'the decisive battle' at sea was the product of nineteenth-century imaginations, not historical experience: very few fleet actions ever resulted in overwhelming victory in terms of enemy ships taken or sunk, and even fewer fitted the description of decisive in that they decided the outcome of a war or rendered the defeated navy incapable of recovery. Even the most superficial consideration of British naval history between 1649 and 1815 would confirm as much. The battles of the Nile and Trafalgar owed the place they received in British naval history to the fact that they were overwhelming victories, and very exceptional, though even in this matter care needs be exercised: ten years after Trafalgar the British fleet was still on station and anticipated a renewed challenge by an enemy which had made good its losses.

The story of the Japanese attack on the US Pacific Fleet at its Pearl Harbor base on 7 December 1941 is the story of sea power and naval powers, while the essential background to the event, which describes and explains how the clash came about, is necessarily concerned with sea power. It was American sea power, in the shape of Commodore Matthew Perry (and often forgotten or

ignored Russian sea power that trailed Perry and stayed on station when he returned home), which had forced Japan to make the limited concessions which marked her first departure from self-imposed exclusion in 1853–1854. It was European and American sea power that in 1863 and 1864, by moving against certain interests in Japan and demonstrating the futility of resistance to western demands, sparked off the last phase of civil war that resulted in the destruction of the shogunate (1863–1868) and paved the way for the Imperial restoration in 1869. And it was warships, Japanese warships, which were to reverse this trend with the landings in Formosa between April and October 1874 – the first attempt by Japan, hitherto an insular and continental nation with no naval and maritime traditions and virtually no history of overseas trading, to assert herself in the international community.

The Imperial Navy, the Kaigun, was formed in 1868. If at the outset it was no more than a 'ragtag collection of vessels thrown haphazardly together', it was also part of that conscious Japanese imitation of western institutions which was deliberately employed as the means of national self-strengthening and whose aim was to ensure that Japan would be able to deal with western powers on the basis of equality. In 1870 an imperial decree established the British

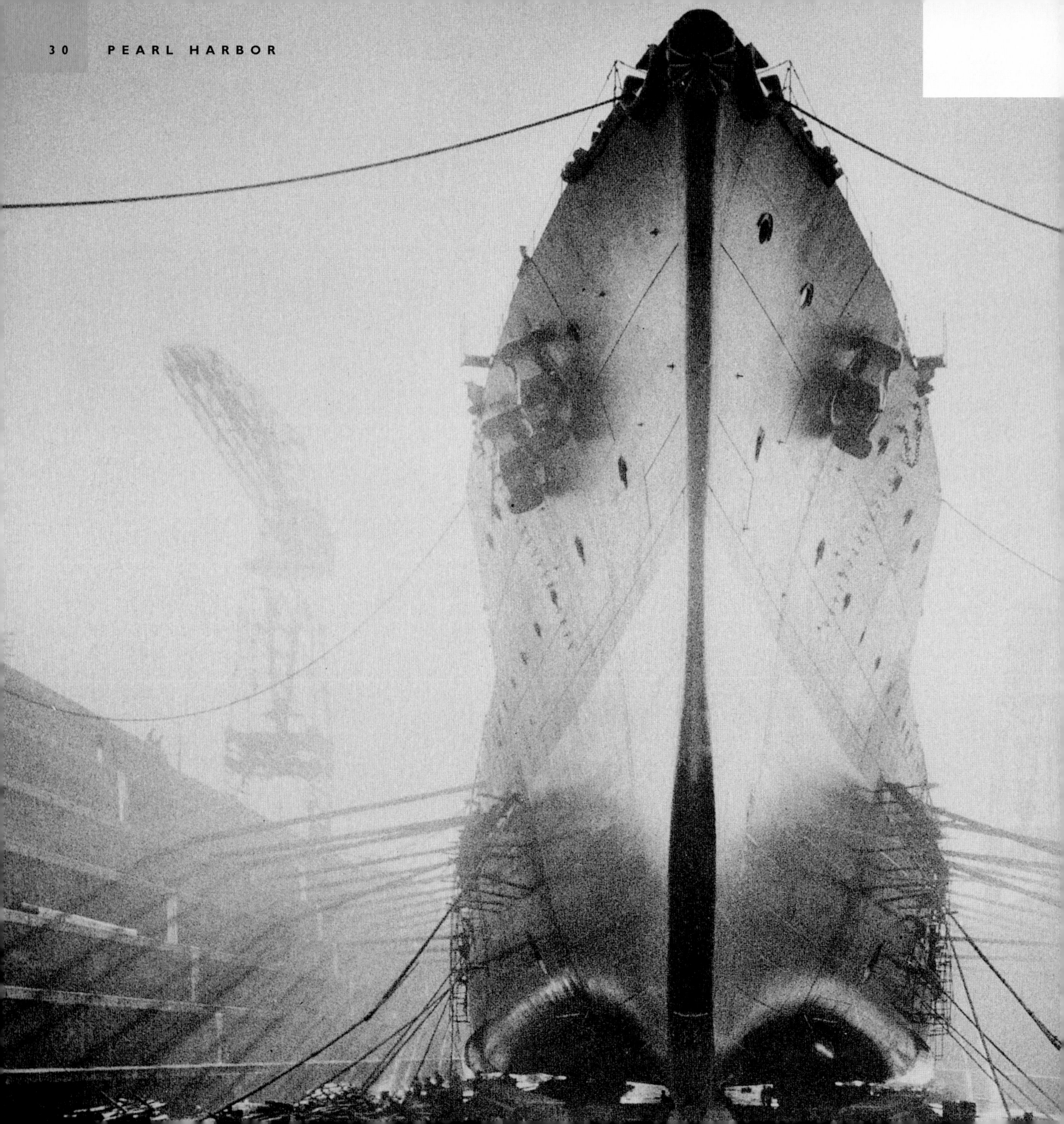

The *Kongo*, nameship of the battlecruiser class, in the dock at Yokosuka navy yard, 29 November 1930. Her reconstruction between September 1929 and March 1931, which resulted in increased range and turret and deck armour, and reduction of fuel and machinery weight, represented a half-way house: it was not until rebuilt a second time that she and her sister ships were able to play the role of fast battleships in the *zingen sakusen*. She was sunk in November 1944 off Formosa.

navy as the model for national naval development and between 1873 and 1879 a resident British naval mission sought to give effect to this decree, though the 1870s were perhaps more notable for the subordination of the navy to the army in the national pecking order and the return of the first Japanese who had been sent abroad to acquire western educations. Other British missions and naval personnel were in Japan between 1879 and 1893, while around 1884, as a result of importing machinery and hiring foreign workers, Japan established the Yokosuka naval arsenal, which was able to build small iron warships. Within a decade this and other yards were able to build steel warships of modest size, and within another twenty years Japan had both state and private yards capable of building the largest warships afloat: the *Kongo*, laid down in 1911 in Britain, was the last Japanese warship built abroad while the *Nagato*, laid down in 1917 at Kure, was the largest and most heavily armed battleship in the world.

In the course of a single lifetime, therefore, Japan was transformed from a mediaeval, feudal kingdom, incapable of resisting small-scale attack from the sea, into a major naval power, and along the way she had recorded overwhelming success in wars with two neighbours. These were the war of 1894 with China and the war of 1904–1905 with Russia. In the second, the *Kaigun* at the battle of Tsu-shima won one of the few truly decisive battles – in the sense of an overwhelming and irreversible victory – ever recorded in naval warfare. The Russian attempt to reach Vladivostok via the Korean Straits resulted in no fewer than 34 of 38 warships and other vessels being sunk, scuttled, captured or interned in neutral harbours, while the Japanese lost just three torpedo boats in the series of actions fought on 27–28 May 1905.

Japan's victory over Russia provided her with admission to great power status. Arguably she had been afforded such dignity in 1902 when she had concluded an alliance with Britain, the two countries promising one another benevolent neutrality in the event of war with one enemy but full belligerence in the event of either being involved in war with two enemies. Accordingly, during the war of 1904–1905 Britain had checked Russia's ally, France, thereby enabling Japan to fight Russia. The same arrangements ensured

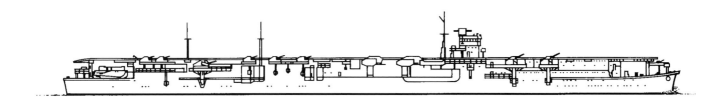

that with the outbreak of war in Europe in 1914 Japan, admittedly after some hesitation, found herself on the allied side. Her main contribution to the allied cause after 1914 lay in the supply of war material and shipping to her entente partners, most obviously Russia, and the war proved very beneficial for Japan in terms of promoting industrial and shipping investment.

By this time, however, a basic unfriendliness between Japan and the United States had emerged. At issue were both international rivalries and an American racial disdain for Japan which manifested itself in the American press and in state laws aimed at Japanese immigrants to the United States. Many of the rivalries focussed upon China, in which the United States had reserved for herself a special place in terms of leading the country to peace and prosperity through example and the Chinese embrace of American institutions, values and practices. Chinese reactions to such American intentions were understandably somewhat bemused but, more importantly, in 1910 Japan and Russia had set aside their past enmity in order to ensure American exclusion from Manchuria, which was then divided between exclusive spheres and influence. Then, of course, in 1915 came the Japanese attempt to ensure for herself a position of overlordship in China with the Twenty-One Demands. This miscarried, but by ensuring support for most of her claims on German concessions

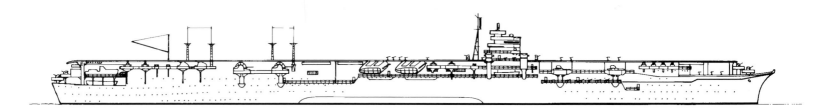

and by imposing upon China recognition of these claims and many of her other demands, this time made *sotto voce*, Japan was nevertheless successful in ensuring for herself a position of local dominance in the Far East. Only a general war could dislodge her.

From the early years of the twentieth century, the US Navy had given much thought to the question of how such a war would be prosecuted and, likewise, the *Kaigun* much thought to the *yogeki sakusen*, the strategy of ambush with which it might break an American advance into the western Pacific. At the same time, the United States was increasingly determined to rival Britain's naval pre-eminence. The combined American 1916 and 1919 programmes would have resulted in the United States having 51 capital ships. Japan responded with the 8–8–8 programme. This envisaged the construction of three forces, each with eight capital ships: three would be laid down and three completed in any year, and thus Japan would acquire a total of 24 very modern capital ships in just eight years. Britain, meanwhile, had found herself caught with a long tail of ageing dreadnoughts.

The three major naval powers therefore had to confront the ruinous prospect of unrestrained naval re-armament programmes. The Harding administration in the United States initiated the search for a means of seeking security through limitations and controls. The result was the Washington treaties. These provided for the ending of the Anglo-Japanese alliance and the banning of forward bases in the western Pacific, for limitations imposed on all the major powers with regard to capital ship and aircraft carrier tonnages, and for further limitations placed on the size of individual capital ships, aircraft carriers and cruisers. Britain and the United States were afforded 525,000 tons of capital ships, Japan 315,000 tons and France and Italy 175,000 tons each. Britain and the United States were allowed 135,000 tons of carriers, Japan 81,000 tons and France and Italy 60,000 tons each. Capital ships of any power were restricted to 35,000 tons and 16-inch guns. Carriers were restricted to 27,000 tons, and while no limit was placed on the number of cruisers the powers could have, these ships were restricted to 10,000 tons and 8-inch guns. Individual powers were allowed leeway on

certain units already under construction, but not at the expense of their totals.

Japan's acquiescence in these arrangements was hesitant, both the country as a whole and the Navy jibing at the treatment afforded them under the main treaties. The internal controversy which attended the 1921–1922 treaties and their acceptance by Japan provided the terms of reference for all the Japanese debates on the subject over the next decade as well as for Japanese ship design and construction in this period. The positive side of the 1921–1922 arrangements for Japan was that she was afforded unprecedented security. Her position of local domination in the Far East was recognised and strengthened by the prohibition of fortified fleet bases north of Singapore and west of Pearl Harbor. More importantly, Japan avoided an unrestricted construction race with the United States, one which she could only lose.

The main supporter of treaty provisions, Admiral Kato Tomosaburo, had ordered an examination of possible limitation arrangements as early as 1919, and his support for limitations was prompted by one very simple calculation: whatever the short-term situation, an unrestricted construction race would see a remorseless erosion of the Japan's position vis-à-vis the United States. For Kato, the only eventuality worse than Japan becoming involved in an unrestricted construction race with the United States was Japan becoming involved in war with the United States. Accordingly, while Kato saw the Japanese fleet as a deterrent rather than the instrument for fighting the United States, he and like-minded naval officers saw Japan's best interest served by arrangements that limited American construction relative to Japan's and by an overall limitation of naval forces on the part of all the great powers.

The problem Kato faced was that tonnage provision for Britain, the United States and Japan had now been set on a 5:5:3 basis and was open to three objections. The first was that there were many who saw Japan's status as insulted by this inequality, even though the majority of Japanese, however, did not dwell upon this point: they recognised that Japan simply was not the equal of Britain and, most obviously, the United States. The other objec-

TOP LEFT The aircraft carrier *Soryu*. Named 'Grey-Blue Dragon', the constellation *Ursa Major*, she was the first of a new breed of medium carrier. Such was the pace of carrier and aircraft development in the second half of the Thirties, however, that by 1941 she was struggling to retain fleet carrier status: she did so by virtue of crew and air group capability. She was sunk off Midway Islands in June 1942.

LEFT The battleship *Fuso*, having completed her reconstruction in the Kure navy yard, 28 April 1933. She and her sister ship were Japan's first battleships to be armed solely with Japanese-made weapons. She was sunk in October 1944 in the Surigao Strait.

BOTTOM LEFT The aircraft carrier *Zuikaku*. Named 'Lucky Crane', she and her sister ship *Shokaku* were perhaps the best fleet carriers built by Japan, a match for the American *Essex* and British *Illustrious* classes. For most of her career she led a charmed life, but was sunk in October 1944 off Cape Egano.

LEFT The battleship *Yamashiro*, almost at the end of her reconstruction, in the Yokosuka navy yard, 20 November 1934. As Japan's first dreadnoughts, she and her sister ship *Fuso* tended to be overshadowed by their successors. She was sunk in October 1944 in the Surigao Strait.

tions were more important, and concerned the impact on the current capital ship programme, which in 1921 seemed to be on the verge of realisation, and the fact that by 1921 the *Kaigun* had adopted the notion that national defence rested on maintenance of a 10:7 ratio relative to the United States. Herein was a double calculation which was the *sine qua non* of *Kaigun* strategic thinking in the inter-war period. The 10:7 ratio was based upon the belief that relative fleet strengths derived from the square of their numbers, and upon the expectation that Japan could hope to wage a defensive war in the western Pacific with realis-

tic hopes of avoiding defeat as long as she maintained her fleet at half the relative strength of an American enemy. Thus the 10:7 ratio offered the Japanese 49 per cent of American strength compared to 36 per cent, or little more than one-third, on the 5:3 ratio.

As far as Kato was concerned, the limitations imposed on American construction and Anglo-American fleet bases was more than adequate compensation for the missing 10 per cent, but there was both within the delegation sent to Washington and at home a vociferous 'Fleet Faction' which strongly opposed the terms of the treaties. As early as 1923,

BELOW The fast battleship *Hiei*. The Emperor's favourite warship, she was reduced under the London limitation treaty provisions to gunnery training status before being rebuilt between November 1936 and January 1940. In November 1942 she became the first Japanese capital ship to be lost, in the first naval battle of Guadalcanal.

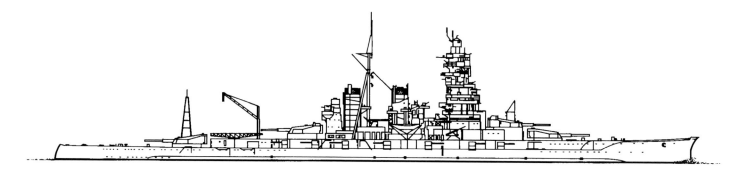

ABOVE The cruiser *Suzuya*. The toughest class of cruisers built by any Second World War navy, the *Mogami*-class were the first Japanese ships to carry triple turrets.

BELOW The fast battleship *Kirishima*. Originally a member of the *Kongo*-class of battlecruisers, she was rebuilt in the Sasebo naval yard between June 1934 and June 1936.

an attempt to have treaty arrangements worked into the current Imperial Defence Policy statement was defeated, and the United States was specifically identified as the most likely hypothetical enemy not simply for the Navy but also the Army. Moreover, with Kato dead by the summer of 1923, the major obstacle to the promotion of his opponents within the Imperial Navy was removed. Obviously Japan and the *Kaigun* remained bound by international treaty, but with Japan all too aware of the often violent anti-Japanese agitation in the western states of the United States, the rules were in the process of being rewritten.

The immediate result of the limitations imposed upon the size and guns of battleships was to pave the way for a race in cruiser construction, but even here there was a complication. The 1927 Geneva conference foundered upon irreconcilable Anglo-American differences, the Americans being opposed to limitation on the size of individual cruisers, destroyers and submarines, and the British wanting higher aggregate totals in order to accommodate their desire for a large number of small cruisers. The Japanese stood by the sidelines in this argument, but in fact their position mirrored that of the Americans. With

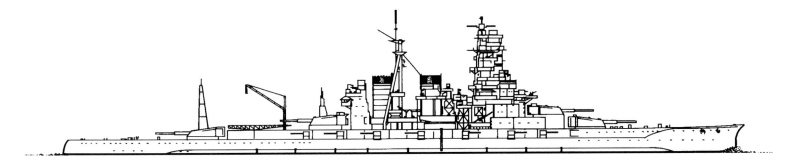

limitations imposed on battleships, the Japanese looked to securing an advantage in cruisers, and indeed by the second half of the Twenties the *Kaigun* was casting its tactical arguments in such terms, almost to the point that it seemed to be making the heavy cruiser rather than the capital ship the arbiter of sea warfare. In fact the Imperial Navy had begun a major heavy cruiser construction programme, but by 1929 the American decision to secure fifteen new heavy cruisers threatened to conjure into existence Kato's second-worse nightmare.

At the naval limitation conference in London in 1930, when the lingering effects of the Depression and empty chancelleries still prohibited major construction programmes, Japan chose to agree to terms that largely repeated the Washington formula. She was afforded 368,340 tons or 69.75 per cent of Anglo-American tonnages, but in the critical heavy cruiser class she was allowed only 108,400 tons or 60.23 per cent of American

tonnage while she was allowed 100,450 tons or 70.15 per cent of American tonnage of light cruisers, 105,500 tons or 70.3 per cent of American destroyer tonnage and 52,700 tons or parity with American submarine tonnage. Japanese bitterness at being denied her seven-tenths heavy cruiser requirement was compounded by the fact that she was afforded such a ratio within the much less important light cruiser category and the fact that she already had more destroyer and submarine tonnage than she was to be allowed under the treaty.

In fact, the London treaty worked very greatly to Japan's advantage because throughout the Thirties the United States made no real effort to build her navy up to treaty limits, with the result that the *Kaigun* stood at four-fifths of US tonnage for most of this decade. But the 1930 arrangements were accepted within the Japanese political and naval establishments only on the basis that Japan would not accept any future limitation agreement: this

LEFT Imperial battle flag and imperial review, probably between January 1933 and November 1936: the gunnery training ship *Hiei*, with either the *Akagi* or *Kaga* beyond her.

BELOW The heavy cruiser *Takao*, off Tokyo Bay, in July 1939. The nameship of a class spawned by the cruiser race of the Twenties, she carried ten 8-in guns, sixteen 24-in torpedo tubes and three seaplanes. She was rendered *hors de combat* as a result of British midget submarine attack in July 1945 at Singapore. Raised, she was scuttled in October 1946.

meant that Japan, in effect, would initiate a naval race in 1937, when the provisions of the treaty were to lapse. At the same time, however, the various elements which were to comprise the defensive, attritional strategy whereby an American fleet entering the western Pacific would be defeated were beginning to materialise, although a full decade was to pass before all aspects of Japanese policy were more or less in place.

In the period immediately after the First World War, and at a time when naval orthodoxy held that a fleet's efficiency declined by some 10 per cent with every 1,000 miles it advanced from its base, the Imperial Navy envisaged the US Pacific Fleet moving forward from its base in the central Pacific in order to give battle in the general area of the Bonins and Honshu. In the early Thirties, this defensive policy was succeeded by what was called 'The Strategy of Interceptive Operations', which differed from previous policy in two respects. The area of operations was extended to include the Marianas and the Carolines, while doctrine and ship procurement policy were harmonised in what can only be described as the Japanese naval equivalent of a de Dondi creation, that majestic clockwork of wheels-within-

wheels which represented the mediaeval view of the universe: ingenious, beautifully crafted, hopelessly wrong.

The defensive battle would be opened off Hawaii by submarines, and three types were built in order to fight an attritional battle as the US Pacific Fleet advanced into the western Pacific. Scouting submarines, equipped with seaplanes, would find the American fleet, which would then be subjected to night surface attacks by cruiser-submarines brought to their points of interception by command-submarines. These cruiser-submarines were endowed with a very high surface speed of 24 knots, the Japanese calculations being that such a speed would allow these submarines to outpace an American fleet advancing at economical cruising speed and thereby to mount successive attacks to the limit of their torpedo capacity during the approach to contact phase.

These operations would be supported, as the American fleet arrived in the western Pacific, by shore-based aircraft. To this end, the Japanese developed in the form of the Mitsubishi G4M Betty medium bomber an aircraft which in its own time possessed a speed and range superior to any other medium bomber in service in the world.

Thereafter the carriers, operating in independent divisions separately and forward from the battle line, would locate the advancing American fleet and immobilise its carriers through dive-bombing attacks that were to smash the enemy flight-decks. With the American fleet thus blinded, it would be engaged by midget submarines laid across its

line of advance, and at the same time it would be engaged by light forces. Japanese fast battleship and heavy cruiser squadrons would sweep aside the enemy screening forces, and then massed light cruiser and destroyer formations, built around massive torpedo armaments, would attack the head of the American line in a series of night attacks. These would be delivered by formations advancing to contact in line abreast and launching perhaps as many as 120 torpedoes in single, scissor-formation attacks.

In overall terms the Japanese expected that these operations would cost the American fleet perhaps 30 per cent of its strength and, more crucially, its cohesion, and at this point action would be joined by the main force of battle-

ships. Between the wars, the *Kaigun* undertook the most comprehensive reconstruction of its capital ships of any navy, stressing the importance of the possession of superior speed, weight of broadside and gunnery range over potential enemies: the counter to American numerical superiority was qualitative superiority of both ships and men. The *Kaigun* anticipated that the battle line would engage its counterpart in a conventional line of battle engagement with such advantages that the Combined Fleet would inflict a crushing defeat upon the American enemy.

Such was the *Kaigun's* basic intent, known as the *Zengen Sakusen* or The Great All-Out Battle Strategy. It invites comment, as do various refinements which were made to

LEFT The element of continuity represented by line formation. Battle practice involving the *New York* and *Texas*: the presence at the rear of the line of the *Wyoming* indicates that this was prior to her being reduced to gunnery training status in 1931.

an attempt to offset any American advantage. But in the inter-war period the Japanese proved unable to complete their own various airfields in the island chains, and it was therefore very unlikely they would be able to complete new airfields in the newly acquired islands of the central and south-west Pacific.

More seriously, and almost incredibly, the basic Japanese plan was never subjected to a fleet exercise before the outbreak of war. Certain parts of the plan – specifically the submarines' role – were subjected to exercise in 1939 and 1940 and found not to work, but the Japanese went to war with their doctrine unchanged, though in a sense this was perhaps unavoidable: there was very little that the *Kaigun* could have done to remedy such a situation at this stage. Nonetheless, the concept of the Great All-Out Battle Strategy dictated ship design and, more critically, *Kaigun* thinking throughout the inter-war period. Japanese warships were reconstructed for battle in the western Pacific, with individual ships possessing only moderate endurance and the Navy itself a very limited capability to refuel at sea: because battle would be joined close to bases in the home islands, ships and formations needed and were given speed, extra guns and better and more torpedoes rather than extra range. As far as the *Kaigun* was concerned, the concept of the Great All-Out Battle Strategy had in effect assumed the character of holy writ.

But there is one last point to make about the *Zengen Sakusen*. It is a simple one, yet it is so obvious and so important that it is elusive. The point is evident in the English translation of the name: the Great All-Out Battle Strategy. What the *Kaigun* had here was nothing more than a tactical plan for the conduct of battle, but by some mysterious process, something akin to transubstantiation, this plan for battle became a plan of campaign and then the basis of national security policy. The Imperial Navy never understood the difference between war and a war, between a war and a campaign, between a campaign and a battle, and instead identified them as one and the same. Be that as it may, herein was the setting within which the plan for the Pearl Harbor attack found its proper context. And the exact manner in which it did so was to become clear between July 1937 and November 1941.

it. In the period after 1939, when Admiral Yamamoto Isoroku was commander-in-chief of the Combined Fleet, the forward defence area was extended eastward to include the Marshalls. By the time that Japan went to war in December 1941, her intention was to occupy islands and island chains in the central and south-west Pacific on which would be hung a perimeter defence where the Americans would be fought to exhaustion. Securing these islands was essential. The Japanese were aware that any attacking American force would possess numerical superiority over either a land-based or a naval force of their own, therefore the *Kaigun's* plans provided for mutually supporting land-based air groups and naval formations in

RIGHT The Pacific Fleet at exercise off Oahu in September 1940: the battle line and the aircraft that were to render such formation obsolete.

Only 60 years have elapsed since the attack on Pearl Harbor, yet the world in which we live has been transformed. It is therefore very easy to lose sight of the extent and importance of the changes which events in Europe between September 1939 and December 1941 represented. At this time democracy was all but extinguished in Europe. The European imperial system was compromised beyond recall. And, perhaps the most important change of all, the defeat of France, and the overwhelming likelihood of Britain's defeat and surrender, forced the United States to look to her own defences. The Two-Ocean Naval Expansion Act, passed on 19 July 1940, provided for the building of eleven battleships, six battle-cruisers, eighteen fleet carriers, 27 cruisers, 115 destroyers and 43 submarines to add to the 358 fleet units in service and the 130 already under construction. It served notice to the rest of the world of the United States' determination to provide for her own security, and its passing was a defining moment in American history, the point in time at which the United States assumed the responsibilities that went alongside the status as the greatest power in the world. And for Japan, the implications were scarcely less significant. The provisions of the Two-Ocean Naval Expansion Act, once completed, would render the *Kaigun* nothing more than an impotent irrelevance, wholly deprived of any prospect of giving battle with any hope of success.

Thus the United States gave notice to Japan of her folly

CAUSE, OCCASION

BELOW The quarterdeck of the battleship *Arizona*, with two Vought O3U-1 seaplanes, one on the catapult ready for launching, 29 March 1931.

BOTTOM The carriers *Lexington*, and *Saratoga*, were opposite numbers to the *Akagi* and *Kaga*, owing their existence to the Washington Treaty.

AND CONTENT

LEFT The Japanese aircraft carrier *Ryujo* was originally conceived with a single hangar deck and a displacement of just 8,000 tons in an attempt to evade Washington Treaty provisions. She had to be provided with an extra hangar deck in order to embark sufficient aircraft with the result that she was unstable and top heavy: her low forecastle caused her to ship water easily, again at risk to stability. Her small size meant that she took longer than other Japanese carriers to launch and recover aircraft.

in ending limitation treaty arrangements, but in so doing the United States failed to appreciate the significance and implications of her actions. The United States, although she did lay down six battleships between 1937 and 1940, had not built to her full treaty allowance even before 1934 and had not responded in full to the challenge presented by the *Kaigun's* Third Programme of 1937. The Two-Ocean Naval Expansion Act marked the point where the

United States picked up the Japanese challenge. It announced the start of an arms race between the United States and Japan which, in the long term, only the United States could win. But, in the short term, Japan possessed a clear advantage. Throughout the Thirties, given the modest American construction programmes, the *Kaigun* stood at 70 per cent or more relative to the United States Navy and possessed clear superiority of numbers over American

ABOVE The American aircraft carrier *Saratoga*, sister ship of the *Lexington* and the only American aircraft carrier to serve in the Indian Ocean during the Second World War.

Imperial Japanese Navy. But the latter's reaction to this development, indeed its anticipation of the passing of the bill by the Congress, was accompanied in June 1940 by the *Kaigun's* beginning full mobilisation, a process which needed eighteen months to complete. What in June 1940 the *Kaigun* expected to happen in December 1941 or thereabouts has never been fully explained, and neither has the fact that over the next eighteen months the number of fleet units undergoing refitting and modernisation was reduced to the grand total of one destroyer. Every other ship in the navy was in service and operationally deployed. But one fact remains obvious: the *Kaigun* could not remain at full mobilisation, if only because of the inroads made by mobilisation into the strength of a merchant fleet already unable to fulfil national import requirements.

These events form the essential background against which were played out a series of diplomatic exchanges that ultimately brought about war between Japan and the United States. These events, of course, followed from the defeat of France in 1940. Within a month of that defeat, and as the Japanese armed services began a re-assessment of the situation in the Far East in light of developments in Europe, the cautious Yonai administration was forced to resign and was replaced by one headed by Prince Konoe Fumimaro which, as a precondition for assuming office, had to agree to the services' demands for a treaty with Germany and Italy, additional credits and provisions for the Army, a non-aggression treaty with the Soviet Union and the adoption of a forward strategy in south-east Asia.

Japan's immediate interests centred upon French Indo-China and British Burma and the supply routes to Chungking and Chiang Kai-shek's nationalist regime through these territories. Within a month of the new administration entering office, Japan demanded the closing of overland lines of communication with Chungking, but in reality this was small change: on 1 August 1940 the *Kaigun* formulated its first demand for the occupation of the whole of French Indo-China. It did so on the basis, which had been explained to the incoming Konoe

ABOVE Japanese, German and Italian flags in the Ginza district of Japan at the time of the signing of the Anti-Comintern Pact in November 1936. Perhaps the most notable aspect of this photograph is the absence of automobiles.

naval forces in the Pacific. Its 1937 programme would be completed by early 1942 while most of the American ships built under the Two-Ocean Naval Expansion Act would be completed between 1946 and 1948. Certainly, by the end of 1941 the *Kaigun* was likely to possess clear superiority of numbers in every type of fleet unit over the US Pacific and Asiatic Fleets.

The significance of these facts was not lost upon the

KεN

MAY 19TH VOL.1. NO.4 1938   UNDERHANDED UNDERGROUND JAPAN   PRICE 25c PER COPY EVERY OTHER THURSDAY

ABOVE The background to a deepening crisis: the portrayal in the U.S. press of the Japanese as bent on seeking any and every possible advantage in the Pacific. The American magazine KEN of 19 May 1938.

treaty governing trading relations between the two countries had lapsed, and from then onwards there were demands in Congress for a total trade embargo against Japan. These were resisted by the Roosevelt administration, but after July 1940 a series of measures, each small in themselves but together of critical importance, deprived Japan of aviation fuel, high-grade scrap and after January 1941, when the ban was extended to copper and brass, virtually every raw material of any importance.

What was happening by January 1941 was that Japan and the United States either had entered or were about to enter the realms of self-fulfilling prophecy whereby their separate actions fed off one another. In November 1940 the Japanese wrung from the French authorities the right to garrison certain key locations in northern Indo-China, and in March 1941 they forced the French to accept a Japanese garrison at Saigon airport and to turn over the whole of Indo-China's rice surplus. One month earlier, Japan had announced her intention to create a new order in eastern and south-east Asia, and had made clear her exclusive interest regarding the raw materials of the East Indies. Subsequently, the Japanese attempt, in April 1941, to secure the northern front by means of a non-aggression treaty with the Soviet Union, and then the German attack on the Soviet Union in June 1941, combined to mark a perceptible quickening of the pace of events in the Far East.

On 25 June, three days after the German invasion of the Soviet Union, the two Japanese services agreed to press south-east Asian matters to a conclusion before turning back to the north in order to deal with whatever situation existed in the wake of the anticipated German victory over the Soviet Union. This decision, largely provoked by the *Kaigun's* determination to tie its sister service to a southern option rather than wait upon events and risk the Army's interest in settling scores with the Soviets being rekindled, was ratified at an imperial conference on 2 July. On 21 July the *Kaigun* formally declared itself in favour of war with the United States in order to secure control of south-east Asia, and three days later was instrumental in forcing through the proclamation of a joint Franco-Japanese protectorate over Indo-

administration, that the prospect of a breach, perhaps even war, with the United States had to be accepted. Moreover, it did so against a background of increasing Japanese attempts to build up reserves of raw materials and of what amounted to the United States' first embargo on trade with Japan. In January 1940, the commercial

LEFT The aircraft carrier *Hiryu*, on trials off Tateyama 28 April 1939. The sixth carrier to enter Japanese service, her commissioning brought the Imperial Navy into possession of a balanced carrier force for the first time.

LEFT The aircraft carrier *Kaga*, soon after completing a reconstruction that increased her displacement by half. Her relative slowness in terms of speed and elevators meant that she always suffered in comparison with the *Akagi*.

China. The next day the United States, followed by Britain and the Netherlands, froze all Japanese assets in territories under their control and imposed a total trade embargo.

What happened thereafter represented the playing-out of a script, a script written in, if not before, June and July 1940. The events that followed – most notably the negotiations in Washington – are well known since they have long been in the public domain, and no single episode is more familiar than the process whereby the Japanese embassy in Washington mismanaged its instructions to deliver its note announcing the end of negotiations to the State Department at 1300 local time on 7 December. What has been less well understood is what was at stake in these negotiations, and certain related matters concerning the outbreak of war.

Formally, what was at issue in the American-Japanese confrontation after July 1941 was Japan's position in both Indo-China and China. The American price for a resumption of normal trading relations between Japan and the United States was the Japanese evacuation of China and French Indo-China, i.e. the abandonment of all the gains Japan had registered since July 1937. At most, Japan was prepared to concede various cosmetic changes, but she could not afford either to give up her holdings within China or to abandon all her ambitions in south-east Asia. On 16 August the *Kaigun* formally demanded the start of war at the end of October, and on 30 August the Army underwrote the Navy's demand. On 4 September the decision for war at the end of October was taken but, with some members of the cabinet seeking some form of accommodation with the United States, there was on the Japanese side a duality of purpose in the negotiations over the next three months.

On the one hand, diplomacy was being used as a cloak for preparations for war, but on the other there was a genuine attempt to find some form of solution which might avoid war. The final part of this effort took the form of a direct appeal for a meeting between Konoe and Roosevelt, and a personal letter from Roosevelt to the Emperor. To a world which over the last 40 years has become familiar, if not over-familiar, with meetings between heads of government or state, this may not seem to amount to very much, but at this time such a meeting would have been unprecedented. Unfortunately, the same basic ambiguity which has typified so many such meetings over the years – meetings held not to settle outstanding questions but to confirm agreement on individual issues – also attended the Japanese initiative of autumn 1941: the Americans would only consider the proposal for such a meeting if the Japanese first committed themselves to an acceptance of American demands. But while the

brought forward, by a matter of months, a crisis that was well on the way to assuming substance and form. Indeed, it is quite possible to argue, quite contrary to what was assumed for so long after the war, that the American action of July 1941 distracts from the real crisis that was taking shape at this time, and that this was a crisis entirely of Japan's own making and for which the Americans were not responsible. As it is, popular perception has long held the United States responsible for the crisis that developed in the second half of 1941, and, of course, that perception

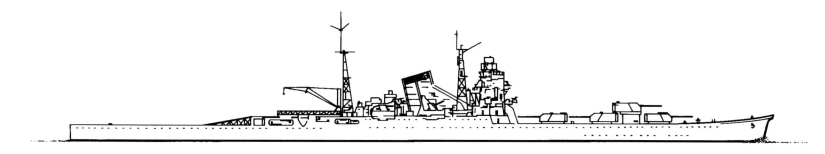

ABOVE Conceived as an improved *Mogami*-class, the *Chikuma*, and her sister ship *Tone*, were provided with a revolutionary design that mounted the main armament forward of the bridge with the area aft providing home for the five seaplanes essential to their role as scouting cruisers for battle and carrier formations. The *Chikuma* was sunk in October 1944 off Samar, the *Tone* was sunk in July 1945 at Kure.

negotiators on both sides clearly viewed such a meeting very differently, there was a certain ambiguity about the American position too, in the sense that there now existed in the United States a belated awareness of national weakness in the short term and therefore of the need to delay the outbreak of war.

Thus there was the unseemly process whereby the United States stated in public that she expected the Dutch and British in south-east Asia to maintain the trade embargo on Japan while in private, in an attempt to give Japan some breathing space, she was urging the Dutch to continue to trade with the Japanese. But Japan's situation was already too critical for this to make much difference. Before the embargo, Japan was trading at a rate, and with trade deficits, which ensured that she would have exhausted her gold and foreign currency reserves some time in early spring 1942. Even if the Americans had done nothing in response to the Japanese move into southern Indo-China in July 1941, Japan would have faced national bankruptcy, and could not have continued to trade, after spring 1942. At worst, the embargo merely

is correct, albeit perversely so: the crisis of 1941 was indeed induced by the American trade embargo, irrelevant, or dubiously important, though it might have been in the wider context of international affairs.

Nonetheless, the crisis, irrespective of its nature and cause, was most unusual in one respect. States as mismatched as Japan and the United States in terms of area, population size, resources and potential military strength very seldom fight one another, and even less frequently do they fight wars initiated by the weaker side. The process whereby Japan induced war in December 1941 has all the hallmarks of a national *kamikaze* effort and provokes as much incredulity as the detail of the process and Japan's final decision itself. Confronted by an inability to win the war in China, in summer 1941 the Japanese leadership accepted the prospect of war with the United States as the price of a move against British and Dutch possessions in south-east Asia, and thereby embarked upon a war with the only power in the world which could defeat Japan and in the process provided the United States with a *casus belli* that she could never have provided for herself.

The process whereby Japan in the course of the Second World War ultimately managed to arraign against herself the world's most populous country and greatest military and industrial power was extraordinary, and in a very obvious sense the process, while easy to describe, is all but impossible to explain. In terms of the war which began in December 1941, explanation, or at least partial explanation, exists on several separate scores. There was the concept of 'the inevitable war' at work. There had been much talk, and not simply in Japan, about 'the inevitable war' and it is difficult to resist the idea that, by its nature, such familiarity lessened resistance to the prospect of war in 1941. There was Japan's continuing resentment of American aggressiveness concerning tariffs and trade and Japanese immigration into the United States in the Thirties. There was the likelihood that in 1941 Japan's national polity would have been destroyed by civil war if she had flinched from the challenge presented by the United States in summer of that year. And there was also, prevalent in the literature of the day, the argument concerning the 'window of opportunity'. The calculations about relative naval strengths, and the September 1941 estimation that by 1944 the *Kaigun* would have been reduced to a level of 30 per cent of the strength of the US Navy, meant that the *Kaigun* really did face a now-or-never dilemma.

All these factors clearly influenced the Japanese decisions which led to war, but there were also two events of immense importance that were to play their part in the process. The first concerned a 7,528-ton Blue Funnel steamer named the *Automedon* which was captured and sunk by the German raider *Atlantis* off the Nicobars on 11 November 1940. The *Automedon* had sailed from Liverpool via Durban and was on her way to Penang, and her voyage across the Indian Ocean had been followed by Italian signals intelligence which reported her position to the *Atlantis*. The *Atlantis*, flying Dutch colours, opened fire on the bridge of the *Automedon*, killing and wounding the nineteen persons there and thus preventing the destruction of various papers the steamer was carrying. Among the captured documents were Admiralty deciphering tables, new fleet ciphers, the merchant navy codes, details of British minefields and the latest Admiralty sailing instructions, plus copies of the British War Cabinet discussions of 15 August 1940 which were earmarked for the Commander-in-Chief Far East. These minutes laid bare Britain's present helplessness in the Far East. They stated that Britain did not have the means to

was given and on 12 December various papers were made available to certain individuals, including the Japanese naval attaché in Berlin and Vice Admiral Kondo Nobutake, Vice-Chief of the Naval General Staff. What subsequently happened to these documents is far from clear, but it is a matter of record that in February 1941 the Imperial Army started jungle training on Formosa and that in the previous month the idea of a war in the Far East being opened with a pre-emptive strike against the US Pacific Fleet at its base in Pearl Harbor was first mooted by Yamamoto.

Only three things can be stated with certainty. The first is that the Japanese high command as a whole knew at this stage that Britain could not oppose Japan in southeast Asia. The second is that in 1942 the captain of the *Atlantis* was presented with a samurai sword, only one of two Germans awarded such signal honour during the Second World War. And the third is that if London did

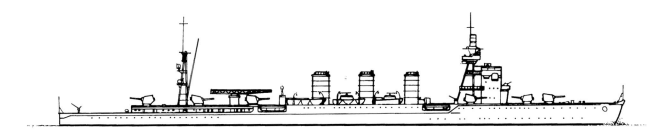

The light cruiser *Abukuma* was of a class designed in 1916 to serve as command ships for cruiser, destroyer or submarine formations.

resist Japanese demands and that Britain, although she might protest, could not oppose any Japanese move against either Indo-China or Siam. With Hong Kong and Borneo in effect written off, the position of Malaya and the Dutch East Indies was summarised in terms that were scarcely any more optimistic.

Why these records had not been sent by aircraft has never been explained but on 4 December the *Atlantis* reached Kobe, and the documents made their way immediately to the German Embassy in Tokyo and to the naval attaché. Then, with the documents dispatched by special courier overland through the Soviet Union to Germany, the embassy, having provided a summary of information to Berlin, asked for permission to pass various documents to Japanese government and service chiefs. Permission

discover the fate of these documents – and the indications are that it did – it did not inform Singapore of what had happened and that the Japanese had knowledge of British vulnerability and weakness.

Of course, by this stage, January 1941, the information was some five months old and Britain had survived the immediate threat to her existence. Moreover, in the months that had elapsed since the cabinet discussions recorded in the documents, British evidence of an entirely different kind had been provided for the Japanese, and indeed anyone who cared to look, in the form of the attack on the Italian fleet at anchor at Taranto on 12 November 1940. In the course of this attack the battleships *Conte di Cavour* and *Caio Duilo* were both hit by single torpedoes while the *Littorio* was hit three times.

All were to be recovered, although the *Cavour* never re-entered service. One heavy cruiser, one destroyer and two supply ships, along with the oil depot, were also damaged. But most significantly, this damage, which had immense strategic repercussions, was inflicted by a total of 21 ageing Swordfish biplanes from just one carrier, the *Illustrious*.

There was a time when in Britain the attack on Pearl Harbor could not be mentioned without reference to Taranto, as if somehow the Japanese could never have thought of such an attack for themselves but had to be guided by a much superior Royal Navy. In reality, by November 1940 the *Kaigun* had little to learn from the British, or any other navy, in the use of carriers and carrier aircraft *en masse* and about pre-emptive attacks on a battle line at anchor.

As is so often the case, the origins of and patents on developments are very difficult to discern. Probably the first serious proposal for such an operation as the one against Pearl Harbor was made in the 1927 war games played at the Japanese naval war college: for the Japanese the result was not very encouraging given that one of two Japanese carriers attacking Pearl Harbor was lost and the two American carriers which attacked Tokyo at the same time escaped unscathed. In 1928 a Japanese officer, Lieutenant-Commander Kusaka Ryunosuke, provided a lecture to senior officers on this subject, and in the same year Yamamoto, having returned to Japan after service as naval attaché in the United States, delivered a lecture to the torpedo establishment on the subject of an attack on Pearl Harbor. Then in 1929 a practical demonstration of the use of carrier-borne aircraft was provided in the form of a widely publicised US fleet exercise which involved a strike by aircraft from the carriers *Lexington* and *Saratoga* against the Panama Canal.

This exercise may well have influenced Hirata Shinsakyu's 1933 book on the subject of the future war with the United States, which had two *Akagi*-class carriers opening proceedings with a strike on Pearl Harbor. It has also been suggested that an American, Hector C. Bywater, in his book *The Great Pacific War* may have been the origi-nator of the idea of proceedings being opened by a

ABOVE The Type B.1 scout-submarine I.17 at its launch in July 1939. She carried one seaplane and had a catapult fitted aft of the conning tower.

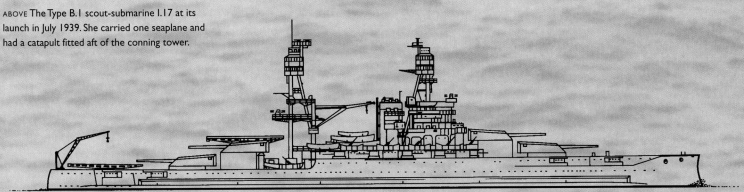

OPPOSITE TOP LEFT AND CENTRE The Type I cruiser-submarines I.1 and I.2. Built in the Twenties with an unprecedented range of 24,400 n.m. at 10 knots and a maximum speed of 19.1 knots. These two submarines belonged to a class that carried supplies for sixty days. With lightly armoured conning towers, these units carried two guns and six torpedo tubes, and were refitted to carry Long Lance torpedoes between 1939 and 1941. The I.1 was lost in June 1943, her sister ship in April 1944. Beyond the I.2 is the purpose-built depot ship *Chogui*, which survived the war.

OPPOSITE BOTTOM The aircraft carrier *Hiryu* in 1939. Supposedly an improved *Soryu*, her island, located amidships and to port proved very dangerous for landing aircraft.

ABOVE The battleship *Arizona* was sunk at Pearl Harbor on 7 December 1941. She was not salvaged and was dedicated as a memorial on 30 June 1962.

Japanese attack on Pearl Harbor. Whatever the case, in 1936 one of the exercises conducted by the Japanese naval war college was an attack on Pearl Harbor, and the US fleet exercise of April 1938 took the form of a strike on Pearl Harbor by aircraft from the *Saratoga*.

Initially it is not evident why the Japanese exercise of 1936 should have commanded any attention because the idea of a Pearl Harbor attack was considered at the Japanese naval war college throughout the Thirties. It was considered negatively, however, in the sense that it was deemed an operation which could not be conducted and thus was never examined in any detail – and the 1936 war game does not appear to have broken this mould. However, one of the officers attending the 1936 war game was Lieutenant-Commander Genda Minoru, generally considered the most gifted and celebrated of the *Kaigun's* pilots of the inter-war period. During his year at the college Genda set out the idea of the use of carriers *en masse*. It was a view that commanded little support, although Genda himself noted that one officer, Captain Onishi Takijiro, was similarly persuaded. In 1938, when he was asked to lecture on the subject of how naval avia-

tion should be organised, Genda returned to the themes of mass and Pearl Harbor, and he found himself and his views denounced violently by a number of naval officers, and his lecturing activity had to be curtailed.

It is not hard to see why Genda should have encountered so rough a reception. In all the major navies in the inter-war period there was a very real gulf between the proponents of air power and those of the big gun, and relations between the two could be very difficult. In the case of the *Kaigun*, however, the central importance of the Great All-Out Battle Strategy to *Kaigun* thinking and concepts of operations, along with the enormous pressure to conform to collective wisdom within the service, meant that the views of such people as Genda and Onishi were frankly heretical and totally unacceptable to the great majority of naval officers. Yet the period when Genda expressed these views was also one in which his ideas began to assume real substance: these were years of change, most notably because of the entry into service of monoplanes with speed, range and weapon loads that were great improvements over those of biplanes.

Certainly, as a result of its experience in the China war,

the *Kaigun* had learnt the importance of massing its aircraft, especially in terms of providing fighter support for its bombers, and Genda, who returned to Japan in November 1940 after service in London, found that the *Kaigun* was now conducting exercises involving as many as 150 aircraft in single missions. The problem, however, was how to keep carriers close enough together to be able to mass such numbers of aircraft, the conventional wisdom of the day stressing the importance of separating carriers from one another. The reason for this was simple: the peculiar vulnerability of carriers gave rise to the belief that a carrier force, once discovered by enemy reconnaissance, would very quickly be overwhelmed. The dispersal of carriers, in single-carrier task groups, therefore offered the best prospect of survival of the whole, but the price exacted was obvious: the concentration of aircraft was rendered extremely difficult.

It seems that the first Japanese exercise involving the use of aerial torpedoes in shallow waters was carried out in Saiki Bay, eastern Kyushu, in 1939: it was conducted by flying boats, presumably the Type 97 Mavis from the Yokohama Air Unit. The specific idea of an attack on Pearl Harbor was not apparently countenanced at this time, even though Pearl Harbor was cited as one of five anchorages where such an attack could be conducted. Yet by the spring of 1940 the Japanese had conducted exercises involving large numbers of carrier-based torpedo planes against warships both in harbour and at sea with full power of manoeuvre, and the success of one of these exercises, ironically one against battleships at sea in either April or May 1940, is said to have prompted Yamamoto to remark on the possibility of launching an attack on Pearl Harbor to Rear Admiral Fukudome Shigeru, his chief of staff until April 1941. It was also around this time that Captain Kuroshima Kameto, Yamamoto's senior staff officer, wrote a memorandum advocating an attack by carrier aircraft against a battle force at the start of an American war. However, the US Pacific Fleet was not in residence at Pearl Harbor at this time: it was only later that it was moved from San Diego as part of a forward strategy employed by the Roosevelt administration in response to the gathering crisis in Europe and the obvious likelihood of trouble in the Far East as a consequence.

All the evidence suggests that both the idea of starting a war with a surprise attack, in exactly the way that the Japanese had opened proceedings in 1904 in the war with Russia, and the twin idea of using carrier aircraft *en masse* and against an enemy force in harbour were both being considered within the Combined Fleet some seven or eight months before the British raid on the Italian fleet at Taranto. But while it is clear that these ideas ran in parallel with one another, it is nonetheless all to easy to forget that, until 1940, no navy, and certainly neither the *Kaigun* nor the US Navy, possessed the numbers to experiment with concentrated carrier divisions. Prior to 1940, when for the first time Japanese carrier numbers reached a total of six, the *Kaigun* at best could deploy three carriers together, more realistically two. The enormous disparity in capability between the *Hosho*, the first Japanese carrier, and the newer *Akagi* and *Kaga* made it very hard for them to work together, while the *Ryujo*, such were her manifest deficiencies, seems to have spent her first three or four years after entering service in 1933 in dockyard hands. It was not until the *Soryu* entered service in December 1937 that the *Kaigun* really had three carriers as opposed to warships with flight decks, but with overhauls, the requirements of training and the demands of the China

war, even this total of three was nominal rather than real. It was only when the *Hiryu* entered service in the second half of 1939 that the *Kaigun* really did come into possession of two properly constituted carrier divisions.

Obviously, the *Kaigun* could never consider the use of carriers and their aircraft en masse until they had numbers enough to use them together, but it proved to be American example that drew the strands together. When he was in London as naval attaché, Genda saw a US Navy cinema newsreel which showed two *Lexington*-class and two *Yorktown*-class carriers together. He immediately realised that dispersal of carriers was not the answer to the problem of their vulnerability: concentration of carriers within a single formation promised to provide unprecedented levels of protection which would be supplied by the anti-aircraft guns of the screening warships and the fighters of the combat air patrol. In fact, it is possible to argue that Genda's solution was wrong, at least in the short term and at least for carriers without radar or the benefit of an Identification Friend or Foe system. Equally, it is possible to argue that the Americans, in the course of their operations in the second half of 1944 and throughout 1945, made the 'Genda package' work. However, the evidence of the first and middle part of the war is not so

One of the 46-ton 78-ft long **2** Type A midget submarines that attempted to sink U.S. warships inside Pearl Harbor on 7 December 1941 clear-cut, and the loss of four Japanese carriers during the battle off Midway in June 1942 would suggest that concentration did not necessarily provide protection against attack.

As it was, when the Combined Fleet established an independent carrier force on 1 April 1941, its logic was very simple: a strike against the US Pacific Fleet at its base in Pearl Harbor could only be staged by a concentrated carrier with enough torpedo-bombers and dive-bombers to have any chance of registering success. It was a point which had been recognised by Yamamoto in a letter dated 7 January 1941 when, in ordering the preparation of a plan for an attack on Pearl Harbor, he told Onishi that both the First and Second Carrier Divisions, the *Akagi* and *Kaga* and the *Hiryu* and *Soryu* respectively, had to be in the attack force – in other words, what in effect was the 'full strength' of the front-line carriers had to be concentrated if a strike was to succeed.

When one considers that the Taranto attack was the largest British carrier operation of the war to date, then the range of Japanese thinking and practical experience can be placed in its proper perspective. By early 1941 air officers such as Genda, who were familiar with operating mixed groups of 150 or 180 aircraft, were thinking in terms of how to operate as many as 300 in a single strike. There were problems enough in trying to handle such large aerial forces simply in terms of the number of carriers required and these ships' ability to maintain so many aircraft in service. There was also the need to standardise training, operating procedures and command between carrier divisions. Yet in trying to provide answers to these questions as 1940 gave way to 1941, the Japanese were light years ahead of the British and US navies at this particular time and most certainly owed nothing to the Taranto example. None of this, however, prevented the Combined Fleet, quite properly, from seeking detailed reports of this operation from its officers in London and Rome.

In the process which led to the attack on Pearl Harbor, the raising of the First Carrier Striking Force on 1 April 1941 was perhaps the most important single development: there could never have been an attack without the existence of such a force. When it was formed, the force consisted of the *Akagi* and *Kaga* (First Carrier Division) with four destroyers, the *Hiryu* and *Soryu*

1 7.57 am: 40 torpedo bombers deliver 40 torpedoes against U.S. battleships at anchor

(Second Carrier Division) with four destroyers, and the *Ryujo* (Fourth Carrier Division) and two destroyers: at this time neither the *Shokaku* nor the *Zuikaku*, the two members of the Fifth Carrier Division, had entered service. But the real story of the attack pre-dates the raising of the carrier force by some months, and in effect began in January 1941 (at a time when the *Automedon's* documents were being subjected to examination within the Japanese high command) when Yamamoto wrote to Onishi, by this time a two-star admiral and chief of staff of the shore-based XIth Air Fleet, outlining his ideas for such an attack. In early February Onishi contacted Genda, who was now a staff officer with the First Carrier Division in the *Kaga*. Genda proceeded to Kanoya and to Onishi's headquarters where, having read Yamamoto's letter, he was ordered to complete a study of Yamamoto's proposed operation 'with special attention to the feasibility of the operation, method of execution, and the forces to be used'. Somewhat surprisingly, Yamamoto indicated in his letter to Onishi his wish to be appointed to command the force that would conduct this attack.

Genda's response, that such an attack would be extremely difficult but not impossible, stated the need for absolute secrecy and the use of all available carriers in order to strike a blow from which the enemy could not recover 'for at least six months'. With the American carriers selected as the primary target, Genda placed no great reliance on torpedoes and stated the need for dive-bombers, even at the cost of altering the composition of the Japanese carrier air groups. According to Genda's own account of proceedings, he gave his response to Onishi after a week or ten days of deliberation, and Onishi forwarded his views to Yamamoto along with his own. At this stage the latter were mildly optimistic but, according to Genda, by September 1941 Onishi had come to doubt the viability of a strike on Pearl Harbor and, as a result, ceased to be consulted by Yamamoto.

After the First Air Fleet was raised, just four of its officers – Vice Admiral Nagumo Chuichi, the commander, Rear Admiral Kusaka, his chief of staff, Commander Oishi Tomatsu, the senior staff officer in the command, and Genda – were aware of Yamamoto's thinking, but nothing was done to develop Genda's February proposal. Within the Combined Fleet staff, however, various aspects of a plan of attack on Pearl Harbor were subjected to detailed study, but it was only in early September, by which time Japan had taken the decision to go to war if all other means of solving the impasse with the United

States failed, that Kusaka gave instructions for flesh to be put upon the bones of the proposals. One week later Genda delivered a plan that he claimed was similar to the plan that was executed – but for the fact that the point of departure was different, there was no liaison with the submarine formations detailed to support a carrier raid on Pearl Harbor, there was no time-slot selected and, somewhat surprisingly, 'the air-raid plan was not worked out in detail'. One wonders just what this offering of Genda's and the actual plan did have in common.

The basic idea of a strike against the American fleet at Pearl Harbor was subjected to a series of war games at the Army War College in Tokyo – the facilities at the Naval War College were too small to house all those who had to attend – between 5 and 17 September. In the course of the games played on 13 September, the plan was deemed feasible, although it was estimated that Japanese losses could extend to two carriers sunk, two more carriers damaged and 127 aircraft lost. After these exercises, on 2 October Nagumo provided air commanders with a special briefing in the *Akagi*. Over the next few days, however, the planners in Tokyo sought to remove the *Akagi* from the Hawaiian operation for service in southeast Asia. As a result there was a series of war games played

by the Combined Fleet staff on the basis of a three-carrier attack involving the *Kaga* and the two carriers of the Second Carrier Division, but this seems to have been less than satisfactory. Representations were then made to Tokyo, with the result that the *Akagi* was restored to the carrier force bound for Hawaiian waters.

This particular issue, however, was but one of three which presented themselves as major problems at this time, in September and October 1941, and which at least in part cut across staff lines. The most important single issue provoked the confrontation of 19 October between Tokyo and the Combined Fleet. This took the form of Yamamoto's despatch of Kuroshima to Tokyo with the demand, backed by the threatened resignation of himself and the Combined Fleet staff, that war should begin with an attack on the US Pacific Fleet at Hawaii, and that this attack should be made with the full carrier strength available to the *Kaigun*. This rather curious episode – and Ugaki for one was unaware of the threat that Kuroshima was authorised to use – is one of the many and real areas of difficulty which litter the process whereby the *Kaigun* settled on the substance of the Hawaiian operation, though in one respect this demand would seem clear. At least on 1 October the First Carrier

(3) Three U.S. battleships were torpedoed by Kate bombers and, it seems, two battleships were torpedoed by one midget submarine.

Striking Force numbered not six but eight units: the *Akagi* and *Kaga*, the *Soryu* and *Hiryu*, the *Zuikaku* and *Shokaku* of the First, Second and Fifth Carrier Divisions respectively, plus the *Ryujo* and *Kasuga Maru* of the Fourth Carrier Division. One assumes that the demand for the use of all carriers in this operation did not embrace these latter two units and indeed it certainly could not have included the *Kasuga Maru*, which was soon renamed the *Taiyo*: when she was completed in September, she did not have her 27-strong air group, and her air personnel were accordingly distributed among groups of the six main carriers.

the war game of 13 September 1941 there appears to have been a furious argument between Kuroshima and Rear Admiral Ito Seiichi, Nagano's deputy, over precisely this question. Genda was told by Ito that neither could the Army release the soldiers nor could the Navy provide the shipping for an operation in the central Pacific which would demand a minimum of three divisions: put very simply, when the military commitments in Manchoutikuo and China, along with the requirements of the various campaigns in south-east Asia, were combined with Japan's lack of shipping, national resources could not be stretched to cover another major undertaking. In dealing with

ABOVE **The Type B.1 scout-submarine I.15.** Seen on trials in Hiroshima Bay in September 1940, she was lost in November 1942.

The commander of the Combined Fleet threatening resignation unless he was allowed to attack the US Pacific Fleet, and this weeks after the Navy's deadline for the start of a war had passed, hardly seems the stuff of which calm, rational decisions – such as going to war and the prior preparation of plans which would be put into effect – are made. It would seem that in mid-October the argument concerned itself with the scale of an attack before the question of whether such an attack should be made had been settled.

The remaining issue concerned the question of why there was no attempt to land on and overrun Oahu at the start of hostilities. Genda claimed that, in his reply to Onishi's request that he consider the problems inherent in an attack on the Pacific Fleet, he stated the need for an amphibious landing and conquest of Oahu, and during

Kuroshima, however, Ito used the argument that a double operation – the *kogeki*, or strike, against the US Pacific Fleet and the *koryaku*, or invasion, of Oahu – represented a combination altogether too complicated and fraught with risk. Ito's argument appears to have been amounted to a tacit acceptance of the *kogeki*.

There were two interesting aspects to this exchange between Ito and Kuroshima. The first was that on September 13 the Japanese realised that there was an opportunity to invade Oahu which would never repeat itself, and that, by allowing the *koryaku* to pass by default, they were in effect resigning themselves to never making the attempt to secure Oahu since, once alerted by an attack, the Americans would prepare defences which would render any invasion problematic. The second was that the argument was settled by Yamamoto, who ruled in favour of Ito, and thus in favour of his superior and against his own staff.

Such matters were not the only ones involving the carrier force under consideration at this time. It is clear from Genda's account that, even as late as the first week in October, the inclusion in the strike force of the *Shokaku* and *Zuikaku* had not been settled. Even more seriously, there appears to have been doubt about the inclusion of the *Hiryu* and *Soryu*. The reason for this particular problem was the range of these two ships, which for the *Soryu* was 7,750 miles at 18 knots. As with so

that war begin with an attack on the American fleet at Pearl Harbor represented one for an operation which at that time could not be executed.

The problem of the *Hiryu* and *Soryu* was overcome but only after a somewhat bizarre sequel. As the various staffs considered the problems of distance and range, it was suggested that the two carriers be deleted from the force sent against Pearl Harbor. Such a proposal does leave open the questions of why they were included in the force in the first place if they lacked the range to reach Pearl Harbor, and of just what force was under consideration in September–October given the reluctance of staffs either

RIGHT The destroyer *Hamakaze*. One of the *Kagero* class, she entered service in 1941 and was a member of the 17th Destroyer Division with the carrier force. She was sunk in the Imperial Navy's last sortie, in defence of Okinawa in April 1945.

many of the *Kaigun's* warships, built with the requirements of the Great All-Out Battle Strategy uppermost, the *Soryu* could not make the return journey from northern home waters to the Hawaiian Islands without refuelling at least once, a characteristic she shared with the *Akagi* (range 8,200 miles at 16 knots) but not with the *Kaga* (10,330 miles at 16 knots) and the *Shokaku* and *Zuikaku* (both 9,700 miles at 18 knots). Moreover, the *Kaigun's* practical experience of and equipment for refuelling at sea were virtually non-existent. In September, when the war games were played, and even probably in mid-October when Kuroshima presented himself and Yamamoto's demand to superior authority in Tokyo, the *Kaigun* could not have conducted an attack on Pearl Harbor because its one and only strike force could not have reached its flying-off position. Yamamoto's demand

to include the *Shokaku* and *Zuikaku* in the force or, if these carriers were included, not to afford them a major offensive role. But in one sense the Japanese problem was obvious. As a nation Japan had just 49 tankers of a total of 587,000 tons to serve alongside the nine fleet oilers available to the *Kaigun*. The extent of the difficulties posed by the refuelling requirements of such units as the *Akagi*, *Hiryu* and *Soryu*, and of the two battleships, two cruisers and two destroyer squadrons that formed the carriers' screen can be understood by the fact that no fewer than eight oilers were to be assigned to this operation, although in the event the last-minute discovery of deficient equipment reduced this total to seven. As it was, three refuelling exercises were held off the southern ports in November, and then all units in the carrier formation took on fuel ten times as they journeyed from the home ports of Kyushu to the Kuriles prior to the operation. But by any standard, these levels of training were minimal.

Such considerations provide the background to two of the more outlandish aspects of Japanese planning. When Rear Admiral Yamaguchi Tamon, the commander of the Second Carrier Division, became aware that planners were considering not including his command in the strike force bound for Pearl Harbor, he became highly intoxicated and physically seized Nagumo and, watched by a collection of officers who made no attempt to intervene, beat his commander until the latter agreed that Yamaguchi's formation would be included in the task force. In another confronta- tion, Yamaguchi threatened to kill Nagumo. Perhaps more immediately relevant, Yamaguchi seriously proposed that the problem of lack of range, and lack of oilers, be solved by abandoning the *Hiryu* and *Soryu* after they had flown off their aircraft. By what standard the Japanese, at the very start of a war with the United States, could afford to write off two of their very best carriers is not clear, but for that matter even less clear was the process by which the *Kaigun* came to any decision given Yamaguchi's behaviour: this should have earned the rear admiral court martial, dismissal and imprisonment rather than the accommodation of his demands. Of Yamaguchi, the least that can be said is that his proposal that second-phase operations should include securing the major islands of the south-west Pacific, landings in Australia, the seizure of the Hawaiian Islands and landings in California and the securing of bases from which air operations across the whole of mainland America could be conducted, strongly suggests that, whatever qualities of leadership he possessed, these in all likelihood were not matched by his cerebral capacity. But he was perhaps the most fervent supporter of Yamamoto's Pearl Harbor proposal within the carrier force, and no doubt that explains a great deal.

But even with this question of carrier numbers resolved, there were three other problems which became increasingly urgent with the passing of time. The first concerned the implementation of level-altitude bombing techniques whereby formations bombed on the instructions of the lead aircraft. Prior to June 1941, the Japanese were achieving a hit rate of less than one in ten with high-level bombers, but in exercises in this month 27 Nakajima B5N Kates registered eleven direct hits against the target vessel *Settsu*, which possessed full power of manoeuvre. Thereafter bombing on the command of the lead aircraft was adopted for all training throughout that summer and autumn and was used at Pearl Harbor, and the seemingly irresistible pressure which had been building up during the spring to dispense with level-altitude bombing was deflected.

At the same time, however, the Japanese were confronted by a seemingly more difficult problem of securing reliable torpedoes which were capa- ble of functioning in water that was no more than 40 feet deep. The Japanese had to ensure that their air-launched torpedoes did not dive below 33 feet, and this meant there had to be a series of experiments with aircraft in order to determine the maximum height and speed at which the torpedoes could be launched, while the torpedoes had to be tested in order to ensure that their special flotation and stabilising devices worked. It was not until the three days of 11–13 November that units from the *Akagi* and *Kaga* at Kagoshima were able to attain satisfactory results with air- craft flying at 150 knots at 65 feet and 100 knots at 35 feet, their torpedoes recording an 83 per cent effectiveness over prescribed distances. In the meantime, however, satis- factory results had been anticipated and Nagasaki navy arsenal had built 50 torpedoes by mid-October and another twenty by the end of the month: by the end of November, it had completed another 50. The first batch of 50 torpedoes was distributed between the *Akagi*, *Soryu* and

LEFT Fleet Admiral Yamamoto Isoroku. Commander of the Combined Fleet, 1939-1943, the originator and architect of the Pearl Harbor attack, he was denied posthumous ennoblement.

OPPOSITE TOP The Mitsubishi A6M2 Type 00 Zeke. The most famous Japanese aircraft of the Second World War, the Zeke was the first carrier aircraft to match or even exceed the performance of land-based counterparts. Its strengths in rate of climb, manoeuvrability and range, however, were purchased in terms of lack of armour and defensive strength. Moreover, her basic design could not be much developed, and her successors proved no match for Hellcats, Corsairs and Lightnings.

OPPOSITE MIDDLE The Nakajima B5N1 Type 97 Kate. Built to a 1935 specification and design, the Kate was quickly rendered obsolescent with the coming of the Pacific war. Nonetheless, she was primarily responsible for whatever Japanese success was commanded at Pearl Harbor and played her full part in the sinking of four U.S. fleet carriers in 1942. Kates remained in service until 1944.

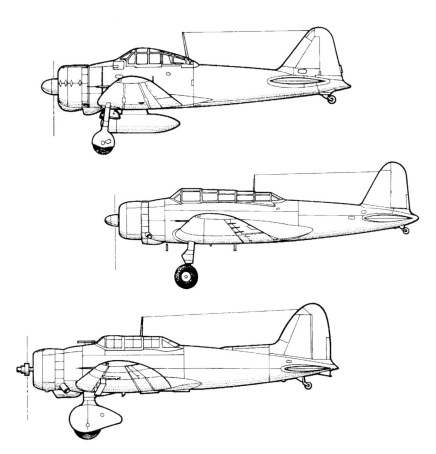

ABOVE The Aichi D3A1 Type 99 Val. The slenderness of Japanese resources can be gauged by the fact that though this dive-bomber first flew in August 1936, just 478 had been built by August 1942. The Val is credited with sinking more Allied ships than any other Axis aircraft of the Second World War.

intended to solve such complicated problems as cruising formation. As a new force, of unprecedented numbers and strength, the First Carrier Striking Force had to determine the number of battleships, heavy cruisers and destroyers in the screen, the distance of carriers from one another, and the distance and position of the units from the screens relative to the carriers. Certain of the answers arrived at were most definitely not to everyone's liking. The allocation of just two fast battleships to the formation invited the criticism that such numbers were essentially irrelevant if the First Carrier Striking Force encountered an alert enemy at sea, but the demands of operations in the south, specifically against British Malaya, ensured that only two of the fast battleships could be spared for Nagumo's demands.

As it was, these and other issues were resolved in the course of autumn 1941, and the First Carrier Striking Force's final plan of attack was completed at the end of October. On 2 November all formation and unit commanders and flying officers attended a massed briefing on the *Akagi* in Ariake Bay. Here, for the first time, they were made aware of the basic idea of a strike against the US Pacific Fleet at its base at Pearl Harbor at the outset of war, their precise role in this plan and the nature of the exercises which were to be conducted over the next two weeks. Then the units of the force quietly slipped away in ones or twos to take on supplies at Kure or Sasebo prior to regrouping at Hitokappu Bay in the Kuriles on and after 22 November. One final briefing in *Akagi* was conducted on 24 November before the formation sailed from Hitokappu Bay on 26 November.

Hiryu in mid-November, when the carriers were in the south. Incredible though it may seem, it was not until 24 November, just two days before it sailed, that the formation received its full complement of torpedoes when the *Kaga*, having been loaded with another 50, arrived at Hitokappu Bay and began the task of distribution.

The Japanese faced other ordnance complications. While aiming showed much improvement during the summer, the fact was that the Kate bomber could not carry and deliver the special Type 5 800-kilogram bomb and the Aichi D3A Val dive-bomber was similarly handicapped with respect to the Type 99 250-kilogram bomb. Both sets of aircraft had to be specially modified in order to be able to carry these weapons, but the various adjustments which were needed could not be completed at Saiki Bay and had to await the gathering of the formation at Hitokappu Bay, prior to the departure for the Hawaiian Islands. And, inevitably, at the same time the First Carrier Striking Force was also involved in exercises

The Japanese planning process and its timetable are a cause for wonderment, though in the final analysis one point has to be made. The fact that in the end everything – everything, that is, except the American carriers – came together in the attack of Sunday 7 December 1941 provides justification of the system: the system worked. Moreover, if the *Kaigun* was left to operate on perilously slender margins then it was not the first service, and Japan most certainly was not unique, in being reduced to such circumstances, though the corollary is obvious: such margins as those on which Japan was obliged to work do not form the proper basis of a plan of campaign, still less a national security strategy. Nonetheless, the detail of events prompts the thought that the basis of whatever success the Japanese commanded on the day derived not so much from the *Kaigun's* ability to surprise the enemy as its ability to amaze itself.

The Japanese planning process came together very efficiently and in a timely manner, but the process and its detail do beg obvious questions and these bear recapitulation. Yamamoto's insistence that war begin with an attack on the American fleet at Pearl Harbor represented a demand for an operation which at that time could not be executed simply because the First Carrier Striking Force could have reached the Hawaiian Islands but lacked the range to return to home waters. The First Carrier Striking Force came within two days of having to sail without its full torpedo complement. It also had no guarantee that its Kates and Vals would be able to carry their designated ordnance and, stretching a point, no guarantee

that its bombers could do anything but miss the target *en masse* while recording only the occasional hit. This was, to say the least, an extraordinary state of affairs.

Such is the background to the Japanese operational plan. Nonetheless, four particular aspects of both the plan and the attack itself still require clarification. These are the lack of agreement about the air group establishments of individual carriers and the carrier formation as a whole; the lack of precision governing the number of aircraft in the two strike formations employed on 7 December 1941; a general failure (with certain honourable exceptions) to define the formations and sub-formations of individual air groups and to relate them to targets; and, lastly, the failure to set out the aims and priorities as defined in the plan. The last of these is perhaps the most surprising, but it is arguably the most important single matter because, naturally, so much of the detail followed from the plan *per se*.

LEFT The extent and thoroughness of Japanese preparations: a photograph captured at the end of the war showing a miniature mock-up of Battleship Row, complete with one oiler in position.

ABOVE A Nakajima B5N1 Type 97 Kate, armed with the Mark 91 torpedo, taking off from the fleet carrier *Akagi*.

In no respect is the absence of certainty more obvious than the definition of operational priority. Western accounts, without exception, note that the Japanese effort was divided into two parts, a first attack force that included Kates with either 800-kilogram armour-piercing bombs or the Mark 91 torpedo, and a second attack force with Vals, both forces being separately completed by aircraft from the *Shokaku* and *Zuikaku* which were directed against airfields on Oahu. Most western accounts suggest that the second attack force, to quote but one source, 'would administer the *coup de grâce* to ships damaged in the first wave and would complete the destruction of US air power beyond the ability to retaliate.' That may well have been what was supposed to have happened on the day, but in fact planning set out very different priorities for the two attack formations.

Japanese operational priorities were defined as battleships and aircraft carriers, in that order, and the Kates of the first attack formation were given the task of dealing with American battleships. Because of the efficiency of their intelligence sources, the Japanese basically knew where individual battleships would be found and had listed them

in numerical order of priority from one to eight. The Kates were under instructions to attack the first four American battleships in order of priority and thereafter, if carriers were in the anchorage, they were then to direct their attention against these. If carriers were absent, the Kates would be free to attack the battleships listed five to eight. The Vals, which were equipped with 250-kilogram bombs, were given the task of dealing with American carriers. If these were absent, or in the event of the first attack formation having accounted for them, the priority of the Vals was to be American cruisers, and only after the cruisers had been destroyed was priority to be afforded to the battle line.

This definition of priorities, provided in the Japanese defence agency's official history, has never been afforded proper consideration in any western source, and nor have two critical facts. The first is that the *Kaigun* went to war with industry having met only 45 per cent of its designated aerial ordnance requirement. The carriers had enough torpedoes to meet most contingencies – they could mount at least two full strikes with these weapons – but in terms of bombs the First Carrier Striking Force was ill-provided. The limited number of Type 5 heavy bombs meant that its main bomb would be the 250-kilogram variety, which would be of limited effectiveness in dealing with major American warships with sea room. The second is that, if refuelling proved impossible in the stormy wastes of the North Pacific in December, Nagumo was to shed his destroyers, the *Akagi* and the *Hiryu* and *Soryu* and to carry out the attack with just the *Kaga* and the *Shokaku* and *Zuikaku*. Given the war games which pointed to the relatively poor results likely to be secured by three carriers, not to mention the Combined Fleet's antics to ensure that the war begin with an attack on the Pacific Fleet with the *Kaigun's* full front-line carrier strength, this directive and arrangement seems more than a little surprising. Indeed, the absurdity of Yamamoto's position is so obvious that it is amazing that no one seems to have noticed it. War had to begin with an attack on the Pacific Fleet by aircraft from all six front-line carriers available to the *Kaigun*, but if the weather was bad the attack could be conducted by three carriers, two of which were held in such low esteem that their aircraft were not tasked to attack warships, and,

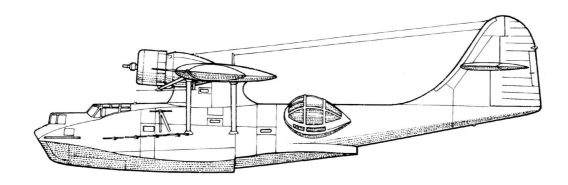

indeed, neither the *Shokaku* and *Zuikaku* carried Type 5 bombs and Type 91 torpedoes. The three-carrier force, so unacceptable when the subject of Ministry and Naval Staff calculations, was seemingly quite acceptable if sanctioned by the Combined Fleet staff. But if the First Carrier Striking Force was reduced to this course of action, its attack on the whole of the US Pacific Fleet would have to be conducted with twelve torpedoes and fifteen heavy bombs. Just what such an attack was expected to achieve is wholly impossible to discern.

Such, at any rate, was the definition of operational priority, but no matter touching upon the *Kaigun* can be handled so simply: this definition, within the terms of the First Carrier Striking Force's own plan, cannot be wholly reconciled with that made by the Combined Fleet in its order to the carrier formation. These orders, specifically Annex 3 of Operation Order No. 1, which was issued on 1 November 1941, stated: 'Targets for attack are airfields; aircraft carriers; battleships, cruisers and other warships; merchant shipping; port facilities; and land installations, in that order.' Such a definition invites three observations. First, one assumes the definition of airfields as first priority stemmed from a fear of American land-based air power and the desire to ensure that the carrier force remained free from effective counter-attack, though this does raise a number of questions on its own account, such as the allocation of the least experienced Japanese formations to this particular task. Perhaps more pertinently, one has to ask whether the devastation of airfields on Oahu was more important than sinking US warships, since that would seem to be the only conclusion of a priority list that lists airfields ahead of warships. Second, the definition of aircraft carriers as priority ahead of battleships

is clear, but one wonders about the basis of the subsequent change in priorities, and whether the reversal in the plan of attack reflected or was a concession to conventional opinion – to gun club pressure – within the fleet and ministry. Third, the definition of priorities by Yamamoto should provide an answer to the criticism made of Nagumo and Kusaka regarding their failure to conduct a third strike against the base facilities at Pearl Harbor. From the time that the first criticism was set down in Morison's third volume of the US Navy's official history of the war in 1948, the fate of Nagumo and Kusaka has been something akin to character assassination by historiographical crucifixion. Yet this criticism would seem to be unfounded, not least that levelled against Nagumo and Kusaka by Yamamoto and Ugaki: it is difficult to criticise Nagumo and Kusaka for their decision, made at a time when the whereabouts of American carriers were unknown, not to attack base installations which Yamamoto and Ugaki ranked as priorities lower even than merchant shipping.

In fact, the whole question of a third strike is extremely vexed, and it is considered in detail in Chapter 5. Here, however, attention must turn to three questions of detail: the air group establishments of individual carriers and the carrier formation as a whole; the number of aircraft in the two strike formations employed on 7 December 1941; and the definition of the formations and sub-formations of individual air groups and their relation to targets. Unfortunately, certain of these questions defy a simple answer, not least that of the air group establishments of formation and units.

Most accounts of the Pearl Harbor attack confine themselves to an estimation of the number of aircraft

ABOVE The Curtiss P-40C Hawk. The most numerous of the American aircraft on Oahu, the P-40 was equipped with a 1,040 h.p. liquid-cooled engine that provided the basis of a long and troubled history. Ultimately some 13,738 Hawks of various marks were built and served in the British, Chinese, Dutch, French, New Zealand, Soviet and Turkish air forces.

employed on the two strikes rather than giving figures relating to the size of individual air groups, and hence the formation as a whole. At least one book, however, has tried to get around such problems by providing different sets of figures. Such ambivalence is understandable because there seems to be no agreement even between official Japanese figures. What is known is that planning prior to the operation indicated that the six Japanese carriers committed to this operation would carry a total of 378 aircraft and 54 aircraft designated as the reserve, a total of 432 aircraft. Japanese official figures, however, indicate that the size of the air establishment was 399 aircraft but, for a number of reasons, this figure would seem to understate the size of the formation's groups by a minimum of ten and maximum of 24 aircraft. It would appear, based upon Japanese figures, that the Japanese carriers together embarked either 411 or 417 aircraft: for the purpose of these pages, the figure is assumed to have been 411.

What is known, however, definitively and beyond doubt, is that the Japanese plan of attack envisaged an opening attack conducted by 189 aircraft and a second attack conducted by 171 aircraft. The first attack formation was to consist of 90 Kate level- and torpedo-bombers, 54 Val dive-bombers and 45 Zeke fighters, and the second attack formation was to number 54 Kates, 81 Vals and 36 Zekes. In the event, the first attack formation was 183-strong while the second attack formation mustered either 170 or 167 aircraft. Why the first attack formation lost six of its numbers is not altogether clear: the second attack formation had one Val, from the *Kaga*, stall and prove incapable of taking off, but two Vals and one Zekes, having taken off, were forced to

return to their carriers with engine trouble and thus did not take part in the attack. In essence, the first wave numbered 50 Kates armed with 800-kilogram armour-piercing bombs and 40 Kates with the Mark 91 torpedo. These aircraft were drawn from the four units of the First and Second Carrier Divisions while 54 Vals from the *Shokaku* and *Zuikaku*, with 250-kilogram bombs, attacked Ford Island, Wheeler and Hickam Fields. Two dozen Zekes, again drawn from the *Akagi*, *Kaga*, *Hiryu* and *Soryu*, were to attack the same three fields, along with Barbers Point, while twelve Zekes, drawn from the Fifth Carrier Division, worked over Kaneohe Field. The second wave was to consist of 81 Vals, again drawn from the four units of the First and Second Carrier Divisions, which were afforded targets of opportunity among American warships while 54 Kates, from the *Shokaku* and *Zuikaku*, were ordered to attack Ford Island, Hickam Field and Kaneohe Fields. In addition eighteen Zekes from the *Akagi* and *Kaga* were to attack Hickam Field while eighteen Zekes from the *Hiryu* and *Soryu* attacked Kaneohe. The balance of aircraft were to be held for combat air patrol over the task force and in reserve. The full organisation of the air component is described on pages 66 and 67.

For the attack on the US Pacific Fleet, however, Yamamoto and the Combined Fleet staff did not rely solely upon the carrier force. One of the lesser known aspects of the attack is the fact that Japan began the war with only 48 modern submarines (plus another twelve suitable only for coastal operations or training) of which over half were committed to complement the efforts of the First Carrier Striking Force: as the submarine service noted, the main attack was to be a surprise attack, sudden and complete, while the submarine attack was necessary to obtain subsequent cumulative effect.

The submarines allocated to the Hawaiian operation were divided into five formations. The first, consisting of the submarines I. 19, I. 21 and the I. 23, was to advance across the northern Pacific ahead of the First Carrier Striking Force. This was to be an advanced reconnaissance force during the advance to contact phase, and during the attack the task of its units was to rescue ditched aircrew and to defend the carrier formation against counter-

First wave aircraft:
43 Zeke fighters,
40 Kate torpedo-bombers,
51 Val dive-bombers and
49 Kate high-level bombers,

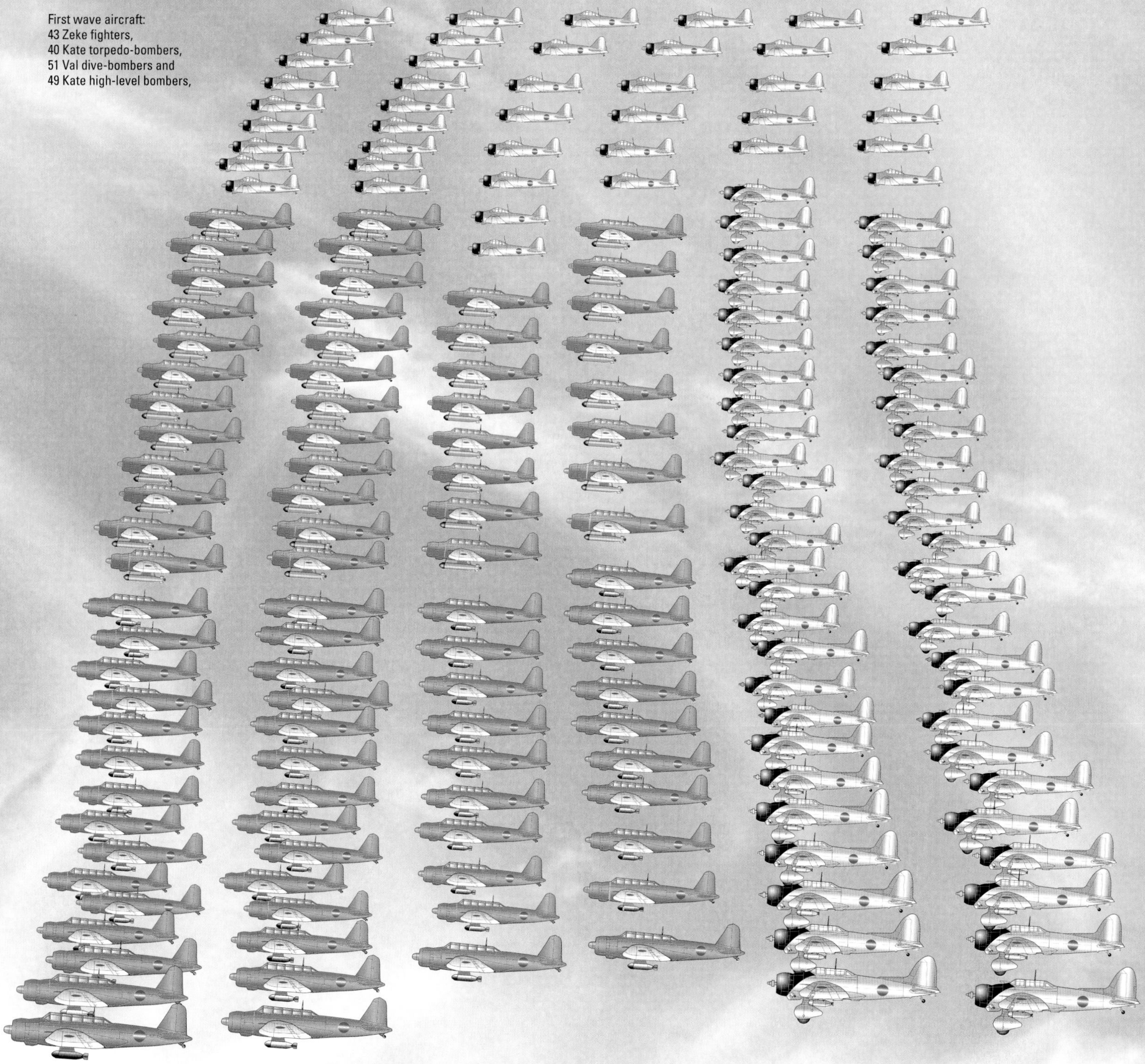

Akagi   *Kaga*   *Sōryū*   *Hiryū*   *Shokaku*   *Zuikaku*

1st Carrier Division   2nd Carrier Division   5th Carrier Division

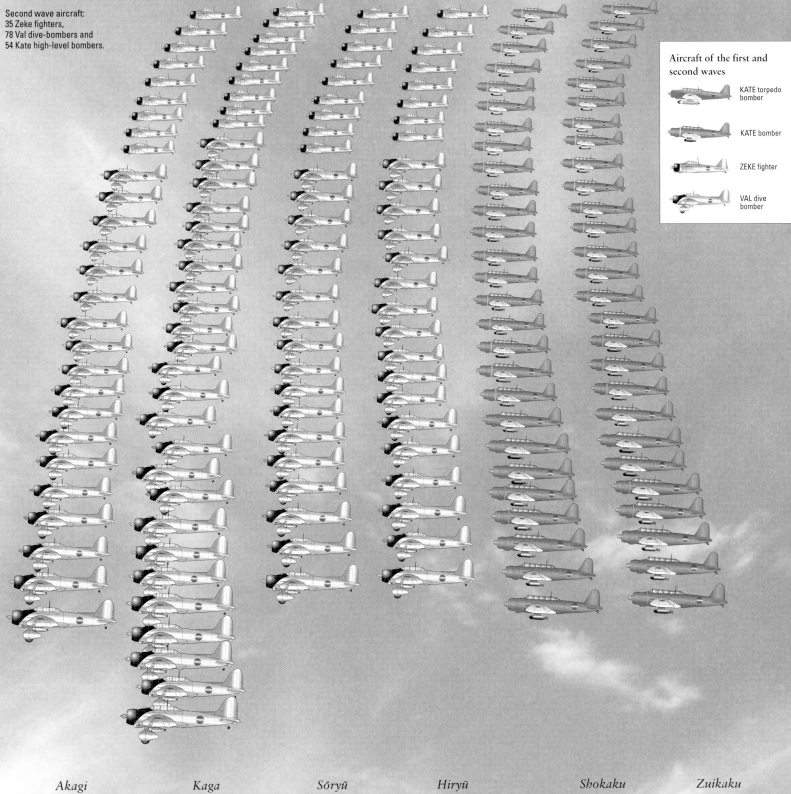

Second wave aircraft:
35 Zeke fighters,
78 Val dive-bombers and
54 Kate high-level bombers.

Aircraft of the first and second waves

KATE torpedo bomber

KATE bomber

ZEKE fighter

VAL dive bomber

Akagi　　　　*Kaga*　　　　*Sōryū*　　　　*Hiryū*　　　　*Shokaku*　　*Zuikaku*

1st Carrier Division　　　　　　　2nd Carrier Division　　　　　　　5th Carrier Division

CLASS OF ITS OWN

One of the most famous pictures of the Second World War: the Mitsubishi A6M2 Type 00 Zeke (or Zero) Model 21 of one of the Imperial Navy's leading airmen, Sakai Saburo, of the 12th Naval Air Group.

attack. Immediately after the raid, with the submarines and carrier force operating in the same area, command of the submarines was to vested in Nagumo: it was anticipated that this arrangement would last three days, after which time control of these submarines would revert to the submarine command. In addition, four submarines, which together formed the First Submarine Group, were ordered to form a picket line to the north of Oahu. These were to hunt down and destroy any American warships seeking either to escape from Oahu or to counter-attack the carrier formation. The four submarines were to form themselves into a picket line stationed about 150 miles north of Oahu, about 50 miles beyond the most southerly point the carriers were to reach.

The third formation consisted of the Second Submarine Group. It consisted of seven units, the I. 1 to I. 7 inclusive. This formation, reputedly, was deployed on a picket line from Oahu to Molokai, across the Kaili Channel. In fact, it seems that the first three submarines were deployed between Kauai and Oahu and the second three between Oahu and Molokai, with the last submarine, which in fact was the command submarine in which the formation commander, Rear Admiral Shigeteru Yamazaki was embarked, deployed to the rear.

The fourth and last formation, the Third Submarine Group, consisted of nine units. These were the I. 8, I. 68, I. 69, I. 70, I. 71, I. 72, I. 73, I. 74 and the I. 75. The I. 8 was a command submarine on which was embarked Rear Admiral Miwa Shigeyoshi. The other eight were cruiser submarines tasked to form a patrol cordon to the south of Oahu, literally a half circle with the I. 72 and I. 73 ordered to scout the Lahaina anchorage. This anchorage had played host to the Pacific Fleet for much of 1940 after it had been moved to the Hawaiian Islands from San Diego, and the Japanese feared that American units might be in the roads and therefore be missed by aircraft striking at Pearl Harbor. The Japanese plan allowed for the two submarines to conduct a reconnaissance of the Lahaina anchorage and, if this proved clear of American ships, to move to positions south-east of Oahu. In the event of major American units being found at the Lahaina anchorage, the Japanese plan provided for the movement of all

submarines eastward, away from Pearl Harbor toward the roadstead, with individual submarines assigned to the three main channels leading to the anchorage. The I. 74 was to be off Niihau on the day of the strike, Niihau having been designated the emergency landing area for Japanese aircraft which incurred such damage that it was unlikely that they could return to their carriers, though as it happens there seems to have been no attempt by I. 74 or any other Japanese submarine to have rescued the one Zeke pilot, from the *Hiryu*, who landed on the island. The I. 8 was deployed well to the south of Oahu.

In addition to these four formations, there were seven more submarines employed as part of the Hawaiian operation. Two of these units, the brand new Type A.1 headquarters/command-submarine I. 10, scouted Suva on 29 November and Pago Pago on 4 December, while the Type B.1 scout-submarine I. 26 conducted reconnaissance of Kiska on 25 November, Dutch Harbor on 27–28 November with her seaplane, and Adak and Kodiak on 30 November. The remaining five submarines, the I. 16, I. 18, I. 20, I. 22 and the I. 24, were responsible for transporting midget submarines to Oahu and then mounting what was in effect the close blockade of the island. With five of his boats detailed to make their way into Pearl Harbor and to use their two torpedoes against units there, the commanding officer of the *Kaigun's* midget submarines, Captain Sasaki Hanku, was embarked in I. 22.

Japanese operational priorities and order of battle for the carrier air groups and submarine formations are easier to set down than the process by which the latter were incorporated into the Hawaiian operational plan. The main force submarines were brought into Yamamoto's proposed order of battle after 29 July when Yamamoto informed the commander of the *Kaigun's* submarine forces, the VIth Fleet, Vice Admiral Shimizu Mitsumi, that certain of his formations and units would be earmarked for the attack on Pearl Harbor. The incorporation of the midget submarines into the plan took place at the end of October 1941, with the result that the five submarines designated as transports had to be taken in hand for refitting. In fact, such was the lateness which surrounded various aspects of submarine readiness that the transports were obliged to proceed to the Hawaiian Islands by taking the shortest possible route between Midway and Johnston. With units under orders to proceed at night on the surface but submerged during hours of daylight, the obvious danger of being discovered by the Americans had to be balanced against what was conceived as operational necessity because, in the last weeks before the attack, the submarines and the midget submarines came to figure increasingly in Japanese calculations.

The initial Combined Staff calculations set no very great store upon submarine operations, but it seems that as a result of Yamamoto's personal insistence submarines were afforded a role in the attack because the submarine was possessed of an operational role and record that carrier aircraft lacked. Clearly, Yamamoto saw the submarine in a belt-and-braces role, but certainly Genda and, it appears, other Combined Fleet staff officers regarded the inclusion of submarines as highly dangerous in terms of compromising the Japanese plan. The basic idea behind the casting of patrol lines around Oahu was that submarines would reach positions roughly 300 miles from Oahu by 3 December and thereafter slowly and surreptitiously close on the island. The basis on which the midget submarines were included was that they would attack after the aircraft and that they would deal with American warships seeking to leave harbour, but as a result of representation from the personnel who would carry out the attack, this was changed, with the result that the midget submarines were given permission to attack American warships inside Pearl Harbor at the same time as the air attack. This had to mean that the midget submarines would have to attempt to get inside the harbour defences before the air attacks materialised. It seems that this change was authorised, by Yamamoto, on the basis that the whole operation carried so large an element of chance that a little bit more would not make much difference. Again, this seems incredible. The two-man midget submarines between them carried just ten torpedoes, and exactly what ten torpedoes could achieve that 360 aircraft could not is hard to fathom. Yamamoto's inclusion of the submarines in the attack would almost seem to indicate a

ABOVE The Aichi D3A1 Type 99 Val. The fixed undercarriage of the Val betrayed the influence of the Heinkel organisation, which was secretly advising the Imperial Navy in aviation design in 1936.

LEFT The readying of Aichi D3A1 Type 99 Val dive-bombers on the flight deck of the aircraft carrier *Soryu*: astern, with island to port, is her companion in the 2nd Carrier Division, the *Hiryu*.

lack of confidence in his carrier aircraft, and must cast doubt upon his strategic judgement.

This last observation invites an obvious question: a lack of confidence on Yamamoto's part in his carrier aircraft to do what? The Japanese plan to attack Pearl Harbor has attracted much comment down the years, and much of it critical. Its obvious weakness was not so much its detail but its context: for Japan to initiate a war with the United States was foolhardy in the extreme. Indeed, the American dimension of the Pearl Harbor plan, in the sense of where the Americans fitted into Japanese plans and intentions, is perhaps the most curious aspect of the whole endeavour. The Japanese attacked Pearl Harbor with the aim of buying themselves six months' freedom from American interference and with the intention and hope of exhausting American resources and will, primarily the latter, in a series of battles fought along the perimeter which was to be cast around their conquests. Leaving aside the fact that hope is a poor basis for planning, Yamamoto's celebrated comment about 'running wild' in the Pacific for six months to a year was matched by other Japanese officers who made similar predictions: Nagano stated on 6 September 1941 that the *Kaigun* could hold its own against the Americans for about two years, while the air-minded Inoue Shigeyoshi expressed the view that Japan could sustain herself in a war with the United States for a year.

It was almost as if the upper reaches of the Japanese high command, in seeking to define national security strategy, refused to properly address the problem presented by the United States since they knew she presented difficulty beyond solution: there was never any statement

of what lay beyond the time limit of Japanese success. It is difficult to resist the conclusion that the *Kaigun* devised the Hawaiian operation on a similar basis: once this operation was successfully concluded and the Japanese were thus granted the time in which to ready themselves, any American fleet that attempted to undo the verdict of a Japanese attack on Pearl Harbor would be overwhelmed by defeat in something like the Great All-Out Battle in the western Pacific – even though, paradoxically, by carrying through the attack on Pearl Harbor, the Japanese Navy had condemned the *Zengen Sakusen* to the rubbish tip.

The best that can be said here is that the parts of the Japanese whole do not hold together very well, and in no single matter was this more obvious than in terms of its aim. In seeking war with the United States, and specifically in attacking the US Pacific Fleet at Pearl Harbor, the Japanese high command sought to ensure the nation against American power. But securing the nation against American power had absolutely nothing to do with Pearl Harbor, the US Pacific Fleet and the First Carrier Striking Force and its aircraft, and most certainly had nothing to do with any of this when the best that was anticipated was six months' unchecked larceny in the western Pacific and south-east Asia. If the best that could be hoped for was American paralysis for half a year then, arguably, the best

course of action open to Japan was anything other than a war with the United States, and the case for a move against the British and Dutch possessions in south-east Asia therefore would seem overwhelming, not least because President Roosevelt would never have been able to take the United States into a war in the Pacific over Singapore and Batavia. That possibility, while favoured by Nagano, had been destroyed by Yamamoto's insistence that war begin with an attack on the US Pacific Fleet.

As it was, the real point about the Pearl Harbor attack is worth repeating: it marked the point when two wars – a German war primarily fought in Europe, the Mediterranean and eastern North Atlantic and a Japanese war primarily fought in eastern Asia – came together in one global conflict. The point of rationalisation behind so much of Japanese policy after 1931 was the urge for autarky and self-sufficiency, to end national dependence on the United States in terms of trade and to overturn a power structure in the Far East that in many ways still reflected a pre-1914 world. In seeking to end such a state of affairs with the attack on Peal Harbor, Japan adopted a formula of action that, if it had been successful, would have made her even more dependent on Nazi Germany, a virulently racist tyranny which, in the final analysis, was never going to be of practical assistance in the conduct of a war against the United States and which, even if it achieved success, would never have been prepared to let Japan keep her conquests. This was the hidden meaning of the Hawaiian operation, and it was so well hidden that no one in the Japanese high command recognised it. They were simply not prepared to give voice to such a conclusion, for to do so would have been tantamount to both a condemnation of those who had been responsible for the conduct of the nation's affairs for the past decade and a recognition of national failure since September 1931.

ABOVE **The take-off of a Nakajima B5N1 Type 97 Kate,** piloted by PO2c Okimura Satpru, from the *Shokaku*: the lead aircraft, piloted by Lt. Ichihara Tatsuo, can be seen in the middle distance.

RIGHT **Pearl Harbor, as seen on** Thursday 30 October 1941. In the centre is Ford Island, with Pearl City on the headland to the right and the navy base, complete with its fuel depots, and Hickam Field to the left.

RIGHT For public consumption. Japanese aircraft about to take off from a carrier, allegedly the attack on Pearl Harbor. From a painting by Shori Arai, who joined the *Akagi* at Rabaul in January 1942.

Before the First Carrier Striking Force conducted the last of its exercises off Kyushu in mid-November and its units sailed for Hitokappu Bay, Etorofu Island, for their final briefings and preparations, the first of the submarines detailed to be on station off the Hawaiian Islands sailed from the Yokosuka naval base. The carrier formation itself sailed at 0600 on 26 November, and in departing from the Kuriles towards what the American military had long regarded as the 'Vacant Sea' of the North Pacific, it was the last of the various formations detailed for the Hawaiian operation to set out. The First Carrier Striking Force comprised six fleet carriers, two battleships, two heavy cruisers, one light cruiser and nine destroyers. In company with it were two supply forma-tions, one with four oilers and the other with three: the two destroyers that were not members of the *Kagero* or later classes, the *Arare* and *Kasumi*, were detailed as single escorts to these two supply groups. The three submarines that were supposed to provide some form of reconnais-sance capability for the carrier force were, and remained, in close attendance because of communications problems. This force was the largest single formation committed to an operation that in total involved twenty warships, seven oilers, 30 submarines and five midget submarines, and it was remarkable in a number of ways.

First, the Pearl Harbor operation was the most impor-tant single undertaking in a synchronised effort that extended across 112° of longitude and which over the

A DATE WHICH WIL

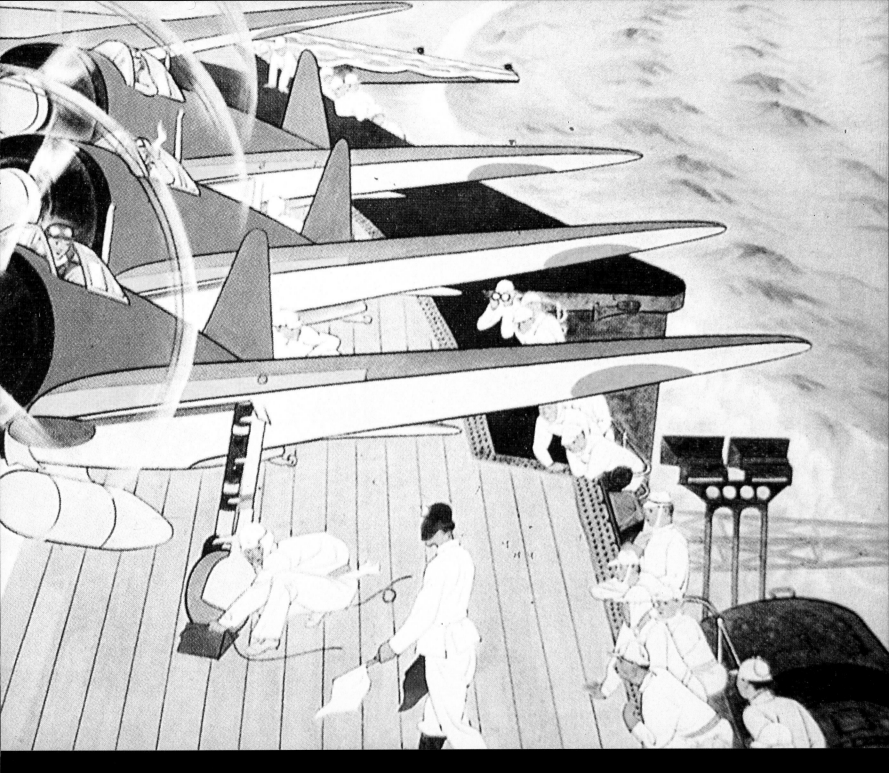

LIVE IN INFAMY

next three months reached across 30° of latitude. In terms of distance and time, and subsequently the economy of effort as formations were used against successive objectives, the overall Japanese offensive that opened the Pacific war probably has no equal. Second, and seldom acknowledged, the attack on Pearl Harbor proved to be the only time when the First Carrier Striking Force operated with its full front-line strength of six fleet carriers. Third, in terms of carrier numbers, the First Carrier Striking Force, as constituted on this one occasion, never had an equal during the Second World War. This operation in 1941

BELOW The task force flagship *Akagi.* with Zeke fighters being readied for take-off.

represented an unprecedented effort, and in its concentration of available force probably represented the most powerful single naval effort of the Second World War relative to its own time. Fourth, with five of every eight of Japan's submarines committed to this operation, this was perhaps the greatest single submarine effort of the Second World War. Fifth, these 57 warships, oilers and submarines conducted an operation which marked the start of a war that none were to survive. Every single warship, oiler and submarine used in this operation was to be lost in the course of the Pacific war. In initiating this conflict the Japanese high command fundamentally erred in its assess-

ment of its American enemy and never understood the nature of the war it initiated in December 1941.

In sailing from Hitokappu Bay on 26 November the First Carrier Striking Force found itself working to a strict timetable. The most immediate consideration was the need to conduct the attack against an unprepared enemy. This meant that the attack was to be conducted on a Sunday, by custom the day of the week when an American fleet and its ships could be expected to be at their least degree of readiness. With the storms of the North Pacific of January and February precluding an approach to the Hawaiian Islands being staged in the winter months, the need for a

ABOVE *Zuikaku's* fighter pilots in a group potrait on 6 December.

teen days to reach its flying-off position 200 miles to the north of Oahu. The slowness of this advance was dictated by the frequency of refuelling and the maintenance of a very low cruising speed of fourteen knots. The destroyer *Akigumo*, which took on fuel no fewer than eighteen times in the one-month round trip from Saiki Bay, eastern Kyushu, to Hiroshima via the Kuriles and the Hawaiian Islands, was refuelled seven times between 26 November and 7 December, and on occasions speeds were as low as nine knots during such operations. Though on 29 November the carrier *Zuikaku* took on 250 tons of fuel in one single replenishment and on 2 December the battleships *Hiei* and *Kirishima* took on 354 tons and 469 tons respectively, the large units of the force were spared having to refuel every other day. The problems presented by the limited range of the carriers *Akagi*, *Hiryu* and *Soryu* were resolved by pumping out ballast and trimming tanks and filling them with oil, and even carrying drummed and canned oil within ships. The *Akagi* carried 1,400 tons of extra fuel in this fashion, the *Hiryu* and *Soryu* that much between them, while the two heavy cruisers *Chikuma* and *Tone* carried 580 tons above their normal load. Such arrangements solved the problem of giving the carriers the range to return to home waters after the raid on Pearl Harbor. The light cruiser *Abukuma* and the destroyers, however, could not be overloaded because their smallness precluded any arrangement that might affect their stability, hence the frequency with which they were refuelled as the force sailed towards Oahu.

During this advance across the northern Pacific, the air groups worked through their respective parts of the plan of attack, with certain changes being worked into the plan as a result of representations made at various meetings either in Hitokappu Bay or at sea. The most important of these changes were the postponement of the attack from dawn, around 0630, until about 0800 on 7 December, and the closing of the gap between the first and second strikes. The first was suggested because of the lack of experience of the Fifth Carrier Division's aircrew in night operations, the change of some 90 minutes meaning that take-off would be before sunrise but as the sky lightened. The second was prompted by the

full moon, for navigational reasons, meant that the attack had to be conducted on Sunday 7 December. This date was chosen in the first week of October, although in fact there was a complementary Army as distinct from Navy calculation in support of a naval deadline of the first Sunday in December. The campaigns which were to be mounted in south-east Asia had to be conducted before the onset of the monsoon at the end of April, and therefore in autumn 1941, as the end of the rainy season approached, so it became imperative for the Imperial Army to begin operations as soon as possible.

Thus the First Carrier Striking Force was allowed thir-

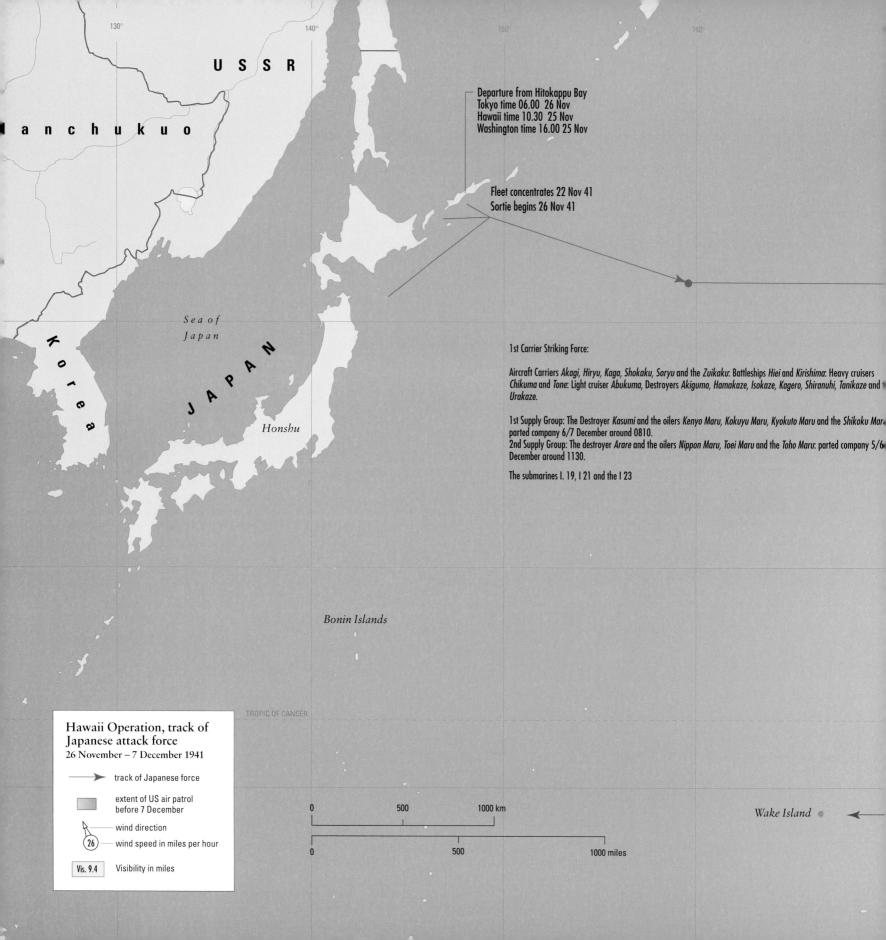

USSR

M a n c h u k u o

Korea

Sea of
Japan

JAPAN

Honshu

Bonin Islands

Departure from Hitokappu Bay
Tokyo time 06.00 26 Nov
Hawaii time 10.30 25 Nov
Washington time 16.00 25 Nov

Fleet concentrates 22 Nov 41

Sortie begins 26 Nov 41

1st Carrier Striking Force:

Aircraft Carriers *Akagi, Hiryu, Kaga, Shokaku, Soryu* and the *Zuikaku*: Battleships *Hiei* and *Kirishima*: Heavy cruisers *Chikuma* and *Tone*: Light cruiser *Abukuma*, Destroyers *Akigumo, Hamakaze, Isokaze, Kagero, Shiranuhi, Tanikaze* and *Urakaze.*

1st Supply Group: The Destroyer *Kasumi* and the oilers *Kenyo Maru, Kokuyu Maru, Kyokuto Maru* and the *Shikoku Maru* parted company 6/7 December around 0810.
2nd Supply Group: The destroyer *Arare* and the oilers *Nippon Maru, Toei Maru* and the *Toho Maru*: parted company 5/6 December around 1130.

The submarines I. 19, I 21 and the I 23

TROPIC OF CANCER

**Hawaii Operation, track of
Japanese attack force**
26 November – 7 December 1941

track of Japanese force

extent of US air patrol
before 7 December

wind direction

(26) wind speed in miles per hour

Vis. 9.4   Visibility in miles

0   500   1000 km

0   500   1000 miles

Wake Island

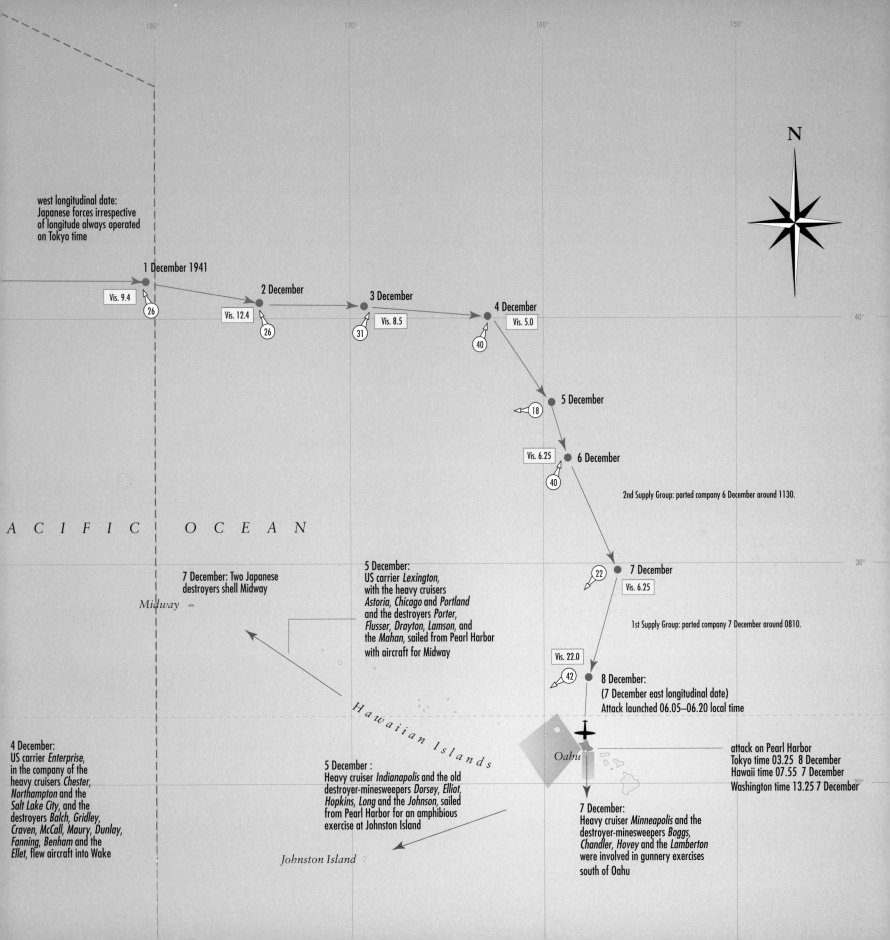

N

west longitudinal date:
Japanese forces irrespective
of longitude always operated
on Tokyo time

1 December 1941

Vis. 9.4

26

2 December

Vis. 12.4

26

3 December

31   Vis. 8.5

4 December

Vis. 5.0

40

5 December

18

Vis. 6.25   6 December

40

2nd Supply Group: parted company 6 December around 1130.

P A C I F I C   O C E A N

7 December: Two Japanese
destroyers shell Midway

Midway

5 December:
US carrier *Lexington*,
with the heavy cruisers
Astoria, *Chicago* and *Portland*
and the destroyers *Porter*,
Flusser, *Drayton*, *Lamson*, and
the *Mahan*, sailed from Pearl Harbor
with aircraft for Midway

22   7 December

Vis. 6.25

1st Supply Group: parted company 7 December around 0810.

Vis. 22.0

42

8 December:
(7 December east longitudinal date)
Attack launched 06.05–06.20 local time

H a w a i i a n   I s l a n d s

Oahu

4 December:
US carrier *Enterprise*,
in the company of the
heavy cruisers *Chester*,
Northampton and the
Salt Lake City, and the
destroyers *Balch*, *Gridley*,
Craven, *McCall*, *Maury*, *Dunlay*,
Fanning, *Benham* and the
Ellet, flew aircraft into Wake

5 December :
Heavy cruiser *Indianapolis* and the old
destroyer-minesweepers *Dorsey*, *Elliot*,
Hopkins, *Long* and the *Johnson*, sailed
from Pearl Harbor for an amphibious
exercise at Johnston Island

7 December:
Heavy cruiser *Minneapolis* and the
destroyer-minesweepers *Boggs*,
Chandler, *Hovey* and the *Lamberton*
were involved in gunnery exercises
south of Oahu

attack on Pearl Harbor
Tokyo time 03.25 8 December
Hawaii time 07.55 7 December
Washington time 13.25 7 December

Johnston Island

180°   170°   160°   150°

40°

30°

20°

realisation that the Japanese dare not allow the Americans time to ready themselves to meet the second strike force. In the event, while the first change was implemented, the second proved impossible: the slowness of the *Kaga*'s elevators meant that the formations for the second strike could not be brought up on deck quickly enough to permit a mere 30 minutes to elapse between the two strikes. A third possible change, however, proved unnecessary. There was the possibility that the Americans used anti-torpedo nets to guard their main units, and it led Genda and Fuchida to think in

December, when it was realised that the carriers would not be in Pearl Harbor next day, was intense. But as the Japanese formation made its way to its flying-off position, it had a more immediate concern – the possibility of its encountering a merchantman, an American warship, reconnaissance seaplane or aircraft. Nagumo, the commander of the First Carrier Striking Force, was under very strict instructions to turn for home in the event of the continuing negotiations in Washington producing an agreement, very unlikely though this seemed to be. In effect, Tokyo was prepared to delay its final decision for

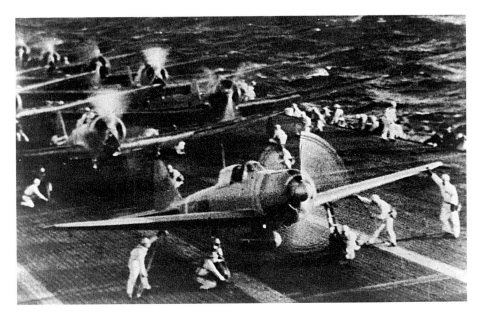

FAR LEFT **A Kate from the** *Zuikaku* leaving Pearl Harbor: in Battleship Row can be seen the *California*, the upturned hull of the *Oklahoma* and the burning *Arizona*. The *Neosho* is entering the base.

LEFT Zeke fighters on the flight deck, awaiting the order to take off.

terms of selecting certain pilots for the task of crashing their aircraft into these nets in order to allow the torpedoes to get to their targets. But the report, received by the carrier force less than four hours before it flew off its strike aircraft, that the American battleships were not afforded protective nets meant that recourse to such a desperate expedient was unnecessary.

A more important concern arose from up-to-date intelligence summaries secured by Tokyo from consular staff at Hawaii, specifically the possibility that the American carriers might be absent from Pearl Harbor. This was a matter on which the Japanese could have no guarantees, and the disappointment registered on 6

war until 1 December, but this schedule left Nagumo's command with obvious difficulties.

The *Kaigun* had sought to ensure itself against the carrier formation being compromised either during its journey across the northern Pacific or being found by long-range American reconnaissance as its approached Oahu by having the proposed course of the carrier force sailed by the liner *Taiyo Maru*, which left Yokohama on 22 October and arrived at Honolulu on 1 November. The *Taiyo Maru* encountered no other ship of any description or nationality during her voyage and was able to report sea conditions which would permit refuelling. While all concerned could take encouragement from the reports –

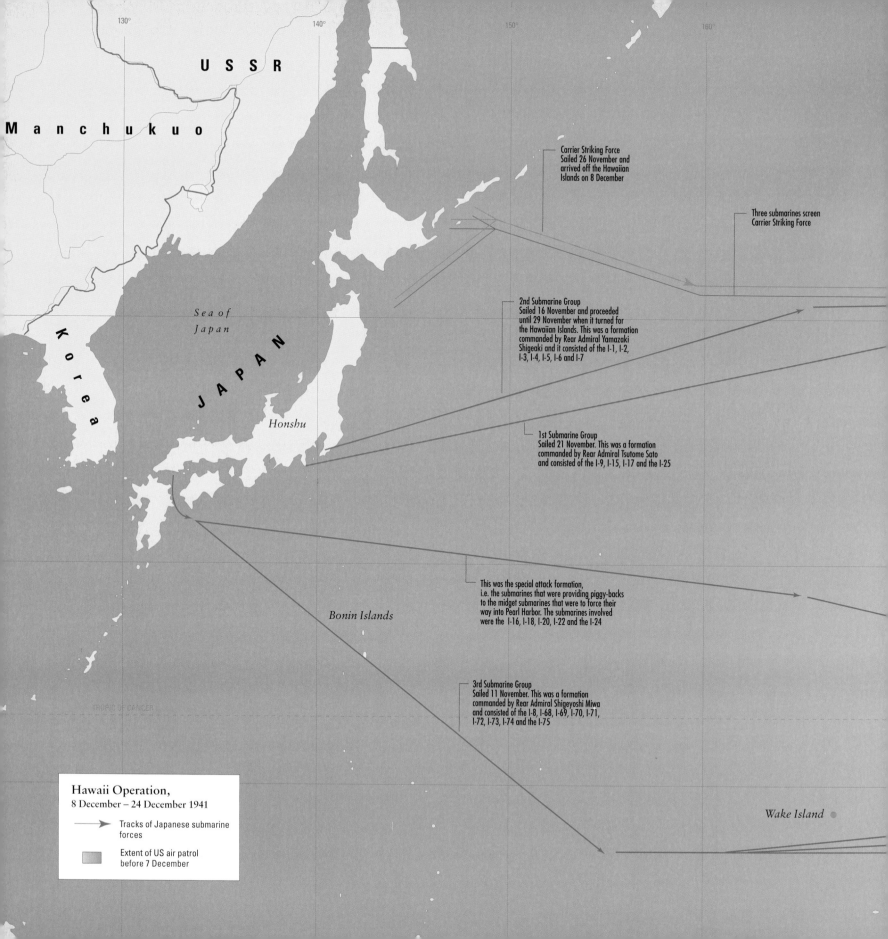

USSR

Manchukuo

Korea

Sea of
Japan

JAPAN

Honshu

Bonin Islands

TROPIC OF CANCER

Wake Island

Carrier Striking Force
Sailed 26 November and
arrived off the Hawaiian
Islands on 8 December

Three submarines screen
Carrier Striking Force

2nd Submarine Group
Sailed 16 November and proceeded
until 29 November when it turned for
the Hawaiian Islands. This was a formation
commanded by Rear Admiral Yamazaki
Shigeaki and it consisted of the I-1, I-2,
I-3, I-4, I-5, I-6 and I-7

1st Submarine Group
Sailed 21 November. This was a formation
commanded by Rear Admiral Tsutome Sato
and consisted of the I-9, I-15, I-17 and the I-25

This was the special attack formation,
i.e. the submarines that were providing piggy-backs
to the midget submarines that were to force their
way into Pearl Harbor. The submarines involved
were the I-16, I-18, I-20, I-22 and the I-24

3rd Submarine Group
Sailed 11 November. This was a formation
commanded by Rear Admiral Shigeyoshi Miwa
and consisted of the I-8, I-68, I-69, I-70, I-71,
I-72, I-73, I-74 and the I-75

Hawaii Operation,
8 December – 24 December 1941

Tracks of Japanese submarine
forces

Extent of US air patrol
before 7 December

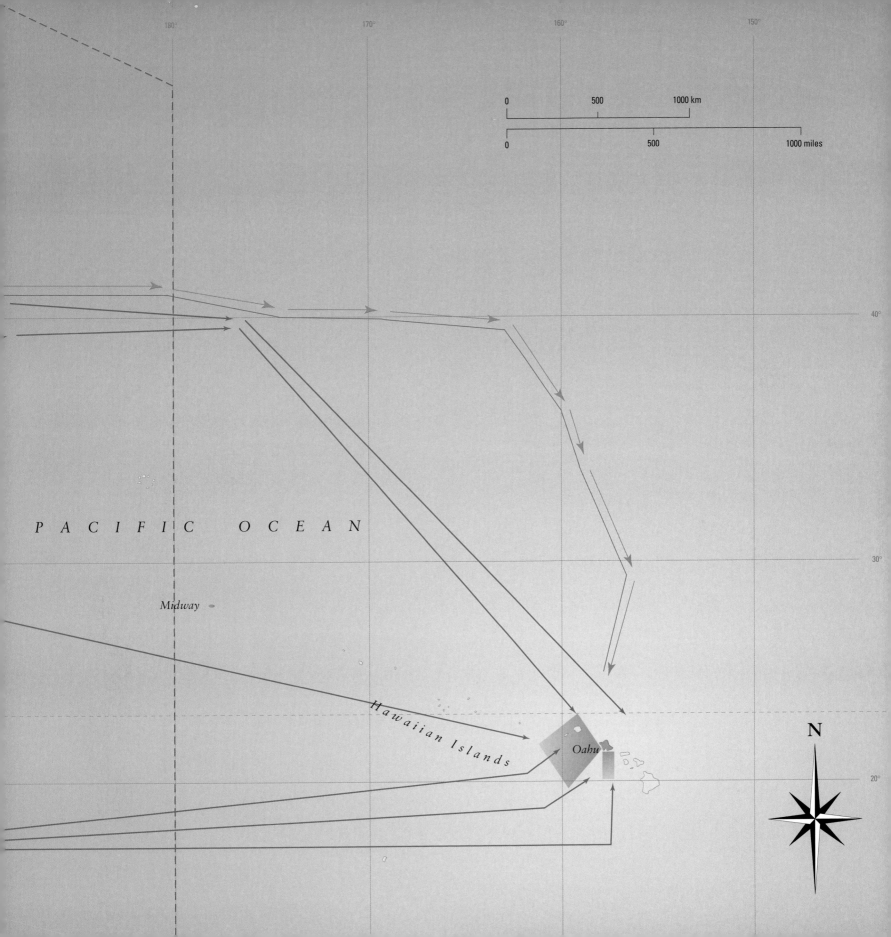

PACIFIC OCEAN

Midway

Hawaiian Islands

Oahu

N

specifically those from the consular staff at Honolulu – which the *Taiyo Maru* brought back with her from Oahu, the fact remained that if the carrier formation's approach was compromised after 1 December, Japan and her Navy faced the all but impossible task of explaining on what business such a force was engaged. As it was, the intelligence reports, which credited the Americans with some 550 aircraft and seaplanes on Oahu, indicated that American air reconnaissance around Oahu was somewhat uneven. It was reported to be good to the south, more or less adequate to the west in the general direction of Midway and beyond, but poor to the north of the Hawaiian Islands. This assessment proved correct and the carrier formation escaped detection, but during the advance to contact there was a realisation that it might be obliged to fight its way to its targets.

Yamamoto had in fact spoken of just this eventuality when he addressed the main personnel from the carrier force on 17 November before the various units sailed for Hitokappu Bay, and in retrospect his comments seem quite extraordinary. It may be that Yamamoto was either simply warning of what might happen or seeking to guard against complacency, but what he said simply does not accord with the rationale and detail of the plan of attack. The *sine qua non* of the Japanese plan was surprise, and it is very difficult to understand the logic underpinning the plan if that surprise were to be lost. But Yamamoto was not alone in this respect. After passing one midget submarine unit leaving for Pearl Harbor, Ugaki

ABOVE **The heavy seas encountered by the 1st Carrier Striking Force during the approach to Pearl Harbor:** in fact on the day of the attack the Japanese force encountered its most difficult conditions to date, and it ran into even worse seas during its return to the home islands.

BELOW **The I. 26 was a Type B.1 scout-submarine. She was not involved in the attack on Pearl Harbor but conducted a reconnaissance of Kiska on 25 November, Dutch Harbor on 27-28 November with her seaplane, and of Adak and Kodiak on 30 November.**

RIGHT **The commemoration to the nine submariners lost at Pearl Harbor on 7 December 1941.They are, in a circle from the left, PO2c Katayama Yoshio I.20; PO1c Sasaki Naokichi I.22; PO1c Yokoyama Shigenori I.18; Ensign Yokoyama Masaharu I.16; Lt. Iwasa Naoji I.22; Ensign Furino Shigemi I.18; Ensign Hiroo Akira I.20; PO2c Ueda Tei I.16; and PO2c Inagaki Kiyoshi I.24.All received posthumous double promotion.Very deliberately omitted, obviously, was Ensign Sakamaki Kazuo, who survived to be taken prisoner. Interestingly, representation of the attack takes the form of the air attack on Ford Island.**

RIGHT **The type 6A submarine I–68: the mainstay class of submarine in Japanese service.**

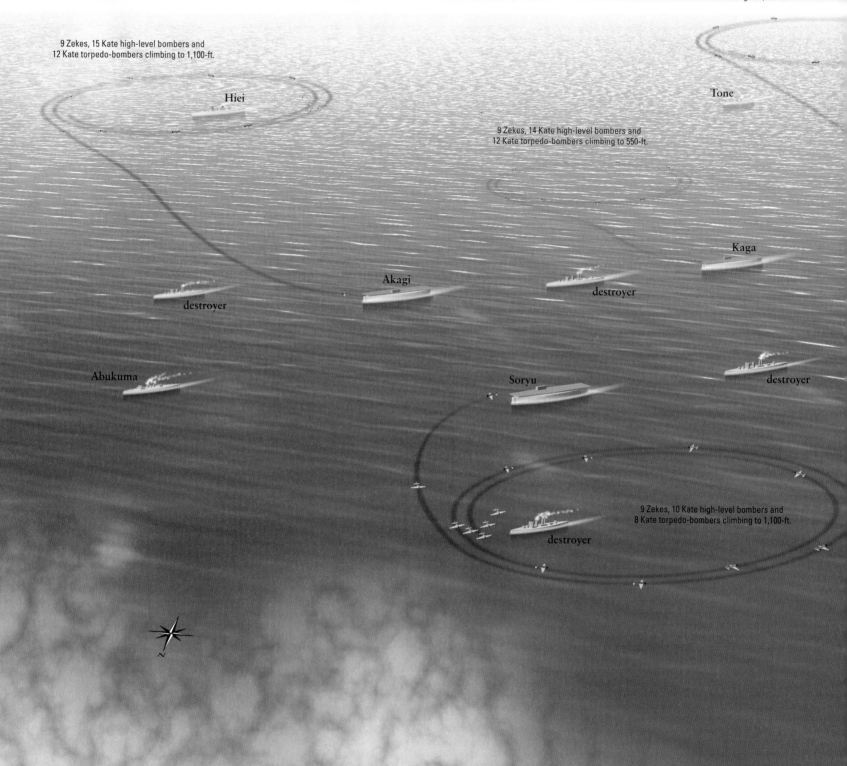

6 Zekes and 25 Val dive-bombers
climbing to 1,100-ft.

9 Zekes, 15 Kate high-level bombers and
12 Kate torpedo-bombers climbing to 1,100-ft.

Hiei

Tone

9 Zekes, 14 Kate high-level bombers and
12 Kate torpedo-bombers climbing to 550-ft.

Kaga

Akagi

destroyer

destroyer

Abukuma

Soryu

destroyer

destroyer

9 Zekes, 10 Kate high-level bombers and
8 Kate torpedo-bombers climbing to 1,100-ft.

Zuikaku

destroyer

destroyer

Shokaku

Hiryu

destroyer

destroyer

6 Zekes and 26 Val dive-bombers
climbing to 1,100-ft.

Chikuma

6 Zekes, 10 Kate high-level bombers and
8 Kate torpedo-bombers climbing to 550-ft.

Kirishima

Detachment of Zekes serving as combat air patrol
as aircraft of the attack formations
flew off their carriers.

LEFT The advance to Oahu: the view from the *Akagi* with the *Kaga* and *Zuikaku* astern.

wrote that 'how much damage they will be able to inflict is not the point' and went on to state with his usual extravagance in matters Japanese that the submariners' 'firm determination not to return alive' pointed to 'the spirit of *kesshitai*' (self-sacrifice) being alive and well. The observations are as surprising as Yamamoto's, given that the purpose of the midget submarines was clearly to inflict loss or damage on the enemy. Whatever Ugaki may have thought, the Pearl Harbor operation was not being staged merely in order to provide certain individuals with the opportunity for self-immolation and martyrdom.

As it made its way to the north of Oahu, the First Carrier Striking Force encountered virtually every possible sea condition and climate change. It experienced violent snow flurries off the Kuriles, then alternating storms, calms and fog before it gained the warmth of sub-tropical waters, although it was paradoxically to meet the strongest winds and worst conditions of its voyage on the morning of the attack itself. In many ways, the weather conditions encountered *en route* to the target reflected events in Washington, specifically the exchanges between Japanese representatives and President Franklin D. Roosevelt and Secretary of State Cordell Hull.

The negotiations in Washington represented the final stage of a process of alienation between Japan and the United States which had been long in the making. At issue was the re-ordering of the international system, specifically in eastern Asia but, by virtue of Japan's association with Germany and Italy, across the world. The immediate conflict of interest between the two countries arose from the economic embargo that the United States had placed on Japan and the latter's occupation of southern Indo-China and subsequent threat to British and Dutch possessions in south-east Asia. The First Carrier Striking Force sailed from Hitokappu Bay one day before the infamous meeting, on 27 November, between Ambassador Nomura, special envoy Kusuru Saburo and Secretary Hull at which Tokyo's final proposals for resolving immediate American–Japanese difficulties were presented. By virtue of the fact that American military intelligence had broken the Japanese diplomatic code, the American high command was well aware of the contents of these proposals, while the tone of Tokyo's despatch was responsible for Washington's issuing of the famous war-warning on 27 November. This message, which indicated that for all intents and purposes negotiations were all but at an end, ordered various American commands, Oahu and the Philippines included, to be especially vigilant, to undertake reconnaissance and other defensive measures, but to avoid firing the first shot. Washington was very specific that if war was to come, then Japan had to be seen to be the aggressor, although by this time the American high command had been made aware of various Japanese moves which over the next few days were to drag American attention to south-east Asia, and away from the Hawaiian Islands and Pearl Harbor.

The various diplomatic messages which were recovered by American intelligence did not give advance warning of the outbreak of hostilities, and most certainly made no reference to an attack on Pearl Harbor. However, certain Japanese precautions, implemented to enhance signals security, inadvertently provided warning of intent. The switching of Japanese codes on 1 December, the second such change in a month when the routine change was six-monthly, was tantamount to a warning that certain – though unspecified – military operations were afoot. Two other measures – the retransmission of signals over many days and the order to various overseas embassies and consulates to destroy codes, ciphers and machines – reinforced this point. American signals intelligence saw through the first attempt at concealment, while the deciphering of the relevant signals and the realisation that Tokyo was abandoning its overseas representatives clearly pointed to the imminence of war: moreover, the fact that fewer 'real' signals were being sent as the days slipped by helped concentrate American efforts on those which were more immediately relevant.

Nonetheless, three factors served to confound the Americans. The first was that the fragmentation of their intelligence effort, between Army and Navy and between Washington and Pearl Harbor, ensured that no obvious pattern emerged and that the individual signals which were recovered did not necessarily receive proper attention and prompt analysis and dissemination. The second, more importantly, was that the idea war would begin with a strike against the Pacific Fleet at Pearl Harbor was simply beyond the imagination of the American high command. Various individuals have been credited with seeing through Japanese intentions while others, along with the Farthing and Martin-Bellinger Reports, anticipated certain aspects of Japan's opening moves. Yet the false sense of security which persisted at Pearl Harbor merely reflected the wider belief that either the Japanese did not have the capability to mount an attack on Pearl Harbor or, even if they had the ability, they would not do so. Indeed, as 7 December drew closer and the extent of Japanese preparations in south-east Asia became increasingly clear, attention turned away from Pearl Harbor. It seemed frankly inconceivable that the Japanese would instigate a move against a base which was 4,000 miles from their home islands, and still less do so in conjunction with a number of offensives staged across the 6,000 miles of ocean from Hawaii to south-east Asia.

The third factor was that on Oahu itself there were insufficient reconnaissance aircraft to cover the approaches to the island properly. There appear to have been about 360 army, marine corps and navy aircraft, of which 139 army and 157 marine and navy aircraft were reputedly operational, front-line units. The Army formations, constituted as the Hawaiian Air Force with the 18th Bombardment Wing at Hickam Field and the 14th Pursuit Wing at Wheeler Field, had patrol aircraft at Bellows Field and one fighter squadron at Haleiwa airfield. The Navy, which had responsibility for long-range reconnaissance, possessed just 69 PBY-3 and PBY-5 Catalinas. All but fifteen of these aircraft had arrived in the previous six weeks and some doubtless needed to be shaken down and tested. Such numbers permitted proper reconnaissance to the south and, with Midway and Wake making their contribution, to the west, but no reconnaissance could be mounted to the north and north-west. In a very obvious sense, lack of aircraft numbers and a failure to perceive the threat fed off one another. There were not enough aircraft to conduct all-round reconnaissance, so no effort was staged in the area where no enemy was expected to be, and the area from which no threat was expected to emerge was not subjected to routine reconnaissance.

1. Tender WHITNEY and Destroyers TUCKER, CONYNGHAM, REID, CASE & SELFRIDGE
2. Destroyer BLUE
3. Light Cruiser PHOENIX
4. Destroyers AYLWIN, FARRAGUT, DALE & MONAGHAN
5. Destroyers PATTERSON, RALPH TALBOT & HENLEY
6. Tender DOBBIN and Destroyers WORDEN, HULL, DEWEY, PHELPS & MACDONOUGH
7. Hospital Vessel SOLACE
8. Destroyer ALLEN
9. Destroyer CHEW
10. Destroyer-minesweepers GAMBLE & MONTGOMERY and light-minelayer RAMSAY
11. Destroyer-minesweepers TREVER, BREESE, ZANE, PERRY & WASMUTH
12. Repair Vessel MEDUSA
13. Seaplane Tender CURTISS
14. Light Cruiser DETROIT
15. Light Cruiser RALEIGH
16. Target Battleship UTAH
17. Seaplane Tender TANGIER
18. Battleship NEVADA
19. Battleship ARIZONA
20. Repair Vessel VESTAL
21. Battleship TENNESSEE
22. Battleship WEST VIRGINIA
23. Battleship MARYLAND
24. Battleship OKLAHOMA
25. Oiler NEOSHO
26. Battleship CALIFORNIA
27. Seaplane Tender AVOCET
28. Destroyer SHAW
29. Destroyer DOWNES
30. Destroyer CASSIN
31. Battleship PENNSYLVANIA
32. Submarine CACHALOT
33. Minelayer OGLALA
34. Light Cruiser HELENA
35. Auxilliary Vessel ARGONNE
36. Gunboat SACRAMENTO
37. Destroyer JARVIS
38. Destroyer MUGFORD
39. Seaplane Tender SWAN
40. Repair Vessel RIGAL
41. Oiler RAMAPO
42. Heavy Cruiser NEW ORLEANS
43. Destroyer CUMMINGS and light-minelayers PREBLE & TRACY
44. Heavy Cruiser SAN FRANCISCO
45. Destroyer-minesweeper GREBE, Destroyer SCHLEY and light-minelayers PRUITT & SICARD
46. Light Cruiser HONOLULU
47. Light Cruiser ST. LOUIS
48. Destroyer BAGLEY
49. Submarines NARWHAL, DOLPHIN & TAUTOG and Tenders THORNTON & HULBERT
50. Submarine Tender PELIAS
51. Auxilliary Vessel SUMNER
52. Auxilliary Vessel CASTOR

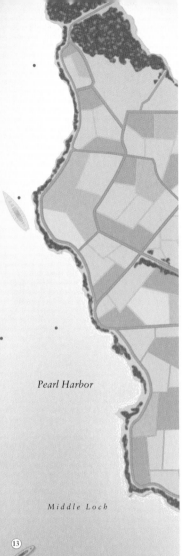

Pearl Harbor

Middle Loch

As the First Carrier Striking Force crossed the International Date Line and then moved south towards its flying-off position some 200 miles north of Oahu, the American naval and military commands in the Hawaiian Islands were concerned primarily with two immediate priorities: the reinforcement of the outposts at Midway and Wake and the protection of installations and aircraft against sabotage rather than direct attack. It was the first of these priorities which helped ensure that the Pacific Fleet's carriers were absent from Pearl Harbor on 7 December.

Therefore one American reconnaissance squadron flew to Wake from Midway on 1 December while a replacement unit was flown to Midway from Pearl Harbor via Johnston Island. Aircraft ferried by the carrier *Enterprise* were flown into Wake on 4 December. The *Enterprise* was accompanied by three heavy cruisers and nine destroyers. The *Lexington* sailed from Pearl Harbor on 5 December with aircraft for Midway. With her were three heavy cruisers and five destroyers. On the same day a third task force, consisting of the heavy cruiser *Indianapolis* and five old destroyer-minesweepers sailed from Pearl Harbor for an amphibious exercise at Johnston Island. The heavy cruiser *Minneapolis* and four destroyer-minesweepers were involved in gunnery exercises just to the south of Oahu, and these were to keep them clear of Pearl Harbor on 7 December. Assigned escort duties were the heavy cruiser *Pensacola*, which was off the Phoenix Islands en route to Manila in the company of one tender and seven transports and freighters, and the heavy cruiser *Louisville* which, in the company of two army transports returning from Manila, was between Santa Cruz and the Ellice Islands. With two submarines stationed off Wake, two off Midway, one destroyer and one submarine south of Oahu, the Americans also had a further three submarines at sea. Thus, discounting the carrier *Saratoga*, which was at Puget Sound navy yard undergoing repairs, and the battleship *Colorado*, two light cruisers, nine destroyers and fifteen submarines which were on or off the west coast, a total of 44 units from the Pacific Fleet – more than one third of its fighting ships and all of its carriers – were not at Pearl Harbor on the last day of peace.

Gathered at the base were the battleships *Arizona*, *California*, *Maryland*, *Nevada*, *Oklahoma*, *Pennsylvania* (in dry dock), *Tennessee* and the *West Virginia*. In total, there was a minimum of 82 warships (eight battleships, two heavy and six light cruisers, 30 destroyers, one gunboat, five submarines, five minelayers and thirteen minesweepers and twelve headquarters ships and tenders) and sixteen auxiliaries at Pearl Harbor. In addition, there was in harbour the turn-of-century, 3,950-ton museum piece *Baltimore*, which had been laid down as a cruiser in 1887 and, as a minelayer, had been decommissioned in 1922, while the stores ship *Antares*, after a round trip to Palmyra and Canton, entered harbour soon after dawn on the morning of 7 December. In so doing, the *Antares* brought about one of two incidents that could, and some would assert should, have compromised the Japanese plan of attack by aircraft of the First Carrier Striking Force.

The First Carrier Striking Force, with all its ships darkened, was some 940 miles to the north of Midway when it received the order from Tokyo that war would begin at midnight 7–8 December. As it came south, it received warnings from Tokyo of the presence of American submarines and, more accurately, reports of the American ships in Pearl Harbor. It received such reports on 3 and 4 December and two on 7 December providing situation reports for 28 and 29 November and 4 and 6 December respectively, and it received another report on 5 December indicating that American air patrols from Oahu were not all that they might have been. On 5 December the formation refuelled from the *Toho Maru*, *Toei Maru* and *Nippon Maru*, the *Hiryu* and *Soryu* being afforded priority. Once refuelling was completed around 1130, the three oilers of the Second Supply Group, in the company of the destroyer *Arare*, turned away in order to make for a designated point where they would rendezvous with the carrier force during the return to the home islands. On the following day the four oilers of the First Supply Group refuelled every unit in the carrier force before they, too, parted company at 0810. They were escorted by the destroyer *Kasumi* and made for a designated point where they would rendezvous with the carrier

1. 15 Kate high-level bombers from the *Akagi*, the first of 49 bombers to attack the four ships successively.

2. Kate torpedo bombers from the *Soryu*.

3. Kate torpedo bombers from the *Hiryu*.

4. Lead Kate torpedo bombers from the *Akagi* and *Kaga*.

5. Follow-up Kate bombers from the *Soryu* and *Hiryu*.

OAHU AND THE PARENT SUBMARINE

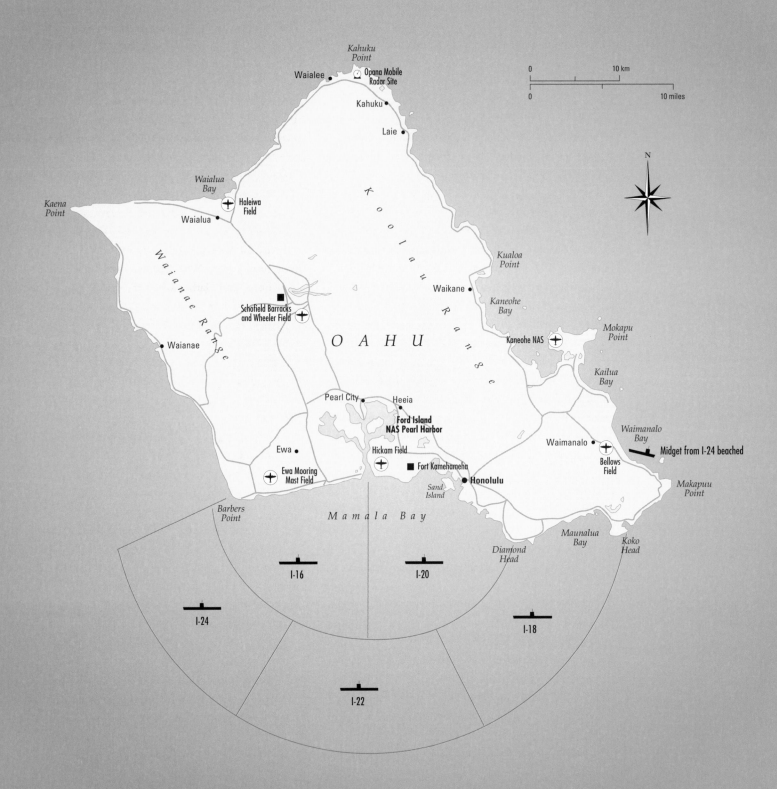

Kahuku Point

Waialee • ⊙ Opana Mobile Radar Site

Kahuku •

Laie •

Koolau Range

Kaena Point

Waialua Bay

Waialua • ✈ Haleiwa Field

Waianae Range

■ Schofield Barracks and Wheeler Field ✈

OAHU

Waianae •

Kualoa Point

Waikane •

Kaneohe Bay

Mokapu Point

Kaneohe NAS ✈

Kailua Bay

Pearl City • • Heeia

Ford Island
NAS Pearl Harbor

Ewa •

Ewa Mooring ✈ Mast Field

Hickam Field ✈

■ Fort Kamehameha

Sand Island

● **Honolulu**

Waimanalo •

Bellows ✈ Field

Waimanalo Bay

⊥ Midget from I-24 beached

Makapuu Point

Barbers Point

Mamala Bay

Diamond Head

Maunalua Bay

Koko Head

⊥ I-16

⊥ I-20

⊥ I-24

⊥ I-18

⊥ I-22

0 — 10 km
0 — 10 miles

N

force on the day after the attack. Once the carrier formation dropped its oilers, speed was increased to 24 knots and the flag signal which Admiral Togo Heihachiro had hoisted prior to the first exchanges in the Battle of Tsu-shima in 1905 was broken out on the *Akagi*. The signal read: 'The rise and fall of the Empire depends upon this battle: everyone will do his duty with utmost effort.'

As the last hours of peace and daylight gave way to night, the carrier force approached its flying-off position in the sure knowledge that its advance was unknown to and unsuspected by the Americans: the fact the local radio station stayed on air through the night gave ample evidence that Oahu, the Pearl Harbor base and the Pacific Fleet had no inkling of what awaited them in the morning. The Japanese also knew by this stage that no carriers were in Pearl Harbor and, as a result of submarine reconnaissance reports, that no units were gathered either in the Lahaina anchorage or off Niihau.

At or just after midnight on 7 December 1941, the first of the five midget submarines was released by its mother craft, the I. 16, some seven miles from the entrance to the Pearl Harbor naval base. Over the next three hours the remaining four boats were similarly released and began to make their separate ways towards the gate and nets at the harbour entrance. At 0342 the minesweepers *Condor* and *Crossbill* were patrolling to the south of the gate when the wake of a periscope was sighted by two members of the *Condor*'s crew. The sighting was reported at 0357 to the duty destroyer *Ward*, which came into the area but could not establish contact with a submarine. The *Ward* was stood down at 0435, and at 0458 the *Condor* and *Crossbill* were admitted to the base after the gate was opened. For some reason, the gate was not closed after the minesweepers and remained open until 0840. Neither the *Ward* nor the local naval radio station at Bishop's Point, which had monitored the conversation between the *Condor* and *Ward*, reported the incident to higher authority. This was not entirely surprising as there had been numerous false alarms in recent months, and with the *Ward* unable to confirm the *Condor*'s sighting, there was really little point in making a report.

At 0630, however, as the *Antares* awaited a pilot to guide her into the base, she sighted what appeared to be a conning tower of a submarine at a range of about a mile. The *Ward*, summoned to the scene, duly sighted the submarine at 0637 and hit her with her second 4-inch round on the waterline at the juncture of conning tower and hull. The midget submarine appeared to slow and sink, and was then caught under the stern of the *Ward* and destroyed by a full-pattern depth-charge attack at 0653. A patrolling Catalina, after initially thinking that the submarine was American, joined the attack with bombs and claimed the sinking for itself. This time, reports to higher authority were made, at about 0720. The American fleet commander, Admiral Husband E. Kimmel, was alerted some twenty minutes later, and the relevant staff officers sought confirmation while they waited for him to arrive at his headquarters. With Japanese carrier aircraft about an hour from Pearl Harbor when the midget submarine was apparently sunk, it was too late to clear harbour, but perhaps there remained time enough to have the units of the Pacific Fleet brought to General Quarters. As it was, not merely was no attempt made to warn the Fleet but the army command on Oahu, and hence its airfields and air formations, was not informed that apparently the Navy had sunk a submarine, nationality unknown, which had been attempting to enter the naval base: the only decision that was made was for the destroyer *Monaghan* to get under way and support the *Ward* at 0751.

If failure this was on the part of the naval command on Oahu, then it was a failure which was mitigated by various factors. The number of false alarms in recent months obviously lessened the impact of this particular episode, and there was perhaps no reason why reports of the sinking of an unknown submarine should have triggered the alerting of the entire army and navy commands on Oahu to the imminence of a general air attack: the idea that somehow or another defences could have been prepared on the basis of this one unconfirmed report must be resisted.

In any event, the approach of Japanese carrier aircraft was duly detected by US Army personnel. On Oahu the army had five radar sites, at Opana, Kaaawa, Kawailoa, Koko Head and Fort Shafter. The Opana radar, generally considered the best, possessed a range of about 130 miles

THE AIR BATTLE

A Kate from the *Shokaku* and the second wave attack over Kanoehe air station. Smoke from the ramp area provided evidence of Japanese success in dealing with aircraft and amphibians at this base (above).

The arrival of B-17 Flying Fortresses in the course of the attack (right) ensured a double vulnerability for these heavy bombers, from both Japanese aircraft and an indiscriminate defence. The Flying Fortress piloted by Lt. Karl Barthelmess was approached by these two dive-bombers, which veered away when a camera was pointed in their direction: the heavy bomber was landed safely at Hickam Field.

and had been operational on the previous day. After closing down overnight, it was to have been returned to service at 0400, but with the two-man crew billeted at Kawailoa ten miles away and the SCR 270B truck-mounted set giving trouble, it was not until 0415 that it was operational again. At 0645, the Opana and Kaaawa sets very briefly picked up aircraft to the north. The Opana set was to be switched off and the watch ended at 0700, but as the crew prepared to shut down, the oscilloscope recorded images suggesting that something was wrong with the set. When a check revealed that nothing appeared to be wrong, Privates Joseph L. Lockard and George E. Elliott had to decide what to do, and on Elliott's insistence what at 0702 appeared to be a major flight of aircraft almost due north of Oahu at a range of 132 miles was reported to the Information Centre at Fort Shafter. The entire conversation took about eight minutes. In the Centre, however, were just two men, Private Joseph McDonald, the switchboard operator who took Elliott's report, and Lieutenant Kermit Tyler. Neither the Controller nor the aircraft identification officer were present, and this morning was Tyler's second duty day, the first having been on the previous Wednesday. Officially the lieutenant was there 'solely for training and observation'.

Tyler was placed in an unenviable position when McDonald gave him the gist of Elliott's reports. He decided to hear what Lockard had to say. As he listened, Tyler thought that the Opana radar might have registered an air group from an American carrier or, more probably, aircraft being flown into Oahu from the mainland. Tyler had been advised that bombers coming to the Hawaiian Islands were afforded the assistance of radio stations playing music all night, and on his way to the Information Centre he had heard Hawaiian music on the radio. A flight of B-17 Flying Fortresses from the mainland was due that morning, and the aircraft which had been picked up seemed to be approaching from more or less the right direction, so Tyler simply told Lockard not to worry. At no stage did he inform Lockard that the B-17s were expected or enquire how many aircraft might have been detected, and at no stage did either Elliott or Lockard volunteer the information that the incoming flight had to comprise at least 50 aircraft. Had this information been exchanged, it is doubtful Tyler could have continued to believe that what had been detected was a flight of American bombers: such numbers of these aircraft were simply not available in December 1941.

The fact that these exchanges between Tyler and Lockard were logged at 0720 clearly indicates that it was already too late for the Americans to do very much. Perhaps the ammunition boxes could have been broken out and perhaps some aircraft on various airfields could have been dispersed, but the moment for preventive action had passed. It was nonetheless to prove unfortunate that the contact was not reported to the Navy, since this meant that after the Japanese attack there was no clear indication of the direction from which the aircraft had come: had the Opana report been available to the Navy, much time and trouble might have been saved later, though probably to no real effect.

Elliott and Lockard continued to track the incoming flight until 0739, when it was recorded to be some twenty miles away. In the meantime, at 0703 or at the very time that the Opana station detected the incoming Japanese aircraft, the *Ward* had obtained another contact with a submerged vessel and subjected it to depth-charge attack. Some three minutes later the destroyer recorded the sighting of an oil bubble some 300 yards astern, and it may well be that she accounted for two of the five midget submarines pitted against the Pearl Harbor base.

BELOW **Target of opportunity: two Japanese fighters circle over the spot, to the north of Ewa beach, where a Dauntless from the aircraft carrier *Enterprise* had crashed after having been shot down. The American dive-bomber was one of three carrier Dauntlesses shot down by Zekes.**

Dramatic representation, with more than a passing resemblance to the Stuka, of the Val in its dive.

At 0500 on 7 December, the Japanese heavy cruisers *Chikuma* and *Tone* each launched a seaplane. The *Chikuma*'s aircraft was to conduct a reconnaissance of Pearl Harbor while the *Tone*'s was to scout the Lahaina anchorage and, assuming it was empty, to search the area to the south of Oahu in the hope of locating any American carrier force which might be in the area. The two seaplanes were ordered not to overfly their initial objectives but to skirt them, and neither would be able to send their reports before the two strike formations had been despatched. On board the carriers, aircraft engines were turned over after 0530, and as aircraft were manned at 0550 the carrier formation turned east into a 30-knot wind and spent some fifteen minutes working up to 24 knots in order to ensure there was sufficient wind speed over the flight decks to lift the Kates laden with bombs of unprecedented size and heaviness. The flight decks of the carriers were rising and falling through some 40 feet and waves were breaking over their decks, and had the Japanese carriers been engaged on an exercise, it would have been cancelled. But operational necessity permitted no such discretion, and the first attack formation, consisting of 185 aircraft, was launched in just fifteen minutes, faster than any time previously recorded, and incurred just two losses, one Zeke fighter that crashed and another which developed engine trouble and could not take off.

The first aircraft launched were the Zekes, which thereafter formed the guard as first the Kates and then the Vals were flown off. The aircraft from the Japanese carriers circled outwards – those from carriers in the port column circled counter-clockwise while those in the starboard column circled clockwise: aircraft from the *Akagi* and *Soryu* and the *Zuikaku* and *Shokaku* climbed to 1,100 feet while those from the *Kaga* and *Hiryu* climbed to 550 feet. At 0620, with all the aircraft which would be taking part in this strike airborne and in formation, Fuchida in his Kate gave the signal for the formation to set course for Pearl Harbor and the aircraft climbed to their cruising altitudes.

The standard cruising formation for Japanese carrier aircraft was for formations to be led by Kates at 13,100 feet, with Vals 1.25 miles astern and 1,650 feet higher,

with Zekes the same distance behind and height above the Vals. For this operation, it seems, the Kate torpedo-bombers flew at 9,200 feet and formed the left side of the Japanese formation. The level-altitude Kates flew to their right, at about 9,800 feet while the Val dive-bombers were stationed on the right at 11,100 feet. The Zekes were deployed at 14,100 feet and were free to range over all the bombers, which were led by Fuchida's 50-strong Kate formation.

As the aircraft from the first strike formation departed, the battleships and cruisers despatched seaplanes to patrol to the east, south and west of a carrier force which turned back onto its previous course to the south and began to bring up on deck the aircraft which would form the second strike force. At 0705 the carriers turned into the wind for a second time, and some ten minutes later began to launch their aircraft, in exactly the same order and with the same procedures as the first wave. Only one aircraft, a dive-bomber from the *Hiryu*, had to be struck because of engine problems, but very quickly two more Vals and a fighter were obliged to turn back with engine problems.

Overall, a total of 350 aircraft – 183 in the first and 167 in the second – were in the two strike formations which conducted the attack on Pearl Harbor, and they were despatched in just 90 minutes. During the approach to Pearl Harbor, the aircraft were afforded the protection offered by thickening cloud at 5,000 feet. Nonetheless, at 0735 the approaching aircraft and the carrier formation were informed by the *Chikuma*'s seaplane that nine battleships, one heavy and six light cruisers were in harbour: three minutes later the seaplane sent a weather report indicating all but perfect attacking conditions. Apart from the small errors of identification on the part of the *Chikuma*'s seaplane and the fact that at 0733 the Lahaina anchorage was reported to be clear, the only matters of note during this phase of the operation were the sun rise, which apparently bore a striking resemblance to the Japanese naval ensign and drew an appropriately mystical response from Fuchida, and – almost a surreal addition – the fact that as the Japanese aircraft approached Oahu, some of the aircrew tuned into the local radio station. It was playing a Japanese song.

According to the Japanese plan of attack, if surprise was achieved, the Kate torpedo-bombers were to lead the assault, but if surprise had been forfeited, the dive-bombers and Kate level-altitude bombers would lead in the hope that by attracting fire they would make things easier for the slow and vulnerable torpedo-bombers. The decision whether or not surprise had been achieved belonged to Fuchida, who was to fire one flare to indicate surprise had been recorded and two that it had not. At 0740 Fuchida, having seen no sign on the ground that indicated an alert defence, fired one flare, but because he thought that one group of fighters had not seen it, then fired a second. The two flares were sufficiently spaced in time to have been interpreted for what they were but, perhaps inevitably, were generally taken as an order for the Vals and Kates to lead the attack. The Japanese formation therefore began to divide, and at 0749 Fuchida gave his own formation of level-altitude Kates the attack order 'To, To, To', the first syllable of totsugekiseyo, which means 'charge', and four minutes later his radioman sent out the famous 'Tora, Tora, Tora' signal, the Japanese word for tiger broadcasting the fact that the attacking aircraft had caught the US Pacific Fleet by surprise. The signal was picked up by both the carrier force and in the battleship Nagato, Yamamoto's flagship in the Inland Sea.

Some two minutes before, at 0751, the torpedo-bombers, led by Lieutenant-Commander Murata Shigeharu of the Akagi, split into their four component groups, with the Kates from the Hiryu and Soryu moving to attack units west of Ford Island while those from the Akagi and Kaga flew to the south-east before turning in a large arc around and across Hickam Field in order to move directly against Battleship Row. As they did so, some of the dive-bombers and fighters reached their objectives, with the result that Ford Island naval air station was attacked before the warships in the harbour: incredibly, the first bomb to fall, aimed at Catalinas at the southern end of the station, missed not just the air station but Ford Island itself. The attack on the air station was witnessed aboard the American flagship, the minelayer-headquarters vessel Oglala, and the battleship West Virginia, with very different results. The Oglala immediately issued an order for all ships to sortie at once, while the West Virginia, thinking that there had been an explosion on board the California, gave the order for rescue parties to make their way to the battle force flagship. The West Virginia's order was overtaken by events immediately, although the marshalling of crew undoubtedly saved lives over the next few minutes. The Oglala's was far too late to be obeyed, however, as the attack by the Kate torpedo-bombers was now materialising.

Kates from the Soryu, through a combination of errors of identification, attacked the target ship Utah and the light cruiser Raleigh, though the group leader, recognising the Utah for what she was, flew across Ford Island and launched his torpedo at the ships which were lying in the berth normally occupied by the flagship Pennsylvania. On 7 December, however, it was occupied by the Oglala and the light cruiser Helena. The torpedo ran under the Oglala and hit the Helena with the result that the latter had one engine room and one boiler room flooded while the old Oglala, which had been commissioned into the US Navy 24 years to the day, lacked watertight doors and bulkheads and had her hull split open by the pressure wave from the hit on the Helena: it was to take another two hours before she finally capsized and came to rest on the bottom on her port side. Four of the Hiryu's torpedo-bombers also appear to have attacked the Helena and Oglala but they missed their targets. The Utah, stripped of belt armour and hit by two torpedoes, capsized at 0810, taking 64 of her officers and men to their deaths. The Raleigh, deprived of power by a solitary torpedo hit that caused flooding to the forward engine room and two fire-rooms, was saved from a similar fate by counter-flooding and the fact that a second torpedo aimed at her missed.

The other Kate torpedo-bombers from the Hiryu and two from the Soryu ignored the Utah and Raleigh on the west side of Ford Island and the Helena and the Oglala on the east side and flew around the anchorage in order to attack the battleships in Battleship Row after the Kates from the Akagi and Kaga had launched their attacks, which began at 0758. It has been suggested that nine-tenths of the damage that was inflicted in the raid on Pearl Harbor was registered by the first strike formation,

THE JAPANESE ATTACK: THE FIRST WAVE

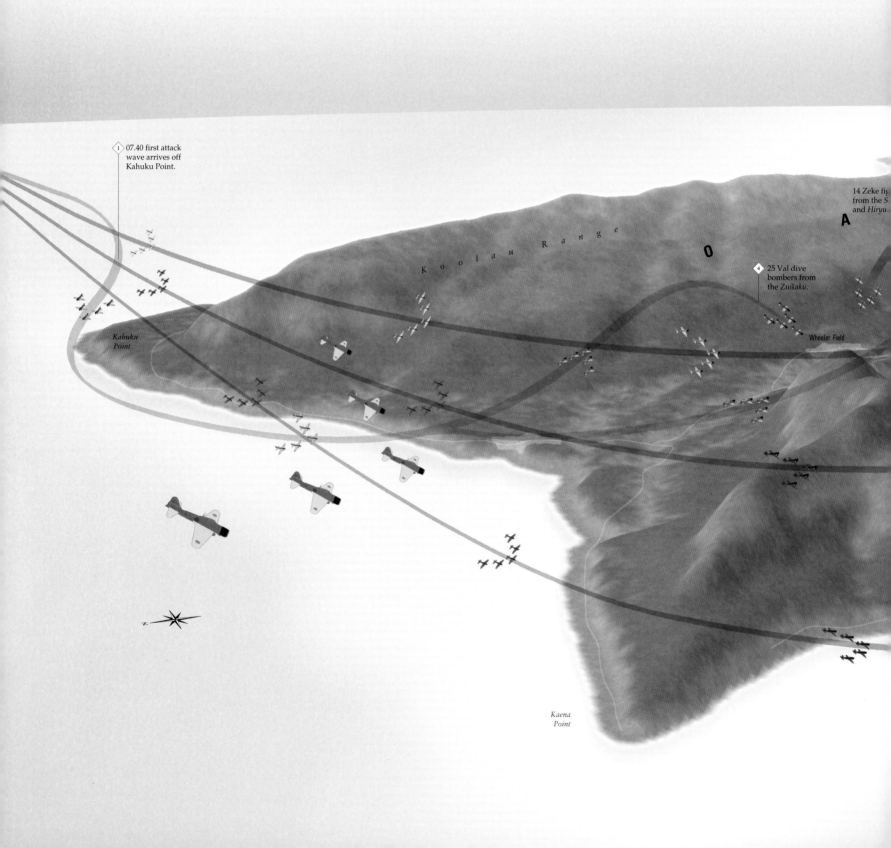

1 07.40 first attack wave arrives off Kahuku Point.

14 Zeke fig[...] from the S[...] and *Hiryu.*

A

O

4 25 Val dive bombers from the *Zuikaku.*

Koolau Range

Kahuku Point

Wheeler Field

Kaena Point

N

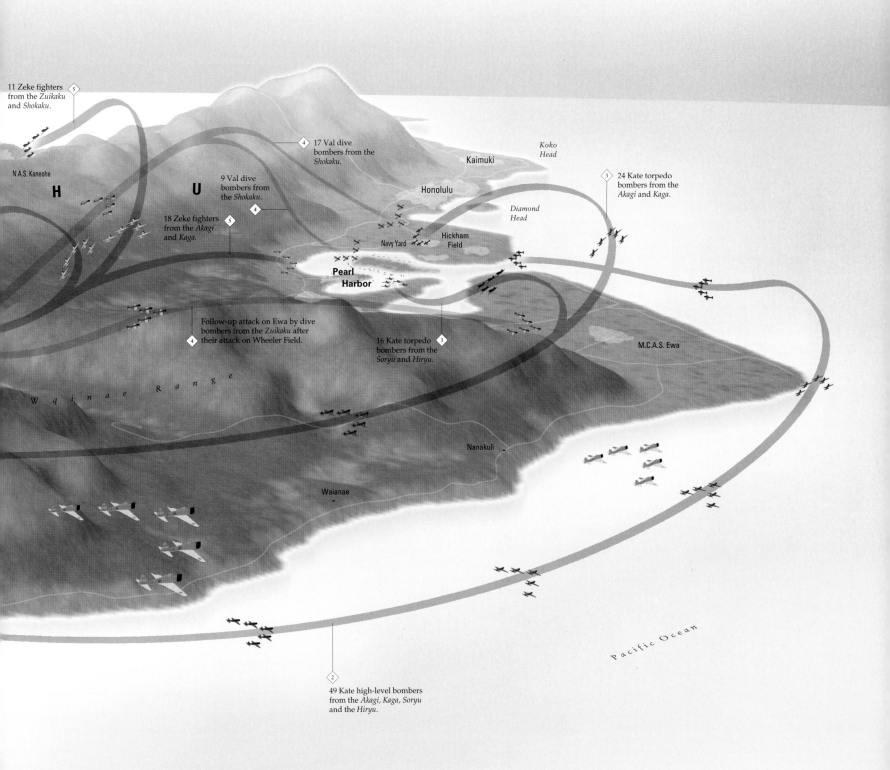

11 Zeke fighters
from the *Zuikaku*
and *Shokaku*. ⟨5⟩

N.A.S. Kaneohe

H

U

⟨4⟩ 17 Val dive
bombers from the
Shokaku.

Kaimuki

*Koko
Head*

9 Val dive
bombers from
the *Shokaku*. ⟨4⟩

Honolulu

⟨3⟩ 24 Kate torpedo
bombers from the
Akagi and *Kaga*.

18 Zeke fighters
from the *Akagi*
and *Kaga*. ⟨5⟩

*Diamond
Head*

Navy Yard

Hickham
Field

**Pearl
Harbor**

⟨4⟩ Follow-up attack on Ewa by dive
bombers from the *Zuikaku* after
their attack on Wheeler Field.

16 Kate torpedo
bombers from the
Soryu and *Hiryu*. ⟨3⟩

M.C.A.S. Ewa

W q i n a e   R a n g e

Nanakuli

Waianae

P a c i f i c   O c e a n

⟨2⟩

49 Kate high-level bombers
from the *Akagi, Kaga, Soryu*
and the *Hiryu*.

FAR LEFT A launch rescues a man in the water as the *West Virginia* settles: beyond her is the battleship *Tennessee*.

In the first minutes of the attack, oil gushing from occupants of Battleship Row. From the top: the *Arizona* inboard of the *Vestal*; the *Tennessee* inboard of the *West Virginia*; and the *Maryland* inboard of the *Oklahoma*, which is in the process of capsizing.

and if this was indeed the case it is only a slight exaggeration to suggest that the greater part of this damage was inflicted in the first ten minutes by the Kate torpedo-bombers. Overall, the Japanese official history claims a total of 23 torpedo hits on five of the battleships in Battleship Row. With the *Maryland* and *Tennessee* shielded from torpedo hits by their less fortunate sisters, the Japanese claim to have hit the *Nevada* with one torpedo, both the *Arizona* and *California* with two each, and the *Oklahoma* and *West Virginia* with nine torpedoes each. Even if a certain doubt attaches itself to the exact number of hits claimed on individual ships – and the final American count on the *West Virginia* suggested she was torpedoed seven times – three things are clear enough.

The first is that the major part of the torpedo attack must have been over by about 0801, and the second is that by this time three of the battleships – the *California*, *Oklahoma* and the *West Virginia* – were *in extremis*. The

RIGHT One of the most famous photographs of the attack on Pearl Harbor: the opening of the attack with, in Battleship Row on the far side of Ford Island, the battleship *Oklahoma* being torpedoed.

BELOW Fires from the *Nevada* (left) as a Val from the *Akagi* flies clear after having attacked *Shaw* and the floating dock.

watertight integrity of the *California* had been compromised by the fact that the battleship had been partially opened in readiness for an inspection which was to take place the following day, and the two torpedo hits posed an immediate and deadly threat to her stability. With sea water contaminating her fuel system and without lighting and power, she was saved from capsizing by immediate counter-flooding but at the cost of settling, which ultimately took more than three days. The *Oklahoma*, which had begun her inspection the previous day and was still partially open, was hit by three torpedoes in very quick succession and even as her crew were making their way to action stations, she began to heel over: with the order to abandon ship given, some of her crew were attempting to move along her blister when she was hit by a fourth torpedo that caused her to settle. With 415 officers and men killed and missing, the *Oklahoma* was held by her masts and superstructure with her starboard keel above water, and it was from the keel that 32 members of her crew were freed two days later.

The *West Virginia* was hit by four torpedoes in very quick succession and immediately took on a list to port,

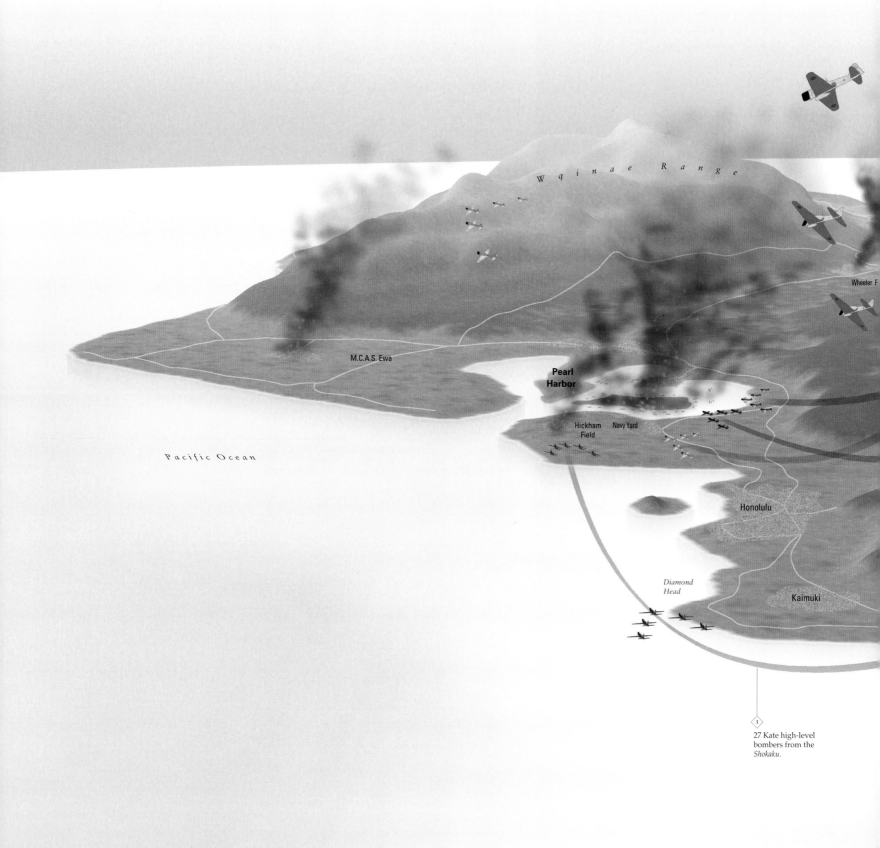

Wqinae Range

Wheeler F

M.C.A.S. Ewa

Pearl Harbor

Hickham Field   Navy Yard

Pacific Ocean

Honolulu

Diamond Head

Kaimuki

27 Kate high-level bombers from the *Shokaku*.

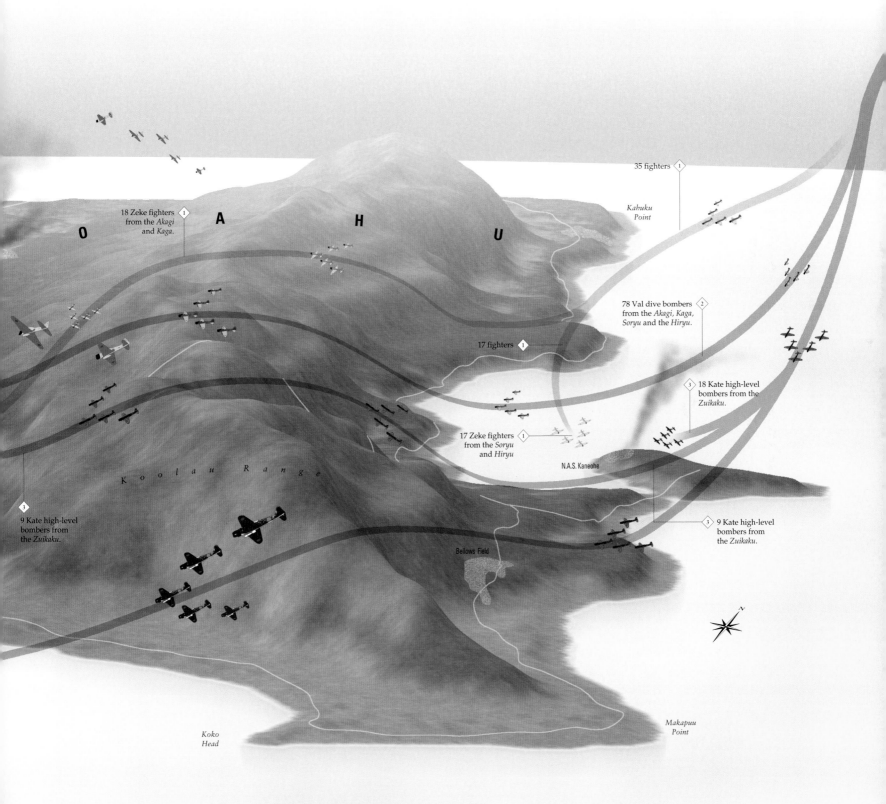

O   A   H   U

Kahuku Point

35 fighters ◇1

18 Zeke fighters ◇1
from the *Akagi*
and *Kaga*.

78 Val dive bombers ◇2
from the *Akagi, Kaga,
Soryu* and the *Hiryu*.

17 fighters ◇1

◇3 18 Kate high-level
bombers from the
Zuikaku.

17 Zeke fighters ◇1
from the *Soryu*
and *Hiryu*

N.A.S. Kaneohe

Koolau Range

◇3
9 Kate high-level
bombers from
the *Zuikaku*.

◇3 9 Kate high-level
bombers from
the *Zuikaku*.

Bellows Field

*Koko
Head*

*Makapuu
Point*

N

THE CALIFORNIA

Shortly before 1000 the battleship *California* was hidden by smoke as burning oil threatened to envelop her. With the *Maryland* in the middle distance, alongside the upturned hull of the *Oklahoma*, the yard tug *Nokomis* can be seen coming astern of the *California* in order to offer assistance.

INSET OPPOSITE The *California* as burning oil threatens to engulf her.

BELOW At or about 1000 the order to abandon ship was given in the battleship *California*: in this picture her crew can be seen going over the side. Within minutes, however, a shift of wind meant that the battleship, as she settled, was kept clear of the threat and she was reboarded.

LEFT One of the most famous pictures of this day: the battleship *West Virginia*, torn apart by torpedoes and bombs, settling with her rear turrets just above water. The battleship *Tennessee* lies between the *West Virginia* and Ford Island.

but as she was hit for the first and second times by torpedoes launched at her by Kates from the *Hiryu*, a torpedo passed under the repair ship *Vestal* and disembowelled the *Arizona*. The force of this explosion and the extent of the problems afflicting the *West Virginia* were apparent even to the fleet commander, Kimmel, who had been answering a telephone call from his command office when the attack began. Told by his staff officer that Japanese aircraft were attacking the naval base, Kimmel ran from his house onto the lawn that overlooked the fleet anchorage. From there, in a state that must have been akin to bewildered helplessness, he witnessed the *Arizona* 'lift out of the water, then sink back down – way down'. As Kimmel watched the *West Virginia* begin to list, his car appeared at his house and, with a submarine commander hitching a lift on the running board, he was taken at breakneck speed to his headquarters.

A third aspect of the torpedo attack on Battleship Row is now equally clear. Research conducted in the last decade of the twentieth century, more than 50 years after the event, very strongly, perhaps conclusively, suggests that one of the midget submarines successfully negotiated the entrance and reached the area near the entrance to the South-east Loch, opposite Battleship Row. This boat is not to be confused with the midget submarine sighted by the destroyer *Zane* at about 0830 and sunk by a combination of shells from the seaplane tender *Curtiss* and ramming and depth-charge attack by the destroyer *Monaghan* in the channel between Pearl City and Ford Island. This particular sinking took place around 0845, and after the midget submarine had fired both torpedoes without hitting anything other than the shore on both occasions. The midget submarine opposite Battleship Row, however, proved rather more successful. From this position, as the Kate torpedo-bombers made their attacks and at a time when four of their torpedoes were in the water, it managed to hit both the *California* and *West Virginia* with its two torpedoes. It was a remarkable achievement, and one which passed unacknowledged for more than half a century. What subsequently happened to this submarine is a mystery, although it is known that at 2241 on 7 December one midget submarine sent a signal to its mother craft, the I.16, claiming a successful attack. Thereafter there was no further contact with this unit.

The midget submarine's attack took place between 0801 and 0803 and by this time, with the first part of the torpedo-bombers' attack complete and the *Oklahoma* in the process of capsizing, the Kates with their 800-kilogram bombs had joined the proceedings. Again, according to the Japanese account, eight of these bombs hit four American battleships, the *California* and *Maryland* each being hit once, the *Tennessee* twice and the *Arizona* four times. Even if one does not dispute the figures, eight hits from a total of 49 bombs was a poor return for a form of attack reputedly registering three in four or even more hits by mid-November, but in truth only one hit possessed real importance.

At 0804 exactly, one of these eight bombs hit the *Arizona* either on or next to her No. 2 turret and penetrated and exploded within the forward magazine. The detonation of the magazine destroyed the forward part of the ship, killing almost 1,000 of her crew, her captain and admiral. The explosion set off a series of fires throughout what remained of the battleship, although its force also extinguished a series of fires in the *Vestal*, which was alongside. The *Vestal* and other ships, however, were bombarded with pieces of the battleship and with parts of bodies. Crew members on the remaining decks of the *Arizona* were burned alive while those thrown into and retrieved from the water of the anchorage were given morphine *en route* to the *Solace*, the base hospital and points beyond. Indeed, one of the most horrific descriptions of the day related to the *Arizona* and her men after the explosion, and as she burned:

'I remembered not to touch the hot ladder rails as I raced... onto the quarterdeck... There were bodies... I'd seen this from above, but it didn't register clearly until I got down on the quarterdeck. These people were zombies... They were burned completely white. Their skin was just as white as if you'd taken a bucket of whitewash and painted it white. Their hair was burned off; their eyebrows were burned off; the pitiful remains of their uniforms in their crotch was a charred remnant; and the insoles of their shoes was

about the only thing that was left on these bodies. They were moving like robots. Their arms were out, held away from their bodies, and they were stumping along the decks...'

The destruction of the *Arizona* was perhaps the most awesome single moment of the day. It was captured on film and has become an event permanently engraved on the American psyche. The battleship has been preserved as a national memorial: she remains to this day in commission and is therefore afforded the courtesies, respect and privileges of a ship in service.

What remained of the *Arizona* and the *West Virginia* were two of the three main targets attacked after this time. American sources suggest that the *Arizona* was hit by no fewer than eight bombs, and these in addition to the torpedoes which hit her, and that the *West Virginia* was hit by two torpedoes from the *Hiryu*'s Kates and by two bombs after the *Arizona* exploded. These bombs were to do massive damage. The *West Virginia*'s three armoured decks forward of the bridge were telescoped together and most of the ship between the forecastle and forward turret was burned out, with four casements destroyed. Nonetheless counter-flooding and the strength of her retaining wires limited her initial list of 28° to 15° and she escaped the fate of the *Oklahoma* as she settled, more or less upright, on the bottom in 40 feet of water and continued to burn until the afternoon of the following day. A total of 105 of her officers and men were killed, the last of those trapped inside the ship dying more than two weeks later, on or about 23 December.

The third of the targets was the battleship *Nevada*. At 0803 she was hit by one torpedo which tore a huge hole in her port bow, and at 0805, as the Kate bombers began

RIGHT The destroyer *Shaw* was gripped by fires that detonated her forward magazine at 0930 in an explosion and fireball of dramatic intensity, heightened by the backgound of black, oily smoke. How the ship survived with only the loss of her bow is one of the mysteries of this day.

RIGHT The scene at Pearl Harbor, sometime after 1000 and probably before 1100. Forward of the capsized *Oglala* is the light cruiser *Helena* alongside the jetty and the *Pennsylvania*, the mast and upper superstructure of which can be discerned against the background of smoke from the *Cassin*, *Downes* and *Shaw*. On Ford Island the buildings at the ramp burn furiously.

BELOW The barrage of AA fire that greeted the second-wave attackers, and the smoke that hindered the efforts of both sides. In left centre, the cloud of thick black smoke was from the *Arizona*, while to the left smoke marks the docks where the *Cassin*, *Downes* and *Shaw* were heavily damaged. The white smoke is from a crashed Japanese aircraft. The repair ship *Vestal*, lower left, can be seen leaving Battleship Row.

A view of the inner loch from a position to the east of Battleship Row. With the attack clearly over, the fires from the destroyers (to the left), from the installations on Ford Island (centre) and from stricken battleships (right) continue to burn. In the distance is the *Nevada*, aground at Hospital Point.

their attack, she started to list slightly to port. Because of the danger of her being trapped by burning oil spewing from the *Arizona*, the decision was taken to get the battleship under way and clear of her present position, but it was not until 0850 that she was able to secure enough power to move. By that time, however, the second attack formation had arrived over Pearl Harbor, and the Japanese concentrated their efforts in an attempt to sink the *Nevada* in the main channel, hitting her with five bombs. At 0907 she came under concerted attack for a second time, and was apparently hit a sixth time before, in a response to a direct order from Kimmel's headquarters, she ran herself ashore at Hospital Point at 0910, where she continued to attract Japanese attention, however ineffective.

Though extensively damaged, the *Nevada* undoubtedly owed her survival to two factors, namely the concentration of the torpedo-bombers against the head and centre of the line and the fact that the bombs which struck her were of the 250-kilogram and not 800-kilogram variety. Had she been sunk in the channel, especially if she had been sunk in the channel between Ford Island and the gate, the ability of Pearl Harbor to function as a base would have been seriously imperilled. In the event, however, she inadvertently distracted attention from the oiler *Neosho*, which had been occupying a berth between the *California* and the *Maryland* and *Oklahoma*. The *Neosho* had discharged half her cargo of aviation fuel to Hickam Field the previous evening and finished delivering the other half to the Ford Island depot five minutes before the Japanese attack. She had started to move astern at 0842 as the second-wave attacks began, and if she had

LEFT The *Nevada*, aground, after the attack, with the yard tug *Hoga* off her port bow attending to one of her fires. Just above the flames and smoke can be discerned her national flag: it was its being caught in the wind as the battleship cleared Battleship Row that was remembered by American survivors who witnessed it as one of the day's dramatic moments.

been hit, the *Maryland*, *Tennessee* and the *West Virginia* might well have been endangered. Nonetheless she was able to get clear of Battleship Row and make her way into South-east Loch and moor next to the *Castor*, where she presented no threat either to battleships or shore installations on Ford Island. As for the *Nevada*, the sight of this one battleship struggling to get under way during the Japanese onslaught and fighting her way down the Channel with her ensign caught in the wind, was generally regarded by those Americans who saw it as the day's most inspiring moment.

But if the Kates had been successful in crippling the US Pacific Fleet in their attack, the Vals and Zekes had been scarcely less successful in a series of strikes on airfields on Oahu. These strikes effectively destroyed any American capacity to organise and co-ordinate effective search and strike operations. Kaneohe Naval Air Station was attacked at 0748, before Ford Island and the battle force were hit, but its attempts to warn the Bellows Field and Hickam Field were simply disbelieved. Kaneohe held three reconnaissance squadrons with 33 Catalinas moored, in hangars or on ramps, with another three on patrol. It was hit in three attacks as well as being strafed by individual aircraft *en route* to or from other targets. The base's fire engine was destroyed in the first attack, and Zekes from the *Shokaku* and *Zuikaku* destroyed about half of the Catalinas and damaged others. By the end of the attack by the dive-bombers from the second-wave, when two hangars were wrecked, 27 of the Catalinas had been destroyed and the remaining six all damaged. Kaneohe was the only base to incur 100 per cent losses.

At Ford Island Naval Air Station, home of Navy Patrol Wing 2, roughly half the number of aircraft and seaplanes at the base, and the hangars, were wrecked inside the first few minutes, the base losing its fire-fighting capacity when the explosion which accounted for the *Arizona* destroyed the water main. The situation on the island was confused by the fact that various naval personnel from the battleships, some hideously burnt, were landed on the island, but the main source of disorder came from the arrival of eighteen Dauntless dive-bombers from the carrier *Enterprise* during the attack, the station playing

RIGHT **After the attack.**
The sunken *Arizona* astern
of the *West Virginia*, which
has settled, and inboard,
the *Tennessee* relatively
undamaged, but trapped by
her less fortunate sisters:
forward are the capsized
hull of the *Oklahoma*
and the *Maryland*.

home to aircraft and seaplanes when these were not with their carriers or ships. One of the Dauntlesses was shot down by American guns at the airfield, and three were shot down by Zekes, one was shot down by Vals from the *Shokaku* and another was destroyed in a mid-air crash with a Zeke. The remainder scattered, with seven putting down at Ewa Marine Corps Air Station: one, attempting first to return to the *Enterprise*, went as far

afield as Burns Field on Kauai in its search for safety. Overall, some 33 of the aircraft, seaplanes and flying boats at Ford Island, including nineteen of the base's 35 Catalinas, were destroyed in the opening attack, though Ford Island's place in the history of this day was assured not by its losses but by the famous signal sent, in clear, from its headquarters at 0758: 'Air Raid Pearl Harbor. This is not (a) drill.'

At Ewa, Zekes made as many as eight passes over parked aircraft in this first-wave attack and exacted a toll of nine of eleven Wildcats, eighteen of 32 Devastators and Vindicators and six of the eight other aircraft at the field. Subsequently the fighters were joined by various bombers which had made their way to Ewa after attacking Hickam and Wheeler Fields and now directed their efforts against buildings and other installations rather than parked air-

craft. Various fighters subsequently made a number of runs over the air base, but virtually all the damage that was done was inflicted in the opening attack. The Dauntlesses from the *Enterprise* which landed at Ewa were ordered out almost as soon as they arrived. Four of them found that the anti-aircraft fire which greeted them at Ford Island was so intense that they returned to Ewa. This time, they were afforded a more considerate welcome

LEFT The death agony
of the *Arizona*.

and, after landing safely, they made their way back to Ford Island later in the day.

At Hickam Field the Japanese encountered B-17 Flying Fortresses both on the ground and in the air. The incoming flight of twelve which had been the source of Lieutenant Tyler's misapprehension chose to arrive over the airfield at the very time it was being attacked: the immediate reaction of many Americans on the ground was to wonder from where the Japanese had been able to fly four-engined bombers. Eleven of the arriving Fortresses were able to land, one on the Kahuku golf course. One was shot down and three were badly damaged. A number of the heavy bombers already on the base were destroyed on the ground and overall about half of the base's aircraft and many of its installations, including the water mains, were destroyed.

At Wheeler Field, the attackers killed hundreds of American servicemen in their barracks and played havoc with the aircraft which had been lined up as a precaution against sabotage and the ground crews had not had time to disperse to the airfield's 125 protective bunkers. The Japanese attacks on this particular field were closely pressed, and some of the Vals that joined the attack flew so low that on their return to their carriers they were found to have telephone wires around their landing gear. A total of 140 aircraft – comprised of 87 P-40B/Cs, 39 P-36s and fourteen P-26s – were on the base, and of this total just 82 aircraft – 52 P-40B/Cs, twenty P-36s and ten P-26s – were operational. The extent of Japanese success in dealing with aircraft at the eastern end of the base – where 30 P-40B/Cs were destroyed – resulted in a series of black fires that provided cover for the collection of obsolescent P-36 fighters at the western end: just four of these 39 aircraft were destroyed. On Bellows Field, where there were just eight local aircraft plus one squadron of P-40s on detachment, the lack of any concerted attack by the first Japanese wave meant that the Americans were able to disperse their aircraft effectively.

The attacks on Oahu's airfields cost the Japanese just four aircraft shot down: put another way, while five Kates was the price exacted for the savaging of the battle line, air superiority over Oahu was won at the cost of one Val and three Zekes. In addition, seventeen Vals, eleven Zekes and a minimum of eighteen Kates were damaged to some degree, and if an overall total of 55 aircraft lost and damaged from a total of 183 does seem to be relatively large, the fact was that the Japanese won an overwhelming victory in the course of their first strike. Within ten minutes of the start of the attack, the Japanese had denied the Americans any means of co-ordinated and effective response as the command system for both the Pacific Fleet and the air formations on Oahu collapsed, its officers either unheeded or helpless, while the only form of resistance that was possible was local, whether by individual ships or bases. Nonetheless, this resistance was very real, and the Japanese aircrew who witnessed the anti-aircraft fire of the American fleet noted that their own could not have matched either the speed or volume of the American response. It was this response which ensured that the 167 aircraft of the second-wave attack lost twenty of their number and had a further sixteen Kates and a minimum of 41 Vals and eight Zekes damaged in the course of their attack, an overall casualty rate of more than 50 per cent. American sources suggest that more than half of the fourteen Vals and six Zekes which were shot down were destroyed by fighters that managed to defy the odds and get airborne rather than by flak.

The second-wave aircraft arrived over Pearl Harbor at 0854, the Americans having been afforded a 25-minute respite with the departure of the last aircraft from the first wave. In that time fires from the *Arizona* all but engulfed the *Tennessee*, the *Oglala* was pulled clear of the *Helena* by two tugs, and the repair ship *Vestal* was cut free from the *Arizona* in order that she might make her way to safety. The *Vestal*, listing to starboard and slowly flooding by the stern, was run aground at Aiea at 0945, some fifteen minutes before the *Oglala* capsized: apparently her admiral stepped from her to the dockside as she did so. More importantly, and as noted earlier, this second phase saw the *Nevada* heavily bombarded and forced to run herself aground at 0910. Subsequently the current brought her stern into the main channel but at Hospital Point she presented no danger and was herself not in danger of sinking.

The battleship *Pennsylvania*, in Dry Dock No. 1, was fortunate in that she was hit twice during the second-phase attack but to no serious effect: she was able to leave to be overhauled on the American west coast on 12 December. The destroyers *Cassin* and *Downes*, which were in dock with the *Pennsylvania*, were not so fortunate. They managed to get their main armaments working within 25 minutes despite parts being in armouries and workshops ashore, but were threatened by fires set off when either a near miss or a hit on the *Cassin* punctured her tanks and spilled burning oil over the two destroyers. An attempt to douse the flames by flooding the dry dock merely saw burning oil riding on the top of the newly admitted water: the result was the bringing of an intense heat across the destroyers' hulls that set off their forward magazines. As she fell off her keel blocks, the *Cassin* rolled over onto the *Downes*, which was little more than a wreck, while just along from this dock their sister-ship the *Shaw* was hit by two bombs in quick succession, one under her forward machine-gun positions and the other through her bridge. These set off a series of raging fires within the ship which forced her abandonment at 0925. Five minutes later the flames and heat set off her forward magazine, thereby inadvertently providing some of the most striking photographs of this or any war on account of the brilliance of the explosion and resultant fires against the sombre background of black smoke.

Curiously, and no doubt quite deliberately, these three destroyers were rebuilt and returned to service. Even allowing for the fact that no navy has ever had enough destroyers, it is hard to resist the conclusion that the US

Navy determined that these three ships were not going to be lost on this particular day. What could be salvaged from the *Cassin* and *Downes* was shipped to Mare Island navy yard at Vellejo, where new hulls and ultimately what amounted to new ships were built around their engines: the *Downes* was recommissioned into service in November 1943, the *Cassin* in February 1944. The *Shaw*, with a new bow, was returned to service in late 1942 and served in the Solomons in the final stages of the Guadalcanal campaign, although fate ensured that she did not survive an encore when she severely damaged herself when she ran aground at Leyte on 2 April 1945: she was never repaired and was scrapped in 1946, while the *Cassin* and *Downes* were scrapped in 1948.

For most of the other ships in harbour, the second-phase attack was a story of near-misses rather than hits. The seaplane tender *Curtiss* had the somewhat unusual experience of being missed by a bomb but hit near the stern by the crashing Val which had aimed it at her. She was then hit a second time in her hangar by a bomb which caused extensive fires and a list and prompted thought of the ship being abandoned or run aground. The *Raleigh* was hit at 0908 by one bomb from a Val from the *Soryu* which pierced the hull under the waterline and exploded outside the ship, missing the light cruiser's 3,000 gallons of high-grade aviation fuel by less than ten feet in the process. Threatened by more flooding, she was saved from capsizing by the throwing overboard of some 60 tons of top weight. The light cruiser *Honolulu* had her hull opened by a near-miss, which resulted in contamination of her fuel, but while twelve other ships reputedly suffered near misses, none suffered any appreciable damage. The heavy cruiser *New Orleans*, the light cruisers *Detroit* and *St. Louis*, the destroyers *Aylwin*, *Cummings* and *Perry* and the tenders *Avocet*, *Dobbin*, *Medusa*, *Tangier* and *Rigel* all narrowly escaped significant damage, the *Medusa* claiming to have been subject to several near misses while the *Avocet* was apparently missed by five bombs which landed within 50 yards of her but did not explode.

Irrespective of the accuracy or otherwise of such claims, and even allowing for the hits which were registered on the *Nevada*, such returns by a total of 78 dive-

bombers afforded targets of opportunity and freedom of action were meagre by any standard. In any event, their efforts were not sufficient to stop a number of warships escaping from the fleet anchorage to reach the open sea. Probably the first to do so was the destroyer *Helm* at or about 0817, and she had a brush with a midget submarine as she did so. The light cruiser *St. Louis* was the largest unit to escape from the harbour, although she had to go through burning oil and, more seriously, survivors in the water off Battleship Row to do so; she also severed a cable holding a dredger to the shore. More prosaically, she claimed at 1004 to have been attacked by a midget submarine whose two torpedoes missed and exploded against the shore: after surfacing involuntarily after despatching her torpedoes, the submarine had then been hit by the cruiser's fire. The *Dale* and *Monaghan* also escaped to the sea, as did the destroyer *Blue*, which at 0950 claimed to have destroyed a submarine apparently trying to make its way into the harbour.

Inside the anchorage, crewmen from the minesweeper *Montgomery* tried to rescue one Japanese pilot whose aircraft was shot down and crashed into the harbour: he resisted all attempts to capture him and was killed. Only one Japanese was taken prisoner, and he was the ensign

ABOVE The destruction of Hangar 6 at the naval air station on Ford Island. The evidence of destruction on the forecourt of the hangar is belied by the fact that on the apron, next to the water, remained a considerable number of Catalinas and OS2U-4 Kingfisher seaplanes from battleships and cruisers, which owed their survival in large measure to the smoke that covered the island and hid them from the view of attacking Japanese aircraft.

RIGHT Saving the Catalinas and seaplanes on Ford Island: in the background is the *California* with smoke still pouring from the *Arizona*.

from the midget submarine which had been brought to Oahu by the I. 24. Throughout 7 December this midget submarine had problems with her gyroscope, and ultimately finished the day not at Pearl Harbor but near Bellows Field, beyond not just Honolulu and Diamond Head but Makapuu Point as well. The two man-crew abandoned their unit with scuttling charges set, but these failed to go off and one man was drowned and the other, Ensign Sakamaki Kazuo, was thrown ashore by the waves unconscious. He was subsequently captured, to become the United States' first prisoner of war. Interestingly, in light of the respectful treatment afforded Yamamoto by history, when reports of this capture reached the home islands, he apparently had what can only be described as a fit of hysteria as he screamed, stamped his feet and denounced an individual who had defiled national and service honour by allowing himself to be taken prisoner.

The attacks on Oahu's airfields in this second phase appear to have caused relatively little damage, while from various bases American aircraft took to the skies in an attempt to give battle. Ford Island seems not to have attracted much Japanese attention, partly because the eighteen Kates from the *Shokaku* were singularly ineffective and only one fighter group was assigned to attack it, and partly because it was shrouded in smoke from Battleship Row. Wheeler Field was also assigned only one attack formation and suffered little damage in this phase. At Hickam Field, where just nineteen bombers remained ready for use, the barracks and fuel depots were very heavily damaged, and American casualties were heavy because of repeated Japanese strafing of the barracks. At Ewa, the the airfield was worked over thoroughly, as was the ramp area at Kaneohe. The Japanese missed Haleiwa Field, and it was from here that five American aircraft managed to get airborne.

LEFT A PBY-5 Catalina, having been secured by a sailor who is still in the water, being pulled to the shore while its wing outboard of its port engine burns. This effort took place during or after the first attack on Kaneohe naval air station, and despite the efforts to save this particular amphibian it was destroyed in the course of the second Japanese strike on the base.

The first two aircraft to take off were credited with six victories over Ewa and Wahialua, but were somewhat fortunate to escape destruction when they were all but caught at Wheeler Field taking on more ammunition. Wheeler Field itself saw five of its aircraft take off: their pilots were credited with shooting down two Japanese aircraft, for the loss of one of their own number. At Bellows Field three American aircraft attempting to get into the air were destroyed, one on the ground and the other two immediately upon take-off: only one pilot survived. The postscript was of similar vein. For some reason, the *Enterprise* chose to fly six Wildcats into Ford Island after darkness fell: three were destroyed by anti-aircraft fire as they tried to land, and another crashed near Barbers Point.

Such is the main part of the story of the Japanese attack on Pearl Harbor. By 1000 or thereabouts, and some ten minutes before the Japanese carriers began to recover the first aircraft to return from Pearl Harbor, the attack was over: Fuchida was the last to leave the scene and did so in the company of two Zekes which would otherwise have been lost had not the Kate been there to act as their guide. The Japanese carriers began recovering aircraft from the second attack force at 1115 and thereafter continued to approach Oahu in an effort to cut down the distance that damaged aircraft would have to fly. Recovery of aircraft was slow because of worsening sea conditions, and a number of aircraft, according to one source as many as twenty, were either written off in heavy landings or were thrown overboard after they had been

BELOW The scene in the dock after the attack: *Downes* (left) having to endure the unwanted and over-familiar attention of her sister-ship *Cassin*. Astern of the two destroyers in the flooded drydock is the fleet flagship *Pennsylvania*.

recovered on the grounds that their battle damage was beyond economical repair. The last aircraft to return did so at about 1214. Thereafter the carrier force recovered its combat air patrol before turning away at about 1300. Working up to 26 knots, their highest speed during the entire voyage, the carrier formations settled on a course of 330 degrees as it headed for Point F at 34° North, 160° West, where the First Supply Group awaited it.

For the Americans, however, the situation was not so simple since it was far from clear at this time that the Japanese effort was spent. The various fires which had been caused were still burning and continued to burn throughout this and subsequent days, while the wounded had to be tended and in certain of the capsized ships work had to start in an attempt to release trapped crew: in addition, the dead had to be buried. Furthermore, the majority of American military personnel anticipated either Japanese follow-up strikes or a full-scale landing, and throughout the rest of 7 December there were numerous false alarms about landings, landings by paratroopers and renewed air attacks. There was at least one case of warships engaging non-existent aircraft and, inevitably, there were reports of non-existent or wrongly identified warships.

Several American warships narrowly escaped being attacked mistakenly, although the heavy cruiser *Northampton* was subjected to a series of ineffectual attacks by a Zeke off Kauai, while on Niihau one Zeke pilot, from the *Hiryu*, put down in the expectation of being rescued by submarine but found himself a prisoner of the local Hawaiian population. Enlisting the help of a Japanese alien and a *nisei*, the pilot sought to recover papers which had been taken from him: the result was an episode in which homes were burned and Hawaiians seized as hostages or shot before the Japanese airman was finally killed and the *nisei* killed himself.

Inevitably, there were extraordinary episodes, not least among them the account by Honolulu's mayor, who stated that he could see fires on the ground, shells bursting in the skies and detonations, and that he watched the attack for some half an hour and 'then I got a little suspicious'. More pertinently, although at first there was either disbelief or a numbness induced by shock and incredulity, the Americans fought back furiously – and angrily. There were unpleasant displays of racial hatred and, all too predictably perhaps, a blind refusal to credit the Japanese with the ability to have carried out such an attack: the Germans were credited instead. Nonetheless, Mess Attendant Doris Miller of the *West Virginia* became the first black American serviceman to be awarded the Navy Cross for what he did this day, while thirteen Medals of Honor were given to Navy and Marine Corps personnel for conspicuous bravery, nine posthumously.

Overall, the story was one of officers and men who were absent from ships and bases making their way to command posts and actions stations which were in fact already functioning, and of an American fighting response which gathered in intensity but nonetheless was fragmented, uncoordinated and largely ineffective. Yet as the hours slipped by, American command and control arrangements re-asserted themselves. They had begun to do so even during the attack itself: the *Nevada* was instructed not to attempt to reach the sea, and Kimmel gave orders that ships were not to attempt to break out because of the danger of their being sunk in the main channel and that air formations should begin the search for the enemy carriers.

But the American command on Oahu did not know the direction from which the Japanese carrier force had come, and its inclination, when given direction-finder readings that suggested the enemy was either due north or due south of Oahu, was to commit its scout and patrol aircraft to the south. The first aircraft thus committed, four A-20 Havoc medium bombers, were sent out at 1127, and soon after noon the first search of the area immediately to the north of Oahu was undertaken after the recovery of a map from a dead Japanese pilot who had been shot down near Fort Kamehameha suggested that the carrier force had come from this direction. The first heavy bombers, two Flying Fortresses, to be sent out covered the southern area, and this was probably just as well: neither was in a fit condition for offensive operations.

The fact of the matter was that for what remained of 7 December 1941 neither American service retained a sufficient number of undamaged aircraft to organise a proper search of the waters off Oahu, and both lacked a balanced strike force capable of attacking the Japanese carrier force had it been found. Under the circumstances, it is surprising and impressive that, according to the Army Air Force's own figures, its aircraft flew a total of 48 sorties in search of the Japanese carriers between 0930 and 1520 on 7 December, although without the information from the Opana and Kaaawa radar sites a considerable part of this effort was wasted.

Unsurprisingly, there are difficulties in properly assessing overall American losses. The naval losses, and the casualties of the day, can be simply stated, but the losses of aircraft are not so easily defined. Eighteen warships and auxiliaries were either sunk or sustained varying degrees of damage on this day, while the human cost for the Americans was 2,008 navy personnel killed, missing and died of wounds with another 710 wounded, 109 marines personnel killed, missing and died of wounds with another 69 wounded, and 218 army personnel killed, missing and died of wounds with another 364 wounded. The total military casualties, therefore, numbered 2,335 killed, missing and died of wounds and 1,143 wounded: civilian losses totalled 68 killed, missing and died of wounded and 35 wounded.

Regarding the American aircraft losses, for many years official figures indicated that 92 naval and 96 army aircraft were destroyed, and various sources supplemented these figures with the total of 159 aircraft (31 of which were allegedly naval aircraft) damaged and 43 left in service. But official figures also suggested that of the Army's total of '123 first-line planes in Hawaii, 63 survived the attack; of the Navy's 148 serviceable combat aircraft, 36 remained', while another set of official statistics, provided in the Army Air Force history, indicated that 87 of a total of 169 naval aircraft on Oahu were destroyed, while 64 of the 231 aircraft assigned to the Hawaiian Air Force were destroyed, although only 79 army aircraft remained operational at the end of the Japanese onslaught.

Despite these inconsistencies, it would seem that the US Navy and Marine Corps lost thirteen fighters, 21 scout-bombers, 46 patrol and reconnaissance aircraft and amphibians, two transports and five other aircraft, while the Hawaiian Air Force lost four B-17 Flying Fortresses, twelve B-18 Bolos, two A-20 Havocs, 32 P-40s, twenty P-36s, four P-26s and three other aircraft. In addition, the Navy lost ten Dauntlesses and Wildcats from the *Enterprise*. A further 81 fighters, six patrol aircraft and 34 bombers from the Army's inventory were damaged to some degree, but only one in five of these had to be written off and the remainder were returned to service. Thus it would appear that 97 naval aircraft and 77 army aircraft were destroyed with another 121 army aircraft damaged, of which 24 seem to have been written off. In other words, after the attack the US Navy retained seven Catalinas and about a dozen Dauntlesses on Oahu fit to fly, while the US Army Air Force had four Flying Fortresses, eleven Bolos and 75 assorted fighters, reconnaissance and utility aircraft.

One naturally risks causing offence by concluding as much, but despite what was said at the time, American losses on 7 December 1941 were slight. The United States was remarkably fortunate in that a number of factors combined to ensure that her losses of ships, aircraft and personnel were not much heavier than was the case. Only two of the battleships, the *Arizona* and *Oklahoma*, and the target ship *Utah* proved total losses: the *Arizona* and *Utah* were left where they had been sunk, while the *Oklahoma* was raised simply in order to clear the anchorage and was sold in December 1946 for scrapping: after all that she had suffered, she chose to sink while under tow to the west coast on 17 May 1947 rather than suffer the final degradation of being delivered to the breaker's yard. The *California*, which had lost 98 officers and men killed, was refloated on 20 March 1942 and in June 1942 was readied for a return to the west coast and a modernisation programme at Puget Sound navy yard that lasted until January 1944. The *West Virginia* was refloated on 17 May 1942 and docked on 9 June: her damage was so extensive that her reconstruction was to take until July 1944. The *Nevada*, which had lost 50 officers and men killed and 109 wounded, was refloated on 12 February 1942. She then returned to Puget Sound navy yard for repairs which enabled her to return to and remain in service until she underwent major reconstruction in June 1943.

RIGHT Weeping for her lost children: the shattered stern and tripod mast of the *Arizona*.

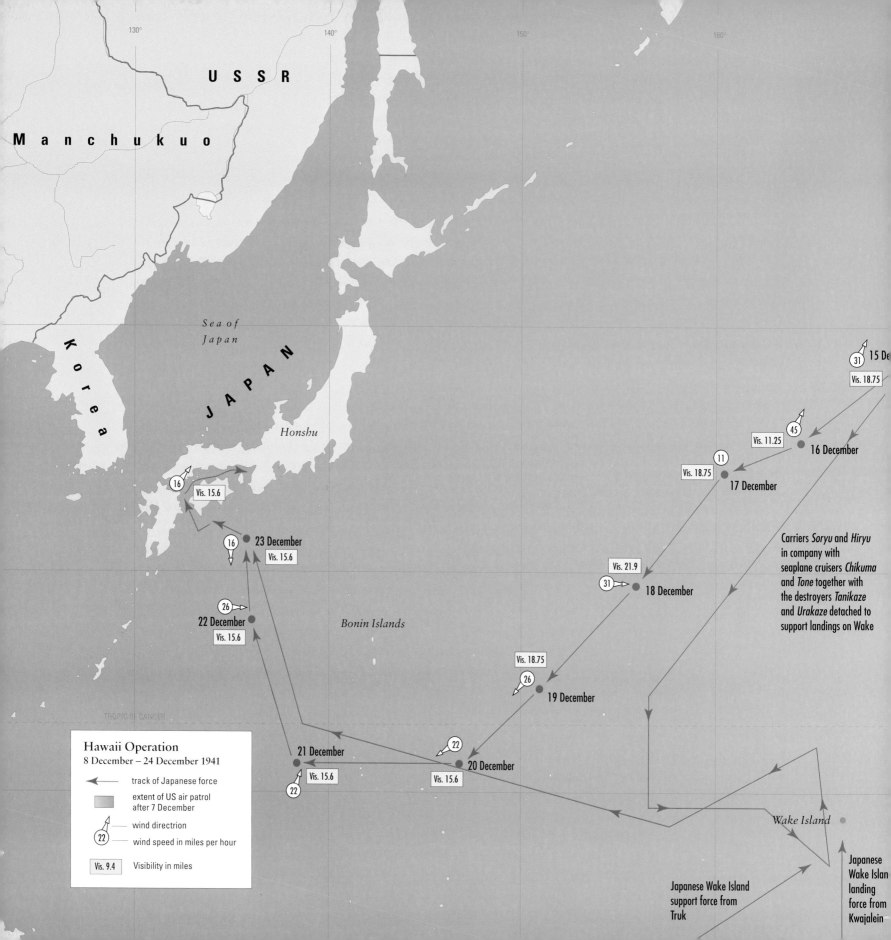

USSR

Manchukuo

Korea

Sea of
Japan

JAPAN

Honshu

Bonin Islands

16 Vis. 15.6

16 23 December
Vis. 15.6

26 22 December
Vis. 15.6

TROPIC OF CANCER

21 December
22 Vis. 15.6

20 December
22 Vis. 15.6

19 December
26 Vis. 18.75

18 December
31 Vis. 21.9

17 December
11 Vis. 18.75

16 December
45 Vis. 11.25

31 15 De
Vis. 18.75

Carriers *Soryu* and *Hiryu*
in company with
seaplane cruisers *Chikuma*
and *Tone* together with
the destroyers *Tanikaze*
and *Urakaze* detached to
support landings on Wake

Wake Island

Japanese
Wake Islan
landing
force from
Kwajalein

Japanese Wake Island
support force from
Truk

Hawaii Operation
8 December – 24 December 1941

track of Japanese force

extent of US air patrol
after 7 December

wind direction

22 wind speed in miles per hour

Vis. 9.4 Visibility in miles

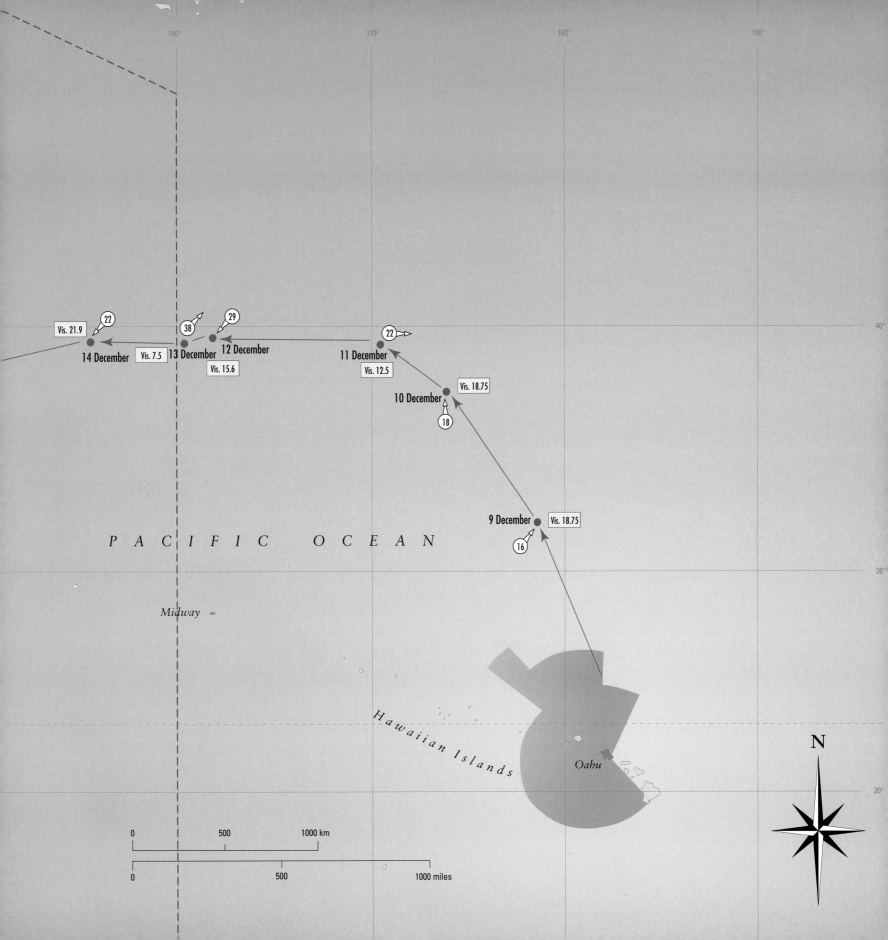

Three more battleships, the *Maryland*, *Tennessee* and the *Pennsylvania*, incurred minor damage. The *Maryland* suffered so slightly that she completed repairs and sailed for the west coast as early as 20 December: she completed a quick overhaul on 26 February 1942 and was returned to training and secondary duties. The *Tennessee*, which had lost just five of her crew killed, was hit by one bomb that penetrated her elevated rear main turret and burned but did not explode, and by a second bomb that hit one of the gun barrels of her elevated forward main turret: splinters from this hit mortally wounded the captain of the *West Virginia*. The *Tennessee*'s main problems, however, were the widespread buckling of her armour belt and plates and the resulting loss of welding and rivets, caused by the heat from burning oil, and the fact that she was trapped until 16 December by the *Oklahoma*, *West Virginia* and the mooring quays. She was returned to Puget Sound navy yard at the end of the year and completed immediate repairs by 25 February before being returned to service: she was recalled for a full modernisation programme in August 1942. The *Pennsylvania*, almost as badly damaged by debris from the *Cassin* and *Downes* as Japanese bombs, had one gun position hit and suffered fifteen killed and fourteen missing. She sailed for Puget Sound navy yard and a quick overhaul, which was completed on 30 March 1942. She returned to Pearl Harbor in the following August and, along with the *Nevada*, saw service in the Aleutians after April 1943.

Almost three years later, on 25 October 1944, the *California*, *Maryland*, *Pennsylvania*, *Tennessee* and the *West Virginia* were to form the American battle line in the Surigao Strait. This action, part of the battle of Leyte Gulf, was the second of only two occasions in the Pacific war when battleships fought their opposite numbers, and in it the Americans overwhelmed and sunk the Japanese battleship *Yamashiro* in a matter of minutes. The *Nevada* missed Leyte because of her service off Normandy and southern France, but she re-entered the Pacific in 1945 with the result that, the *Arizona* and *Oklahoma* excepted, all the battleships sunk or damaged at Pearl Harbor on 7 December 1941 were present in the final actions off Iwo Jima and Okinawa in 1945.

Of the other ships sunk and damaged, the light cruisers *Helena* and *Raleigh* were both quite badly damaged, but the *Honolulu* so slightly that she was escort to a convoy to the west coast as early as 12 January 1942. After completing repairs at the Pearl Harbor and Mare Island navy yards, the *Raleigh* entered the south-west Pacific theatre in July 1942, while the *Helena*, which was repaired at the Mare Island yard, entered the Solomons in September 1942: she was sunk at the battle of Kula Gulf in July 1943. The destroyer *Shaw*, despite her lost bow, sailed for San Francisco under her own power as early as 9 February 1942: she was returned to service in June 1942 and fought at the battle of Santa Cruz in October. As noted elsewhere, her two sister ships, the *Cassin* and *Downes*, were rebuilt: both returned to operational status in 1944.

Of the auxiliaries, the *Vestal* fittingly set about her own repairs even as her men worked on more heavily damaged ships, and she was sent to Tongabatu in August 1942 where she provided support for warships involved in the fight for Guadalcanal. The *Curtiss* sailed for repairs in San Diego which lasted just four days with the result that she was back at Pearl Harbor on 13 January 1942: she was in the south-west Pacific after June 1942. The minelayer-headquarters ship *Oglala* was raised only to sink again not once but twice, and having been raised a third time she suffered a fire before she managed to reach dry dock. She was refurbished and recommissioned in February 1944 and served out what time was left to her as a repair ship and PT-boat tender. She was decommissioned at San Francisco in July 1946 and discarded in March 1947.

In real terms, therefore, the United States lost just two battleships and one target ship, and the services of fifteen other warships and auxiliaries for periods of anything from a couple of weeks to 30 months. The battleships which were recovered and then subjected to modernisation or reconstruction programmes would anyway have been liable for such work even without the treatment they were afforded at Japanese hands on 7 December 1941. As it was, none of the battleships which were lost or damaged on 7 December 1941 were modern and capable of operating with carriers, and therefore had to be assigned secondary duties. Their being lost or damaged at Pearl Harbor was not of major consequence, and in effect their loss resolved the

ABOVE Her fires extinguished, the destroyer *Shaw* lies helplessly in YFD-2. The drydock had partly sunk, and was listing at about 25 degrees.

conflicting claims of the battleship and carrier to be at the heart of tactical formations. From the time that the Japanese struck at Pearl Harbor, the US Navy had no option but to make the carrier task group its key tactical formation.

But to put these losses into perspective and to underline the problems facing the Japanese after they had initiated a war with the United States, one must consider American industrial performance. Three sets of statistics, chosen from any number of similarly daunting American achievements, seem salient here. The first is that in the course of the Second World War, the United States, which herself raised 100 army and marine divisions, provided military aid to allies which in financial terms equalled the sum needed to raise 2,000 infantry or 555 armoured divisions, and this at a time when the average American income was less than $1,000 per annum. The second is that one shipyard alone, the Kaiser yard at Vancouver, Washington, launched its 50th escort carrier one year and one day after launching its first. And the third is that between 7 December 1941 and 15 August 1945, the United States Navy commissioned into service no fewer than eighteen fleet carriers, nine light fleet carriers, 77 escort carriers, eight battleships, thirteen heavy and 33 light cruisers, 349 destroyers, 420 destroyer escorts, 73 frigates and 203 submarines – and to these fleet units must be added the phenomenal output of amphibious and support shipping. It is totals of this order which put the loss of two battleships in context.

American aircraft losses at Pearl Harbor were likewise modest, not least because so many of the aircraft destroyed were obsolescent or worse. But at peak production in March 1944, when her factories were producing one aircraft every 294 seconds, the United States would have been able to replace all that were lost on Oahu on 7 December 1941 in something like sixteen hours – and every single aircraft lost or damaged on that day could have been replaced in less than 36 hours.

The human losses suffered by the Americans at Pearl Harbor have also to be set in perspective. Between 22 June 1941 and 12 May 1945 the Soviet Union in her war with Nazi Germany lost 19,014 dead a day, every day: in other words, the USSR in any week of her Great Patriotic War lost in terms of dead the equivalent of American dead in the whole of the Pacific war. Such was the price of victory in continental warfare, a form of warfare the United States was largely spared.

The American losses, however, were understated, and by one person, Admiral Husband E. Kimmel. The fleet commander at Pearl Harbor could only watch as his great ships died along with officers and men whom he knew as members of an extended naval family rather than a naval service. When he was in his office and looking towards Battleship Row, Kimmel's window was shattered and he was struck in the chest by a spent machine-gun bullet. Very quietly he said to himself, 'It would have been merciful if it had killed me.' It is hard to disagree, but in another sense Kimmel had died already.

ABOVE The long and difficult task of recovering lost ships: the area near the captain's quarters in the *Oklahoma*, 1944.

The flooded drydock and heavily damaged destroyers *Cassin* and *Downes*, with the largely undamaged fleet flagship *Pennsylvania* astern: the light cruiser *Helena*, alongside the jetty, was in the position normally occupied by the battleship. In the distance is the battleship *California*.

Over the years, the question of a follow-up, or third, strike by the First Carrier Striking Force on Pearl Harbor has been the subject of considerable comment, specifically along the lines that the Japanese should have staged another strike which singled out the oil depot, the docks and the power station at the American base for destruction. Either during or immediately after the war, senior American admirals went on record with the view that the Japanese missed an opportunity to inflict telling strategic damage by their failure to conduct such a strike, and such was one of the four main conclusions drawn from the operation in the official history, S.E. Morison's *History of US Naval Operations in World War II, Volume III: The Rising Sun in the Pacific, 1931–April 1942* (1948). The main thrust of argument has been that, had the Japanese set about the shore installations on Oahu and so denied the Americans a base from which to conduct operations, they might have inflicted damage considerably greater than that they had exacted on American warships. In fact, Morison was extremely loud in his condemnation and wrote:

It would be impossible for anyone to find in the annals of history an operational precedent having brought about a more fatal blow upon the aggressor himself than this attack. Tactically speaking, the Japanese committed the blunder in the Pearl Harbor attack of concentrating their attacks only on warships instead of directing them on land installation and fuel tanks. Not only was it strategically a folly, but politically, too, it was an unredeemable blunder.

Although they succeeded in destroying the battleship fleet and wiping out the land air force, they overlooked various naval installations in Pearl Harbor. Amongst them were repair shops which later were able to repair those ships damaged in the attack within an astoundingly short space of time. They furthermore did not make attacks upon power facilities and fuel tank dumps which were stored

Kusaka Ryunosuke

Genda Minouru

THE FOLLOW-UP STRIKE CONTROVERSY

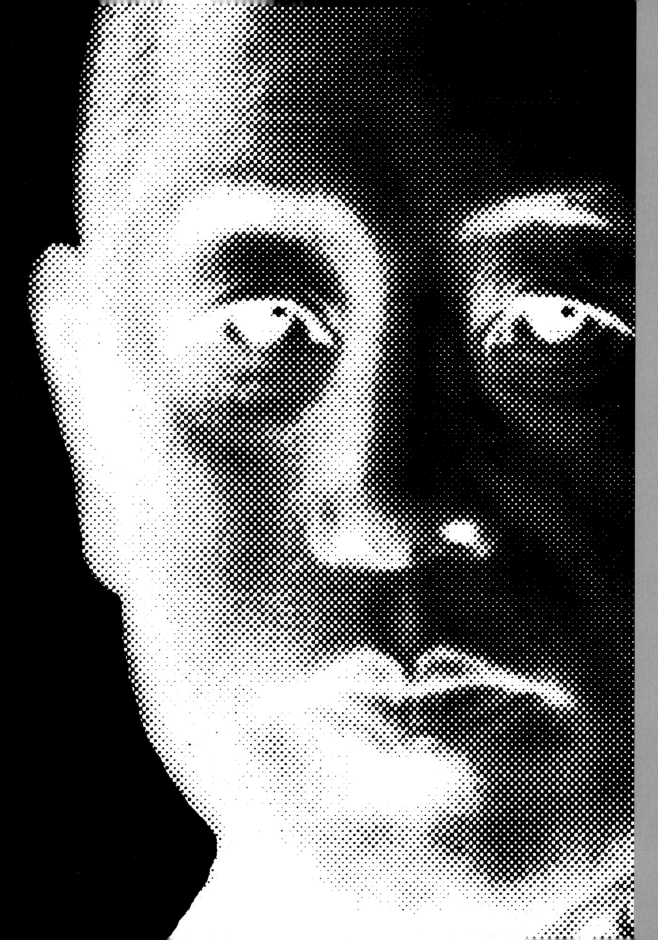

TOP LEFT Rear Admiral Kusaka Ryunosuke, chief of staff of the 1st Carrier Striking Force until October 1942, thereafter air formation commander before being sent to Rabaul as chief of staff to local command. In 1944 chief of staff to commander of the Combined Fleet, he assumed command of 5th Air Fleet in August 1945 and was responsible for post-war demobilisation.

BOTTOM LEFT Genda Minouri, by common consent the leading Imperial Navy pilot of the inter-war period. He survived the war as a captain and commander of a naval air group, and became head of the air force after the Japanese services were reconstituted in 1955.

up to their huge capacity. As duly expressed in the opinion of Admiral Thomas S. Hart, commander-in-chief of the Asiatic Fleet, at the time, the loss of those installations would probably have delayed the US counter-offensive in the Pacific more than did the actual damage to the US vessels.

These comments have been the starting point of much subsequent writing about Pearl Harbor. It has been generally conceded that the Japanese passed up a great opportunity, one which never repeated itself, to inflict significant strategic loss upon the United States. This belief, for the most part, has travelled hand in hand with either the assumption or explicit assertion that Nagumo, the commander of the First Carrier Striking Force, and Kusaka, Nagumo's chief of staff, must bear prime responsibility because it was they who refused to mount a third strike when presented with Fuchida's demand for one when he returned to the *Akagi* after leading the First Attack Force in his Kate.

There are three issues here. The first, simply, is the timing of a third strike given that the Japanese carriers

ABOVE Battleship Row at about 0940 as the light cruiser *St. Louis* headed for the open sea after leaving her berth in the repair basin. Beyond her the destroyer *Bagley* was backing into the main channel in order to follow the example of her senior. The fires that were to cause the *California*, left, to be abandoned within some twenty minutes seem neither fierce nor close enough to be a threat.

Any criticism of Nagumo and Kusaka really has to square a circle in explaining how these two officers could have inverted the list of priorities governing their conduct of operations and attacked targets which Yamamoto and Ugaki simply did not consider worthy of serious consideration and effort. The orders given Nagumo did not grant discretionary powers and freedom of action, and they certainly did not identify the base facilities at Pearl Harbor as the proper target of offensive operations. In such circumstances, the raising of the question of follow-up operations by members of the Combined Fleet staff, the dismissive attitude shown towards Nagumo by Yamamoto and Ugaki, and the staff's attempt on 8 December to get Yamamoto to order Nagumo to carry out follow-up strikes all seem most bizarre. Why was it not until Nagumo was withdrawing his formation that the question of follow-up operations suddenly became so important for the Combined Fleet staff? Why had there been no provisional orders issued before the operation? And just why should the Combined Fleet staff have presumed that it could read the First Carrier Striking Force's situation better than that formation itself? The answers are far from clear. For if the Pearl Harbor objective was important enough to demand a follow-up or series of offensive operations, then it was important enough to be the subject of an assault landing, and the separation or otherwise of the *kogeki* and the *koryaku* raises entirely different issues. Quite incredibly, on the following day, Yamamoto gave orders for his staff to prepare a plan for landings on and the seizure of Oahu.

In terms of the timing of a third strike, one has to admit that it seems the Japanese had to conduct such an operation on the afternoon of 7 December or not at all. But the more one looks at the Japanese situation, the more one is convinced that a third strike at this time was never feasible. The first aircraft to take off did so at about 0605 Hawaiian time and the last aircraft were recovered around 1215. Presumably because of the need to recover and fly off aircraft from the combat air patrol, it was not until about 1300 that the carrier force reversed course and sought to put distance between itself and Oahu. From the despatch of the first aircraft of the first wave to

completed the recovery of their aircraft relatively late on 7 December and that, had this strike been delayed until the following day, the escorting destroyers would have found themselves in a critical situation as regards oil. The second, which is a little more complicated, is when a follow-up strike could have been conducted given the aircraft available. The third is the question of whether, despite various claims which have been made and accounts of proceedings written, a follow-up or third strike was ever considered on the *Akagi* once the recovery of aircraft was completed.

THE NAVAL BASE

The navy base at Pearl Harbor with the oil depots and Hickam Field. The main docks and repair facilities were within the sheltered area opposite Battleship Row.

the carriers turning round to get clear of the area thus occupied almost seven hours.

A follow-up strike on the afternoon of 7 December could not have been a two-wave affair, and therefore once can assume that a strike would have needed less than six or seven hours. But in conducting its two strikes in the morning, the carrier force had not retained a reserve force capable of offensive operations. A third strike could only have been mounted from aircraft which had returned from the morning's strikes, and would have had to have drawn primarily on Vals, refuelled, re-armed and, in many cases, repaired, after they had returned from their morning's missions. But two problems would have confronted any attempt to mount a third strike. The returning aircrews would have had to have been properly debriefed and then briefed anew in readiness for a third attack, and the basic requirements of this plan would have had to have been passed from the *Akagi* to the other carriers. This transfer of information would have been vital because any attempt to mount an attack on the afternoon of 7 December would have depended on the air groups from the *Shokaku* and *Zuikaku*, since they alone possessed the number of Vals required for a follow-up strike.

It is very difficult to say with any certainty how long these processes would have taken. The planning would have run in tandem with the refuelling, re-arming and repair of recovered aircraft. Nonetheless, no details of a plan could have been settled before it was known how many aircraft, and from which groups, would be available for further operations. Given that at Midway the Japanese needed 70 minutes to re-arm aircraft retained for a second strike and were caught by American dive-bombers when five or ten minutes from these aircraft being launched, one would suggest that the two processes might well have needed between two and three hours. At best, this would mean that the Japanese carriers would not have been able to launch their aircraft until 1500. If one allows four hours for an attack – a duration that might be considered too short for a process which had to stretch from the launch of the first to the recovery of the last aircraft – one comes to 1900. Yet sunset on 7 December 1941 was at 1712. Civilian twilight – the last

time when the horizon would have been discernible – was at 1737, and nautical twilight, with the very last traces of daylight in the western sky, was at 1805. Put at its simplest, it is inconceivable that Nagumo and Kusaka would have been prepared to undertake a third offensive operation which exposed their aircrews to the lottery of a night landing. They would not have risked the possibility

American carriers which had been absent from Pearl Harbor on the previous day. Again, it is inconceivable that the Japanese would have mounted another attack against the Pearl Harbor base without first searching for the missing US carriers. But arguably the real question which arises is whether the Japanese formation would have had the administrative margin to mount such an operation.

LEFT The stern view of the flooded drydock and the wrecked *Cassin* and *Downes*.

RIGHT The battleship *California* settling with various rescue and support ships moving to her assistance.

of losing a high proportion of aircraft and highly trained aircrew at the very start of a war. Nor would they have taken such chances after an operation which seemed to have achieved a wholly unanticipated degree of success. Therefore it would appear that a follow-up strike could not have been carried out until the following morning. By that time, however, other factors would have infringed upon any such intention.

The most pressing of these other factors would have concerned the numbers of aircraft either held for air combat patrol or committed to searching for the

The war diary of the destroyer *Akigumo* gives the following entries:

4 DECEMBER: The *Akigumo* was supplied with 95 tons of oil by the *Toho Maru* ...

5 DECEMBER: The *Akigumo* was supplied with ten tons of oil by the *Nippon Maru* ... At 1130 the three oilers and one destroyer of the Second Supply Group parted company...

6 DECEMBER: The *Akigumo* was supplied with twenty tons of oil by the *Kokuyo Maru* ... At 0830 the four oilers and one destroyer of the First Supply Group

parted company ... At 1130 the First Carrier Striking Force set itself on course for its flying-off position and increased speed to 20 knots.

7 DECEMBER: At 0618 the carriers began to fly off the first-wave attack. By 0722 the second-wave attack had been despatched successfully and the carrier force resumed its course to the south. The first aircraft from the first-wave attack to return to the carriers did so at c. 1010. The first aircraft from the second-wave attack to return to the carriers did so at c. 1115. By 1300 the last aircraft had been recovered and the carrier force was set on a course of 330° at a speed that varied between 20 and 26 knots.

8 DECEMBER: According to the signals log of the destroyer formation, the *Akigumo* and *Tanikaze* left the main formation and set a course for a rendezvous with the First Supply Group. The two destroyers were then to refuel and lead the oilers to a main force that would follow at a steady 26 knots. The *Akigumo* war diary refers to the formation maintaining the previous day's course at 'a speed of 26 knots throughout the day', before meeting with the First Supply Group 'in the evening'. In 90 minutes, ending at 0400, the *Akigumo* took on 250 tons of oil from the *Kyokuto Maru*.

The *Akigumo*'s fuel capacity was 600 tons, but on the assumption that the refuelling of 5 December from the *Toho Maru* left her more or less full and the next couple of days' steaming made only marginal demands which were more or less made good, it must follow that some 22 hours of steaming at 20 knots and then something like 42 hours of steaming at or about 26 knots left the destroyer a little over half full.

If the First Carrier Striking Force had been unable to conduct a follow-up strike until the morning of 8 December, then one would have to assume that throughout 7 December the formation, once it had recovered its aircraft, would have continued to steam at high speed away from Oahu before turning back, under cover of night, to make a second high speed run to its flying-off position and, after it had launched its aircraft, would then continued to approach Oahu and so facilitate the

return of its aircraft. It would subsequently have been obliged to repeat the previous day's performance in withdrawing at high speed from the scene.

A third attack, conducted on the morning after the main attack, would therefore have committed the carrier formation to a complete day's high-speed steaming, but throughout this extra day and attack, however, there would have been one critical difference from the events of the previous day – the Americans would be looking for the enemy, and certainly one US carrier would be nearing Pearl Harbor. The Americans would have had little in the way of real firepower with which to attack a Japanese formation, but an additional 24 hours of steaming at 26 knots would have meant that the *Akigumo*'s needs would have been in the region of 400 tons, perhaps as much as 450 tons, and if the Japanese attack had to be delayed until the afternoon of 8 December, then the demand would have been higher. With

RIGHT What purports to be a photograph of Battleship Row but which seems to be disinformation. In the foreground of this photograph is the wreck of the *Arizona*. Beyond are the masts of five battleships, first the *West Virginia* outside the *Tennessee* and then the *Oklahoma* outside the *Maryland*, and beyond them the masts of the *California*. But if the *Arizona* had been destroyed then the *Oklahoma* had capsized, a state of affairs that prompts the suspicion that this photograph had been doctored for press release to show that only one battleship had been lost.

a capacity of 600 tons, the *Akigumo* presumably could have coped: the problem was not so much a third strike but the subsequent run to the north-west with the destroyers' tanks at least two-thirds empty. Clearly, such a prospect could not have recommended itself to Nagumo and Kusaka, who from the outset always showed themselves in favour of the single, two-phase attack.

Whichever way one looks at the position of the First Carrier Striking Force, a follow-up strike on 7 December or the next morning seems highly improbable, in real terms impossible. There is also the question of what type of aircraft and size of force were in fact available for an attack on the base given that the Japanese carrier formation would have been obliged to retain a combat air patrol and, presumably, a reserve strike force in order to guard against the possibility of being subjected to attack. Here one confronts the problem of defining both Japanese losses incurred in the course of the two attacks of the morning of 7 December 1941 and the state of their carrier air groups thereafter.

The conventional accounting of Japanese losses suggests that the first strike lost a total of five Kates, one Val and three Zekes while the second strike lost fourteen Vals and six Vals, a total of 29 aircraft, of which five were torpedo- or medium-altitude bombers, fifteen were dive-bombers and nine were fighters. As far as individual carriers were concerned, the *Akagi* lost four Vals and one Zeke, the *Kaga* five Kates, six Vals and four Zekes, the *Hiryu* two Vals and one Zekes, the *Soryu* two Vals and three Zekes and the *Zuikaku* just one Val.

In terms of aircraft damaged in the course of operations on 7 December 1941, however, the situation is more ambiguous. The number of aircraft damaged is seldom afforded any consideration in accounts of this attack, and in the account which is generally regarded as representing the final word, *At Dawn We Slept*, the authors give a total of 74 aircraft damaged, this consisting of 23 fighters, ten torpedo-bombers and 41 'bombers', a definition which one assumes refers to Vals. But any consideration of the Japanese record, as given in *The Pearl Harbor Papers*, which was compiled by two of the authors of *At Dawn We Slept*, will reveal that the *Kaga* had seven Kates, eighteen Vals

and three Zekes damaged while between them the *Hiryu* and *Soryu* had three Kates, 23 Vals and twenty Zekes damaged. Thus the two authors common to *At Dawn We Slept* and *The Pearl Harbor Papers* give the same figures for the number of aircraft damaged incurred by the whole force of six carriers (*At Dawn We Slept*) and for just three of its carriers (*The Pearl Harbor Papers*).

Incomplete Japanese returns indicate a total of 111 aircraft damaged, and such a total, given the statement that 265 aircraft remained intact and ready for operations after all aircraft had been recovered, must mean that 210 of the aircraft which had taken part in the morning's offensive operations could have been made ready for a third strike, if ordered. Of this 210 total, it is possible to deduce that 104 were Kates, 56 were Vals and 50 were Zekes: the balance of 25 aircraft consisted of seven Kates, twelve Vals and six Zekes. The same Japanese returns indicate that 86 aircraft could not have been made ready for a third strike on 7 December, which must mean that 25 – seven Kates, twelve Vals and six Zekes – in fact could have been. Therefore one must assume that 235 of the aircraft which returned from the morning's strike would have been available had a follow-up strike been ordered in the afternoon, and this total would have consisted of 111 Kates, 68 Vals and 56 Zekes. But the 86 aircraft which were unavailable for a third strike on 7 December could presumably have been made ready for one the next day. Of this 86, 27 were Kates, 46 Vals and thirteen Zekes, which means that on 8 December – and probably during the afternoon rather than the morning – the Japanese carriers would have had available for a follow-up attack 138 Kates, 114 Vals and 69 Zekes from the previous day's strike operations. The problem with such figures is their neatness: the figures are exact, with no margin which might represent aircraft in various stages of disrepair. A set of statistics which indicates that on December 8 the carriers had 135 Kates, 108 Vals and 63 Zekes available from the previous day's strike operation – and that therefore fifteen aircraft were 'adrift' – would seem to be much more realistic.

Given Genda's decision that a third strike, should one be ordered, would not include Kate torpedo-bombers because of the intensity of the anti-aircraft fire which greeted the second wave of attackers, one would suggest that the small number of Vals immediately available precluded any third strike being mounted on the afternoon of 7 December. Admittedly a strike against shore installations would not have exposed the Kates to the worst of American anti-aircraft fire, but the fact that so few Vals – probably no more than half the number which had been committed to the two attacks of the morning – would have been available for an immediate follow-up strike places obvious question marks against the viability of such an attack. Moreover, with perhaps more than half of the available Zekes held with the carriers' strengthened combat air patrol, and with only 63 Vals available for operations, it is very hard to see how a third strike could have been on the afternoon of 7 December against a defence which expected the Japanese carriers to launch another assault.

If the Japanese position regarding a strike on the afternoon of 7 December would appear at best problematical, the situation aboard the Japanese carriers late in the afternoon of 8 December would not have been much better. Admittedly more aircraft would have been available – the *Shokaku* would have been able to deploy 25 Kates, 25 Vals and sixteen Zekes and the *Zuikaku* 26 Kates, 26 Vals and seventeen Zekes – and these figures indicate that the First Carrier Striking Force would have possessed a sufficient number of aircraft to have undertaken a follow-up strike, perhaps even strikes, on 8 December. With perhaps 243 Kates and Vals, the Japanese nominally had enough bombers to mount a two-wave attack, as they had the previous day when they had used 272 bombers offensively. But in reality the First Carrier Striking Force would have been limited to a single effort: anything more would have dramatically increased the risk of discovery by either the American carriers or the aircraft and ships from Pearl Harbor which would now be searching the waters around Oahu.

It would therefore appear, *prima facie*, that the real choice lay between a third strike on the afternoon of 7 December or none at all, and that there was never any realistic chance of the Japanese being able to mount such an attack given the hours of daylight available. An attack could have been

The staff of the Combined Fleet, with officers of the aircraft carrier *Akagi*. Yamamoto is shown seated between Kuroshima and Ugaki, eighth from the right in the front row mounted on the morning of December 8, although such an attack would have presented very real difficulty. An attack on the afternoon of 8 December would have been easier in terms of preparation and aircraft numbers, but these considerations would have to be balanced against the requirements of a combat air patrol, reconnaissance capability and reserve, not to mention the critical question of the destroyers' fuel reserves. One should also note that a third strike could have been made much later, after the force had proceeded to its rendezvous with its oilers, refuelled early on 9 December and then steamed back towards a flying-off position nearer Oahu. But 11 December is the earliest date such a strike could have been made, and the best which could be said about Japanese defensive and administrative obligations is that they were unlikely to have eased in the meantime. The fact is that if the Japanese were ever going to strike the base facilities at Pearl Harbor and seek to paralyse or immobilise the Pacific Fleet or prevent its using the base, then they should have concentrated against these facilities in the first-wave attack on 7 December, and then moved against the warships and aircraft in the second-wave attack. One might be able to glimpse the reaction if such a suggestion had been made, and if one has both imagination and a maliciously developed sense of humour. Such a suggestion is nonsensical, and would never have been entertained for a minute by any navy.

There remains, however, one more aspect of the question of a third strike which demands attention, and that is the source of the demand for a third strike. Prange, in *At Dawn We Slept*, points to a basic ambiguity on Nagumo's part, noting that while the First Carrier Striking Force's commander gave orders that the Japanese force would withdraw to home waters after the attack to await redeployment in the war's second phase, his Operation Order No. 3 states that during the attack preparations would be made for further offensive operations. Nagumo also stated that torpedoes would be used in follow-up operations, and that if American land-based air power had been eliminated, 'repeated attacks will be made immediately in order to achieve maximum results. However, if a powerful enemy force (moves) to counter-attack, subsequent attacks will be

"I am looking forward to dictating peace to the United States in the White House at Washington"
— ADMIRAL YAMAMOTO

What do YOU say, AMERICA?

ABOVE The first casualty of war: as is so often the case, whatever Yamamoto had said was remembered, altered and used in evidence against the accused.

Collier's

DECEMBER 12, 1942   TEN CENTS

DECEMBER 7, 1941

ABOVE The outbreak of war unleashed rabid racism in the United States, as witnessed in this savage caricature of the Emperor one year after Pearl Harbor.

had given the question of follow-up operations much thought, and continued to do so until the morning of the attack. Genda had toyed with four different options. The first two barely differed from one another and made provision for the carrier formation to stand to the north of Oahu for several days and to mount attacks on American warships wherever they might be found, whether at Pearl Harbor or at sea, over several days. The third option was not too different from the first two but incorporated an attack on Midway as the carrier formation made its way home, while the fourth option, the most interesting of all, was for the carrier formation to come east of Oahu before moving to the south of the island, repeated attacks being staged on successive days as the Japanese formation sought the utter annihilation of the Pacific Fleet. But while Genda had these options in hand, he knew on 6 December if not before that Nagumo had little interest in anything other than one double strike against Pearl Harbor. The basic aim of this attack was to inflict such damage on the Pacific Fleet that the Japanese would win a six-month respite in which south-east Asia could be conquered and the defensive perimeter could be created on which the Americans would be fought to a standstill. Nagumo and Kusaka were confident that their carrier air groups, if blessed with the element of surprise, would be able to inflict such damage and would not need more than the one double strike.

It is obvious, though, Genda hoped that his superiors could be persuaded otherwise, and that they would agree to a series of attacks. Yet any careful reading of Genda's options indicates that he was not necessarily thinking in terms of attacks on port facilities, shore installations and the like. He was thinking primarily in terms of inflicting crippling loss upon the US Pacific Fleet. Indeed, on the morning of the attack Genda limted himself to the proposal that returning Kates should be armed with tropedoes to meet any American forces which tried to mount a counter-attack, but that if none materialised, the Kates should be armed for the normal bombing role. Such deliberation amounted to no more than normal staff procedure, and there seems to be little evidence to suggest that Genda believed a follow-up attack would be

directed against it'. Prange states that the idea of 'repeated attacks' was a concession to Genda and Fuchida (p. 374).

It is not exactly clear that Fuchida made representations in favour of 'repeated attacks' prior to this order being issued by Nagumo. It is clear, however, that Genda

necessary, and on his own admission he made no representation to his superiors which suggested he was convinced of the need for such an operation. The only individual of any standing who thought outside the terms of reference supplied by warships and victories seems to have been Onishi, although it appears than even he had not foreseen the desirability of strikes against the port facilities and shore installations at Pearl Harbor. Onishi had commented on the importance of strikes against auxiliary shipping as the means of lowering the operational capacity of the enemy's fighting ships and seems to have been the only senior commander to have recognised this dimension of operations. But this argument carried little weight: Japanese carrier aircraft were never going to attack auxiliary shipping ahead of warships.

Nonetheless, the idea of the follow-up strike against Pearl Harbor's port facilities remains firmly implanted in the public's mind: it was, after all, one of the defining moments in the attack as depicted in the film *TORA! TORA! TORA!* Prange, of course, was historical adviser

in the making of this film, yet any consideration of this episode must encompass three salient facts. First, Fuchida was subsequently to claim that, as he flew back to the *Akagi*, he 'mentally earmarked for destruction the fuel-tank farms, the vast repair and maintenance facilities, and perhaps a ship or two bypassed that morning for priority targets'. But there is no evidence he had ever considered such targets for destruction before, and yet we supposed to believe that Fuchida had anticipated post-war criticism of the Japanese failure to attack these facilities and in fact proposed a course of action that would have forestalled it. Second, the account of this one incident and various other asides, particularly on Nagumo's deportment, have been provided solely by Fuchida. There is, or at least there seems to be, no independent confirmation of this version of events – one which was actually given by Fuchida on 11 December 1963. In other words, Prange passed off as fact an account of events given by Fuchida after an interval of 22 years, and in eighteen of those years Fuchida had had ample opportunity to provide his account of proceedings yet had failed to do so. Third, and most interestingly, Kusaka gave his account of proceedings in *The Pearl Harbor Papers: Inside the Japanese Plans* and makes absolutely no reference to Fuchida demanding a follow-up strike against the base facilities at Pearl Harbor (p. 162), while Genda, in his own memoirs penned at the end of the Sixties, makes absolutely no mention of any episode involving Fuchida demanding a follow-up strike on his return to the *Akagi*. Indeed, Genda categorically denied that such a demand was ever made.

Genda, writing in *Shinjuwan sakusen kaikoroku* (Recollections of the Pearl Harbor Operation: Tokyo, Yomiuri Shimbunsha, 1967; reprinted, Tokyo, Bungei Shunjusha, 1998) (pp. 300–301), stated:

According to Dr Prange's book *Tora, Tora, Tora* and others, a fierce argument took place on the bridge of the *Akagi* [after the recovering of second-wave aircraft] as regards the proposal for a second strike [i.e. the third wave]. This not true. The author [Genda] had been on the bridge for some eight hours before the start of operations and remained there over the following four days . . . Such a proposal was never made.

LEFT The real meaning of Pearl Harbor: 'We here highly resolve that these dead shall not have died in vain, that this nation, under God, shall have a new birth of freedom, and that government of the people, by the people, for the people, shall not perish from the earth.' President Abraham Lincoln, at Gettysburg, Pennsylvania, 19 November 1863.

I of course did not make such a proposal myself. The day before the attack [i.e. 6 December] I suggested [to Nagumo] that a second strike would be necessary should the first strike fall short . . . This is all that I did, but . . . Nagumo seemed to have no plan to implement a second strike. Later . . . Kusaka told me that, even before the start of the operation, he and . . . Nagumo had decided not to carry out a second strike.

There can be little real doubt that Fuchida was engaged in blatant and shameless self-advertisement in his deliberately false representation of an episode which never took place – and Fuchida inadvertently gave the lie to his subsequent account of events in his interrogation by US naval officers on 10 October 1945. Conducted under the terms of the strategic bombing survey, and subsequently written up as Appendix III to the *Campaigns of the Pacific War*, to the direct question of why there was no follow-up attack, Fuchida answered that the extent of Japanese success in neutralising American air power on Oahu was not realised until all reports were finally gathered together and analysed, some three or four days after the attack. Fuchida also stated that the knowledge that the attack had accounted for four battleships was also a factor since it seems the Japanese high command regarded this number as the guarantee that the Americans would not be able to contest Japanese moves throughout the western and central Pacific. If ever Fuchida had the opportunity to reveal his insight, albeit one of December 1963, then one would suggest that this was it. Yet there appears to be no indication whatsoever that during this interrogation he gave any inkling of what he subsequently claimed to have happened.

All this aside, there is the matter of what ordnance the carriers would have had in their magazines for use in follow-up strikes. One hundred torpedoes were delivered to the First Carrier Striking Force for this operation, which must mean that there were 60 left, presumably with the *Akagi*, *Kaga*, *Soryu* and *Hiryu*. One assumes, therefore, that further attacks could have been made against warships whether inside Pearl Harbor or at sea, but the Japanese carrier force appears to have had no Type 5 heavy bombs other than those used by Kates in the first attacking for-

mation. And for sustained operations against major warships and industrial targets, specifically the docks and power station but not necessarily the oil depot, the smaller 250-kilogram bomb lacked real destructive power.

Furthermore, it is very hard to see how Genda's fourth option – to stage repeated attacks on successive days – could have been pursued given that the Japanese carrier force had dropped its oilers two or three days short of Pearl Harbor. The first three options would have been difficult enough with the oilers separated from the carrier force by more than a full day's steaming: how the carrier formation could have continued to operate by going forward after the attack on Pearl Harbor and then carrying out successive attacks over the next three days is a mystery – again, it is not so much the major units as the destroyers which would seem to be the problem. One accepts that Genda might have wanted to have attempted such a course of action, but this sort of refuelling capability belonged not to 1941 and the Imperial Navy but 1944–1945 and the US Navy. In December 1941, the Japanese simply did not possess the oilers, the supply ships and, most critically, the manpower to undertake such operations.

Perhaps it is significant that the general opinion within the carrier air groups and in the formation as a whole was divided on the merits of a follow-up strike. There would seem to have been three different lines of argument working against a third strike, namely that the two strikes to date had done all that had been asked of them, and the six-month respite had been won; that there could be no question of a follow-up strike while the whereabouts of the American carriers was unknown; and that other operations awaited the carrier force. There appear to have been relatively few aircrew who favoured further offensive operations unless these were directed against American carrier formations, while the question of whether there would be further operations seems to have elicited different responses in different ships. In the *Shokaku*, for example, it was expected that there would be further follow-up operations after the first two attacks, although the evidence for this view is perhaps quixotic: the meal for returning aircrew was prepared and set out without beer or *sake*. On such small matters might historical argument turn.

RIGHT **Waiting for battle: a Wildcat on the deck of an American carrier.**

In seeking to properly assess the result of the Japanese attack on Pearl Harbor and to explain what followed in its wake one faces the legacy of decades of popular prejudice. The Japanese crippling of the Pacific Fleet, the elimination of the threat presented on the flank, left the Japanese free to overrun south-east Asia, and between December 1941 and April 1942 the various enemies of Japan were individually and collectively routed. In reality, the fact that Japanese landings on the Kra Isthmus were staged some minutes ahead of the attack on the Pacific Fleet points to the fact that the staging of the assaults on British, Dutch and American possessions in south-east Asia was not directly dependent upon events at Pearl Harbor. Japan's success in her various opening moves was the result of a number of factors, and the apparent success achieved at Pearl Harbor was the result of these factors coming together, not the cause of success elsewhere.

Genuine perspective, a proper reading of the attack on Pearl Harbor, exists in two forms. The first lies in an accurate appreciation of the balance of power which existed in the Pacific on 6 December 1941, and the fact is that on this date Japan possessed clear numerical superiority over the US Pacific and Asiatic Fleets. The margin of superiority that the US Navy possessed relative to the *Kaigun* was its Atlantic Fleet, and this had been gathered in another ocean in response to the situation in Europe. In virtually every class of ship, but most obviously in terms of numbers of aircraft carriers, battleships and cruisers, the *Kaigun*

ASSESSMENT AND

AFTERMATH

Three advertising posters, though only the first, being visual, really translates very easily: the irresistible force of the *samurai*. The second, inset, reads 'We would like you to become a strong man of the sea.'

The third, on the right, reads: 'Hurry to join the battle at sea and in the sky.'

海の強者になるためだ
鍛へよ強く逞しく
海軍志願兵徴募中

青少年諸君
急げ！
海の空の決戦

possessed a clear advantage over the US Pacific and Asiatic Fleets: even if the Japanese had chosen not to move against the Pacific Fleet in its base in the Hawaiian Islands at the outbreak of war, it is doubtful if the Pacific Fleet could have moved to contest the various Japanese moves in the central Pacific, still less Japanese moves in the western and south-west Pacific and south-east Asia. Any American fleet gathered for such a move would have possessed a local superiority relative to a Japanese fleet which would have been dispersed for the purposes of staging its various amphibious operations. But in terms of numbers and quality, no force the Americans could have gathered from the units in the Pacific before the outbreak of war could have offered battle on the basis of equality, still less superiority, and with any real prospect of success.

The second is the complete reverse of this argument. If the First Carrier Striking Force had managed to sink every single unit in the US Pacific Fleet, including the carriers, at the outbreak of war and then the Imperial Navy had not lost a single warship over the next 30 months, the *Kaigun* would still not have been able to offer battle on the basis of numerical equality either at the Philippine Sea in June 1944 or, more obviously, at Leyte Gulf in the following October. While the Japanese would not have been outnumbered in each and every ship type, an understanding of the forces at work is provided in the simple fact that in the battle of Leyte Gulf, the greatest naval battle in history, the US Navy had more destroyers than the Japanese had carrier aircraft.

Thus it would seem that any attempt to assess and evaluate the result of the Japanese attack on 7 December 1941 incorporates paradox and contradiction. In fact this is not the case. An understanding of the war which was unleashed on this day, depending on how evidence is presented, may contain paradox and contradiction, but in terms of this one single action the outcome can be stated very simply. Despite the losses the Japanese inflicted on the Americans, the attack was a failure. For all the appearances to the contrary, and even allowing for the fact that the world was accustomed at this time to measure states and navies against one another in terms of battleship numbers rather than any other single naval unit of cur-

rency, the Japanese attack on Pearl Harbor miscarried, and for two basic reasons.

The first is this. The Japanese attack was directed against the tools, and not the basis, of sea power. Left intact by the Japanese at Pearl Harbor were the power stations, docks and, critically, the oil farms, facilities which alone provided the means whereby a fleet could both stay on and operate from that station. Had the Japanese set about the destruction of just the oil farms, which were located above ground and could not be defended, an intact Pacific Fleet, even if it suffered not as much as a single loss, would have been forced to withdraw to San Diego, and if the Japanese had been able to devastate the dockyards and power sources, much time would have passed before the US Navy could have returned in strength to the Hawaiian Islands. But given what we know of the American industrial effort in the Second World War, this might have been sooner rather than later, and it is quite possible that the final outcome of the war in the Pacific would not have been affected overmuch: there is little doubt that the American national determination to see this war through to victory would not have been diminished or destroyed by the elimination of Pearl Harbor as the forward base in the first part of a war with Japan. And this is, of course, the second reason why the attack was a failure.

Whatever the Japanese did at Pearl Harbor, the Americans would have reversed it by virtue of their massive and irresistible industrial and demographic advantage over the Japanese. At some time or another, and again most likely sooner rather than later, the Americans would have sought and won a battle and a campaign which pointed to the certainty of overall victory. Indeed, one could plausibly identify the American campaign in the Gilbert and Ellice Islands in November 1943 as the point in time the Pacific war effectively ended. On this occasion the Americans moved in such strength that their ability to isolate and overwhelm individual garrisons, and to break any Japanese attempt to support these garrisons, was assured from the outset. This was a campaign in which the Americans could determine where and when it would take place and what level of force would be used: all the Japanese were allowed was merely the right of ineffective response. Thereafter, with the Americans possessing such overwhelming advantages, the decision of the war itself had been determined and all that remained to be answered was the exact nature and form of Japan's final defeat and the cost that would be exacted in the process.

There is only one possible objection to this portrayal of events: what would have been the situation if the Japanese had adopted the *koryaku* rather than the *kogeki*? A certain cynicism suggests that if the Americans could build frigates at Duluth in Minnesota and at Superior in Wisconsin – both locations which were further from the North Atlantic than Newfoundland is from Ireland – then they would have been able to move to recover Oahu easily enough. Moreover, if the Japanese had gone for the invasion of the island rather than the strike against the

base, they would have left themselves with an impossible logistical problem. One way or another, it is hard to see how either the outcome or timing of events would have been much effected.

The great irony of such a situation resides in the fact that at least part of this reality had been appreciated within the Imperial Navy even before the attack on Pearl Harbor. In its pre-war planning, the *Kaigun* had appreciated the critical importance of the Pearl Harbor base, but commitments in south-east Asia precluded any possibility of the opening of hostilities being accompanied by an amphibious operation aimed at securing Pearl Harbor. In the immediate aftermath of the raid, however, the realisation of the error of omission began to impress itself upon senior *Kaigun* officers, but it did so even as the demands of other theatres and the claims of various operations vied for attention and

endorsement. With the Imperial Navy having gone to war with the aim of completing its conquests by April 1942, when the next phase of a protracted war with the United States would be put into effect, Japanese officers found themselves confronting the conflicting claims of the Indian Ocean, operations designed to secure either northern Australia or Australia as a whole, and operations intended to cut American lines of communication with that country.

Only when these alternatives were on the table did the idea of an offensive in the central Pacific emerge in mid-January 1942, and for the best part of three months this option, the central Pacific option, appeared to take second place to the south-west Pacific option. The latter, based on the calculation that the forces needed for any direct move against Australia simply were not available and that the logistical burden of any such operation would prove impos-

TOP LEFT The Doolittle Raid. One of sixteen B-25 Mitchell medium bombers preparing to take off from the aircraft carrier *Hornet* 18 April 1942.

LEFT The first of the B-25 medium bombers takes off.

RIGHT The aircraft carrier *Shokaku* dodging bombs and torpedoes at the battle of the Coral Sea, 8 May 1942. The *Shokaku* was hit by three bombs and sustained damage that rendered her unable to be readied in time for the operation designed to secure Midway Islands.

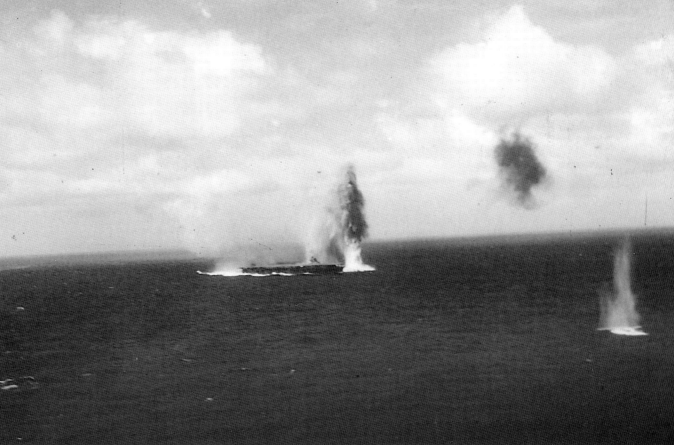

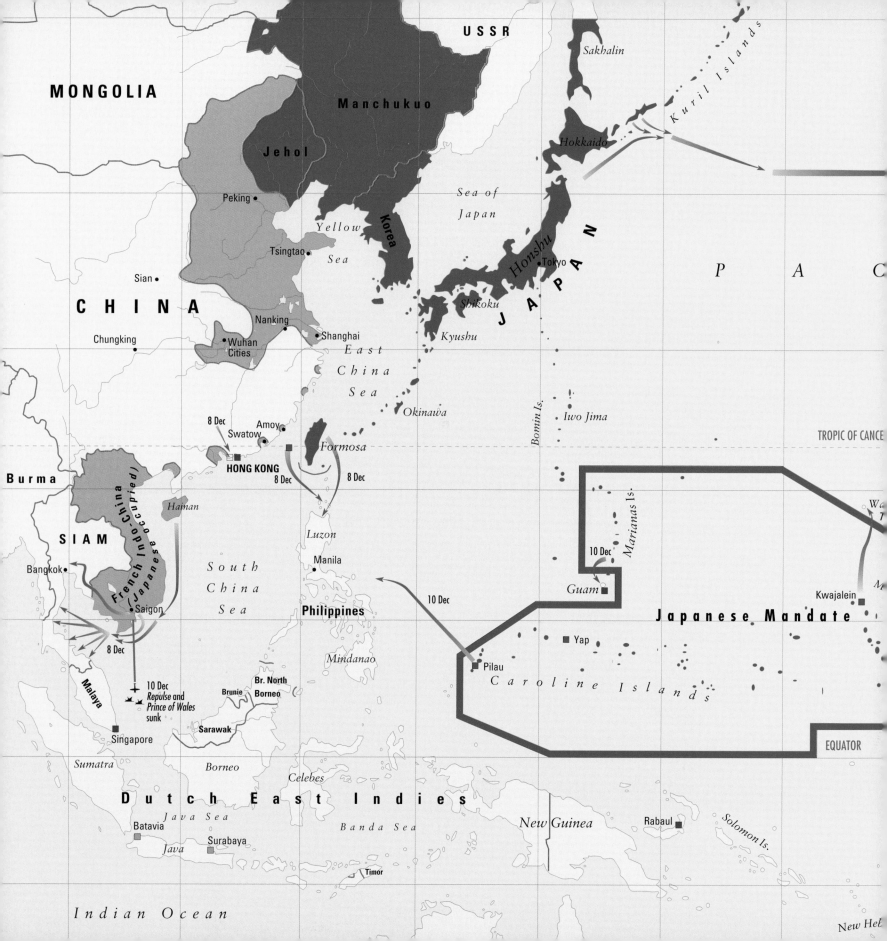

MONGOLIA

USSR

Manchukuo

Jehol

Peking •

Sakhalin

Hokkaido

*Sea of
Japan*

Korea

Kuril Islands

Yellow

Tsingtao •

Sea

CHINA

Sian •

Nanking

• Shanghai

Honshu • Tokyo

JAPAN

Chungking

• Wuhan
Cities

*East
China
Sea*

Shikoku

Kyushu

P A C

Okinawa

Bomin Is.

Iwo Jima

TROPIC OF CANCE

8 Dec
Swatow

Amoy •

Formosa

HONG KONG

8 Dec

8 Dec

Burma

Hainan

French Indo-China
(Japanese occupied)

Luzon

SIAM

Bangkok •

• Manila

10 Dec

Marianas Is.

Wa
7

• Saigon

*South
China
Sea*

Philippines

10 Dec

Guam

10 Dec

Kwajalein

M

8 Dec

Japanese Mandate

Malaya

10 Dec
Repulse and
Prince of Wales
sunk

Mindanao

Brunie

Br. North
Borneo

■ Yap

• Pilau

Caroline Islands

Sarawak

Singapore

Sumatra

Borneo

Celebes

Dutch East Indies

Java Sea

Banda Sea

New Guinea

Rabaul ■

Solomon Is.

Batavia

Surabaya

Java

EQUATOR

Timor

Indian Ocean

New Hel

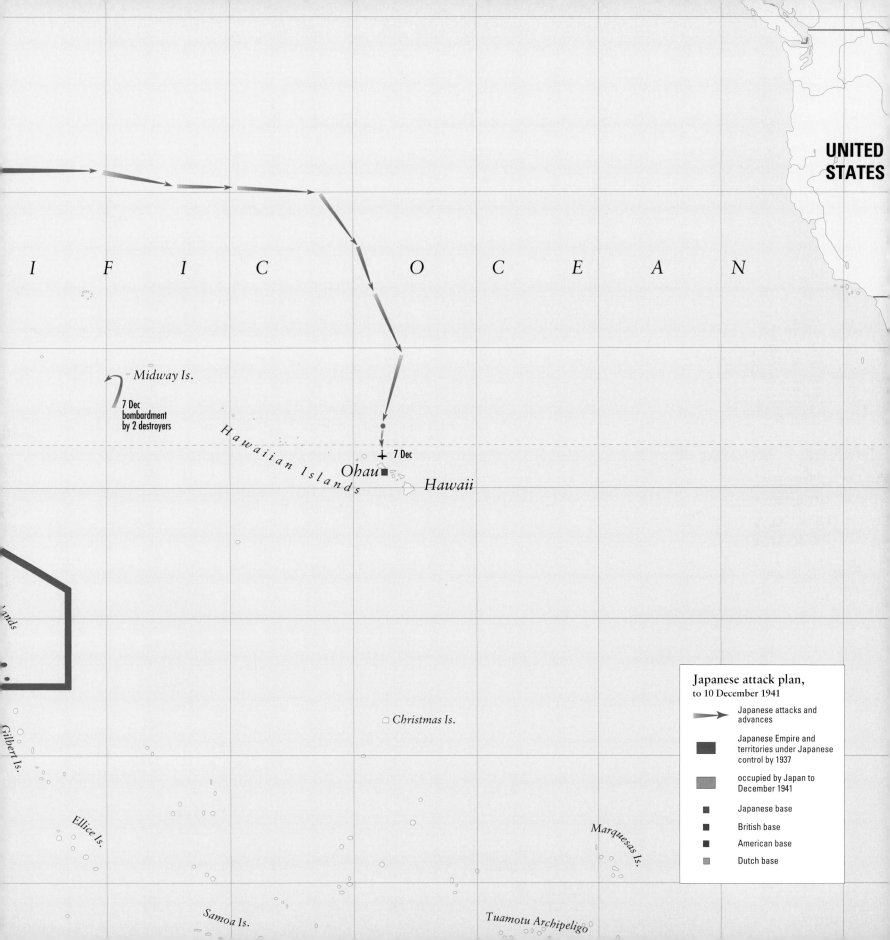

UNITED
STATES

I F I C   O C E A N

Midway Is.

7 Dec
bombardment
by 2 destroyers

H a w a i i a n   I s l a n d s

＋ 7 Dec

Ohau ■

Hawaii

...ands

○ *Christmas Is.*

Gilbert Is.

Ellice Is.

Marquesas Is.

Samoa Is.

Tuamotu Archipeligo

RIGHT Eleven Devastators gathered on the flight deck of the American aircraft carrier *Enterprise* prior to the battle of Midway Islands in June 1942. In the battle just four of fourteen torpedo-bombers from the *Enterprise* survived the attack on the Japanese 1st Carrier Striking Force, the *Kaga* evading those torpedoes aimed at her with ease.

sible, in effect had two parts. It was concerned initially with securing Port Moresby in eastern New Guinea and various small bases in the Solomons, but mainly with securing New Caledonia, Fiji and Samoa, bases from which the Imperial Navy could set about the isolation of Australia.

It was not until the first week of April that, after the high commands of the Army and Navy had agreed on an offensive into the south-west Pacific, Yamamoto and the Combined Fleet staff formally presented the demand for a central Pacific offensive. To Yamamoto what was important at this stage of proceedings was not the securing of various islands of the south-west Pacific from which American lines of communication could be attacked, and not even the south-west Pacific as such, but the bringing of American carriers to battle and the central Pacific theatre. The latter took precedence over the south-west Pacific in the thinking of the Combined Fleet commander because he calculated that only by crossing the 180th meridian, into the western hemisphere, could the Japanese hope to force battle upon the Americans, and it was his calculation that such a battle, specifically such a battle with American carrier formations, had to be provoked and won at the earliest opportunity. For Yamamoto the basis of national security had to be the elimination of the main threat, American carrier forces, in the immediate future, when the initiative and advantage of numbers still remained in Japanese hands.

The problem facing the Japanese in a central Pacific offensive, however, was that in the wake of the attack on Pearl Harbor there could be no repeat of a move against Oahu and Pearl Harbor: realisation that the garrison had been strengthened and, critically, that the Americans had introduced comprehensive radar and reconnaissance capability in order to cover the base, meant that Combined Fleet attention was fixed on the tiny atoll of Midway with its two square miles of islands, Eastern and Sand, and six square miles of lagoon. Yamamoto's intention was that the Combined Fleet should move with one task force initially against the American base at Dutch Harbor in the Aleutians before a second task force attacked Midway. Yamamoto's logic insisted that, with amphibious forces detailed to secure Midway, the Japanese move would either force the American carriers to give battle in defence of or for Midway. And if the Americans declined to be so drawn, then the Japanese would gain an important asset on the defensive perimeter they intended to cast around their conquests in the south-west Pacific and south-east Asia.

To say that the Yamamoto proposal and much of its detail left something to be desired would be an understatement: there was little real evidence that an attempt to secure Midway would force battle on the Americans. As it was, the Combined Fleet calculated that, if Midway were to attacked on 4 June, any carrier and battle forces brought to the islands could not remain on station, in order to fight and win 'the decisive battle' their action was to provoke, beyond 13 June. And this was hardly enough time make success a certainty. Moreover, the Combined Fleet also estimated that any reconnaissance force stationed at Midway would lack the numbers and the capacity for dispersal to ensure both its own security and that of any garrison, and that maintaining a force on an atoll 2,591 miles from Tokyo but only 1,323 miles from Pearl Harbor would prove impossible. Indeed these fundamental calculations involving time and distance were sufficient to destroy the whole reasoning of the plan of campaign, but what was at issue here was not simply a question of future policy but one of authority and power.

In this situation, the Combined Fleet naturally held the whip hand. In October 1941, the chief of the naval staff and the head of the planning division had agreed to the attack on Pearl Harbor when confronted by the threat of resignation on the part of Yamamoto and his staff. Now the naval staff were faced with the same threat, and this time from a Combined Fleet endowed with the prestige and standing gained by four months of victories. It had no real basis of opposition to Yamamoto's demands, and in these circumstances the agreement with the Army on a south-west Pacific priority and commitment counted for nothing. The great tragedy for the *Kaigun* and, more seriously, for Japan was that these realities were more influential than the arguments of the naval staff, which for the most part were more right than wrong, and certainly more right than the arguments of Yamamoto and the Combined Fleet staff.

Critical in the process whereby Yamamoto and the Combined Fleet imposed a central Pacific offensive for mid-1942 on superior authority were the activities of American carrier forces in the aftermath of the Pearl Harbor attack. Their basic role was defensive, covering the approaches to and the defence of Pearl Harbor. Nonetheless, with the outbreak of war, and the enforced abandonment of the American garrison in the Philippines, the prime American strategic interest after Oahu was the establishment and defence of lines of communication across the south-west Pacific to eastern Australia. American carriers thus found themselves committed to the covering of various military convoys in this theatre, and indeed by March 1942 the American commitments in the south-west Pacific, along the evidence of Japanese intentions in this theatre, had resulted in American carrier forces being evenly divided between the central and south-west Pacific stations. No less significantly, the carriers, in addition to their defensive missions, had begun to peck around the edges of Japanese conquest, most notably off Rabaul on 20 February, at Marcus on 4 March and, crucially, at Huon Gulf, eastern New Guinea, on 10 March. Off Lae and Salamaua, a total of 104 US aircraft from the *Lexington* and *Yorktown* flew through the Owen Stanley Range to attack the shipping gathered there after the Japanese landings two days earlier: two transports and two escorts were sunk and one light cruiser, two destroyers, two minesweepers and one transport were damaged extensively.

The US Pacific Fleet war diary recorded on 11 March that it was doubtful if the enemy would be greatly inconvenienced by a raid whose outcome was generally regarded as disappointing. In fact, the Americans did far better than they realised. With no forward base within easy reach, the damaged units were forced to return to Japan for repair, while the loss of the two transports was critical for a command that, because of the slenderness of its resources, had been obliged to use the same transports, troops and escorts for successive operations. But the real point for the Japanese was not their losses but the fact that the Americans were in the south-west Pacific, and with two carriers. This fact was to result in a change which worked

The Japanese aircraft carrier *Kaga* under attack off Midway Islands, 4 June 1942. She was wrecked over her length by four bomb hits at about 1024 and was abandoned about 1700: a series of detonations blew the ship apart and she sank at about 1925, the first of the first-line Japanese carriers to be sunk during the Pacific war.

itself through the Japanese decision-making system over the following four weeks as the local and national commands sought to maintain the offensive in this theatre despite the evidence of the Americans' presence.

Initially it was decided that the *Kaga* should make her way to Truk to support the operations aimed at securing Port Moresby and bases in the Solomons. Then, when it became clear more than a single carrier needed to be deployed to a sector where two enemy carriers were known to be, it was decided that the two carriers of the Fifth Carrier Division, the *Shokaku* and *Zuikaku*, along with their escorts, were to be despatched to the South-west Pacific command preparatory to their being involved in the main offensive in the central Pacific against Midway. Thus during the first half of April the Japanese plan of campaign and its timing fell into place. With the bulk of fleet units which were then in the Indian Ocean scheduled to return to the home islands for quick overhaul before the central Pacific operation, Port Moresby and bases in the Solomons were to be secured in the first week or so of May 1942, after which time the *Shokaku* and *Zuikaku* were to return to Japan. Then, in the last week of May, various formations were to sail for the Aleutians and Midway, and after 13 June, whether a decisive battle had been fought or not, the main formations were to retire, the battle forces to Japan and the carrier forces to Truk. The south-west Pacific priority was then to come to the fore with Japanese forces moving to secure New Caledonia, Fiji and Samoa before the main forces were again committed to offensive action in the central Pacific, this time against Johnston Island and in August.

Although Japanese plans were not developed beyond a general intention, it is clear that the operation against Johnston was seen as the means of again seeking 'the decisive battle' if such an engagement did not materialise off Midway. It is also clear that, with Midway and Johnston under their control, the Japanese planned to move directly against Oahu: the basic plan of campaign would seem to make very little sense unless this was the general intent.

So Yamamoto and the Combined Fleet marked out the path that was to lead the Imperial Navy, and the US Navy, to battles in the Coral Sea in May and off Midway

LEFT A Kawanishi H6K5 Type 97 Mavis flying boat under attack. The Mavis was used for very long-ranged reconnaissance and in fact bombed Pearl Harbor, to no effect, in March 1942. There was no reconnaissance of Pearl Harbor before 7 December 1941, and prior to the battle of Midway in June 1942 the ability to read Japanese signals enabled the Americans to station units in French Frigate Shoals, therefore denying the Japanese a sheltered place where submarine-tankers could refuel the flying boats.

Islands in June, but in the planning process three American operations were of considerable importance. The importance of the raid on Japanese shipping in Huon Gulf has been noted, and for Yamamoto the relevance of this episode lay not in the theatre – the southwest Pacific – but in the reality of American carrier activity. The raid only confirmed the implications of the earlier American attack on Marcus, although in truth from the beginning of February 1942 Japanese concern caused by the pinprick raids on the Marshalls and Gilberts on the first of the month led to the *Shokaku* and *Zuikaku* being ordered to patrol the approaches to Tokyo while the other carriers were involved in operations in the Indies. But it was the Doolittle Raid of 18 April 1942 that was to have the greatest influence on Japanese policy, not in terms of decision because the Port Moresby/Solomons-central Pacific-south-west Pacific formula had been adopted before this attack, but in terms of silencing opposition to Yamamoto's *diktat* and in ensuring *Kaigun* concentration of attention on this seemingly all-important operation in the central Pacific.

The Doolittle Raid, which for propaganda purposes the Japanese tried to dismiss with some cause as The Do-Nothing Raid, first took shape between 10 and 15 January 1942 when Captain Francis S. Low suggested a bombing raid against the Japanese home islands using army medium bombers operating from the deck of a carrier. He and Captain Donald B. Duncan, another staff officer in Washington, were detailed to work out an operational plan. For the next two months, however, the US Pacific Fleet was too committed to consider this option, but in February 1942 the fleet carrier *Hornet*, after four months of exercises in the Caribbean, entered the Pacific. After more exercises she came north, arriving at San Francisco on 1 April.

The *Hornet* was five feet wider in the beam than her sister ships and, in the course of her first set of exercises before she entered the Panama Canal, had shown that she could embark and operate the B-25 Mitchell bomber. As it was, when she left San Francisco on 2 April with sixteen Mitchells on board, her crew assumed that months of training and preparation were to be rewarded by relegation to ferrying duties. Instead, eleven days later the

Hornet, which sailed in the company of two heavy cruisers, four destroyers and one oiler, effected a rendezvous with the carrier *Enterprise*, one heavy and one light cruiser, four destroyers and one oiler in latitude 38° north, longitude 180°. With the Mitchells on her flight deck because they could not be stowed in the hangars, the *Hornet* could not provide herself with combat air patrol, hence the presence of the *Enterprise*. The combined formation, Task Force 16, would reach a planned position some 450 miles to the east of Tokyo from where it was to launch the Mitchells on the afternoon of 19 April.

The Japanese detected radio traffic in the central Pacific after 8 April, when the *Enterprise* group left Pearl Harbor, and this was correctly interpreted as indication of an impending raid on Honshu. What the Japanese could not anticipate, however, was that the American carriers were to stage such a raid with medium bombers committed to a one-way flight: the aircraft would make their way to airfields in China after striking at various targets on Honshu. However, on the morning of 18 April and at a distance of some 750 miles from Tokyo, Task Force 16 blundered into a picket line of fishing boats deployed specifically for the task of providing early warning of any American approach toward the capital. As the carriers' escorts accounted for four of the picket boats one, the *Nitto Maru*, was able to transmit a warning before being sunk.

Thus precisely forewarned, the Japanese naval authorities concluded that, assuming the Americans did not abandon their obvious intention, many hours would pass before they came into range. For Task Force 16, the unwelcome contact with the Japanese boats suggested that an attack be launched immediately, and the fact that some of the bombers would be very unlikely to reach friendly airfields in China was accepted. Accordingly, when the Mitchells struck at various military, oil and industrial targets in Tokyo, Kube, Yokohama and Nagoya, and even hit the aircraft carrier *Ryuho* in dock in the Yokohama Navy Yard with one solitary bomb, the Americans encountered no fighter opposition and very little flak. As the Japanese never considered that the enemy aircraft were to make their way to China, the Mitchells were able to make good their escape. Four successfully reached airfields in China and one made for the safety of Vladivostok: the remaining aircraft crashed over China as they exhausted their fuel. Apart from one man killed during the landings, all but eight of the American personnel were led through Japanese lines by Chinese peasants. Of the eight that were captured, three were executed on the spurious charge of having bombed civilians, while the Chinese peasantry paid an immediate and savage price for sheltering and helping the American airmen.

Strategically the Doolittle Raid was of little account: indeed staging it threatened to cripple the US Pacific Fleet because it needed the use of three fleet carriers in the central Pacific – the two carriers of Task Force 16 plus the *Lexington* in a covering role – at a time when the Americans became aware of Japanese intentions towards Port Moresby and the Solomons. In the event, the early launching of the raid meant that the *Lexington* was freed two days earlier than anticipated and was able to return to the Coral Sea just in time to meet the *Shokaku* and *Zuikaku* and the other enemy forces gathered to secure the capture of the main allied base in eastern New Guinea. Thus was fought, between 5 and 8 May 1942, the first naval battle between ships that did not sight one another and the first fleet action since the battle of Jutland in 1916 – an engagement with which it is usually contrasted on account of Jutland's being the last in a line of battles which reached back to the age of sail.

In fact, Jutland and the Coral Sea share numerous points of similarity – more perhaps than they do points of difference. Both battles were fought with weapons which were untested in combat, and both sides faced unknown dangers without possessing any body of experience and combat knowledge on which to draw. Both sides had to contend with either uncertain or poor communications and they were fighting battles whose areas had grown far beyond that of past experience and in which speeds (of ships, not to mention those of aircraft) had increased to an even greater extent. Thus time was compressed, specifically decision-making time. Intelligence varied between the scarce and the abundant, but irrespective of its quality, it was invariably misapplied and its full value went unrealised. In both battles what might now be termed 'target

identification' and 'fire distribution' were more often wrong than right, and in both actions there were probably as many bad decisions as good on the part of commanders who, for a variety of reasons, had only incomplete knowledge of what was happening around them and where the enemy might be. In both actions light, wind, sun and, above all, night played very important parts, and in both actions defensive concerns, the safety of costly ships, were very important in helping to ensure what seemed at the time to be indecisive outcomes. And finally, in both battles the defence prevailed and decisively so, even though their losses were the greater. In both battles the defence prevailed in part because of a intelligence advantage which enabled them to fight, or at least attempt to fight, the type of battle that accorded to their strategic interest and advantage.

In the battle of the Coral Sea the Americans lost the *Lexington*, one destroyer and one oiler, while the *Yorktown* was damaged. The Japanese lost the light carrier *Shoho*, which had been assigned a covering role, while the *Shokaku* was damaged severely enough to force her immediate withdrawal from the battle area and the *Zuikaku*'s air group was so mauled that the carrier herself was as good as *hors de combat*. Strategically, the battle resulted in a clear American success because the Japanese, faced with unreduced enemy air groups around Port Moresby and in northern Australia, chose to abandon their planned assault on Port Moresby, deciding instead to mount it – as it should always have been – after the Midway operation. In fact, far more serious than the local matter of ownership of Port Moresby was that the damage incurred by the two carriers of the Fifth Carrier Division cost the First Carrier Striking Force what should have been its margin of superiority at Midway.

With the *Shokaku* and *Zuikaku* eliminated from an early June schedule, although the latter could have been readied in time for a postponed offensive, the First Carrier Striking Force had just four carriers with which to lead the assault on Midway, a total which was wholly inadequate given that the Americans had four carriers in the Pacific and the *Yorktown* had not been sunk. In fact, the *Yorktown* was able to operate aircraft and return to

RIGHT One US battleship restored to health. The *Tennessee* was in dockyard hands between August 1942 and May 1943, emerging to take part in the Aleutian campaign. With a wholly new superstructure, her old secondary armament gone and with new radars and secondary and tertiary armaments, she took part in every major landing operation in the central Pacific after November 1943. She was hit by a *kamikaze* off Okinawa and extensively damaged. The difference of silhouette between this and her pre-1941 state is remarkable: she looks a different ship

Pearl Harbor under her own power and without assistance despite the damage she incurred in the Coral Sea, and herein of course was the stuff of which heroic legend is made. With an estimated 90 days needed for the carrier's overhaul and refit, she was allowed just three days in order to be made ready for battle, after which she could be afforded full and proper treatment befitting her condition. Events, of course, conspired to deny her such treatment, but not before she had played her full part in the battle off Midway on 4 June 1942. But that is another story.

Over the last decade we have heard from our national leaders that recourse to the use of force has been made in order to solve specific problems, be it the Iraqi occupation of Kuwait or Serbian atrocities in Kosovo. War

judgement which the Statesman and General exercises is rightly to understand [the nature of] the war in which he engages, not to take it for something, or wish to make of it something, which it is not... and it is impossible for it to be' and that wars invariable assume courses and outcomes very different from that intended by their authors.

The Japanese attack on the US Pacific Fleet at its Pearl Harbor base on 7 December 1941, whether alone or in the company of the Japanese plans which led to the battles in the Coral Sea and off Midway Islands, certainly provides evidence of the correctness of Clausewitz's dictum, and also of von Moltke the Elder's famous observation that no plan ever survives the first contact of battle. Such matters as plans, organisation and doctrine are merely the common basis of change, and the application

seldom if ever solves problems. Problems are changed or transposed by war because man made war in his own image, complete with all the elements of human frailty and misjudgement therein. No summary of war better illustrates this than the statement drawn from Clausewitz that 'The first, the grandest, and most decisive act of

of force is not liable to any simple or predictable cause-and-effect relationship. Pearl Harbor specifically and the Pacific war in general provide evidence of this fact. As the Pacific war ended, the American power to arrange the peace as she would wish, most obviously with respect to the situation within China and her desire to exclude the

RIGHT The futility and folly of the attack on Pearl Harbor. Few illustrations better demonstrate the difference between battleships of different generations than this photograph of the *Oklahoma*, having been salvaged, alongside the battleship *Wisconsin* in 1944. The *Iowa*-class battleships were in a class of their own, and certainly represented a better investment than the *Yamato* and *Musashi*, but the smallness of the *Oklahoma*, and the obvious indications of inferiority relative to a member of a successor class, is potent evidence that the Japanese, in striking against an ageing battle force, attacked the wrong targets, ships that very much belonged to another time.

Soviet Union from the Japanese war, was less than it had been at any time over the previous three and a half years, and yet this statement takes no account of the achievements of the United States during that time.

Those achievements were awesome. In the Pacific, in the ocean where the Japanese hoped to begin proceedings with an assault that would cripple American power and will, US warships recorded in Operation Hailstone, at Truk on 17 February 1944, the most destructive single day in merchant shipping history and at Leyte Gulf, on 25 October 1944, the most destructive single day in naval warfare. In February 1945 American carrier forces raided the Japanese home islands with five groups with sixteen fleet and light fleet carriers, nine capital ships, seventeen heavy and light cruisers and 77 destroyers: of these vessels, just two carriers, four battleships, two heavy and two light cruisers had been launched before the outbreak of war. In the course of the raids on the Japanese home islands in the last weeks of the war, American carriers were committing more than 1,000 aircraft to single offensive operations and their fighters were mounting combat air patrol over Japanese airfields. And lest the logistic effort needed to maintain a fleet on station be forgotten, it bears recounting that off Okinawa between March and July 1945 American carrier formations used more oil than did Japan as a nation in 1944. So much, then, for a war begun at a date and in a way of Japan's own choosing, and in this failure is one fact that permits this story to be brought to its close. It concerns the fate of just one of the Japanese warships which took part in the attack on Pearl Harbor, the heavy cruiser *Tone*. The *Tone* was the very last of the warships of the First Carrier Striking Force to be sunk, and it is difficult to resist the idea that her fate, cruel as it was, was nonetheless an appropriate comment on both the attack on Pearl Harbor and the Japanese war effort per se. The last survivor of the force which had conducted the attack on the US Pacific Fleet at its base at Pearl Harbor, she was caught and sunk at her moorings at Kure, in the Inland Sea, in the great raid of 24 July 1945 when American and British carrier groups put 1,747 of their aircraft over the Inland Sea, its bays, its harbours and its islands.

Once a thing is done .

. a fool sees it

THE PEARL HARBOR ATTACK
ASPECTS OF JAPANESE PERCEPTIONS

TOHMATSU HARUO

When the first news of the success of the attack on Pearl Harbor, and the destruction of the American battle force, reached the Japanese public, a sense of euphoria swept the country: even liberal intellectuals, who might have been expected to harbour misgivings, were caught up in the prevailing elation. Iwanami Shigeo, the owner of the famous publishing house that symbolised liberal progressive elements in pre – and post-Second World War Japan, recorded an enthusiastic entry in his diary: he was uplifted by the belief that the strike against the American fleet would change the nature of the conflict in China.

At a distance of some 60 years, such logic may seem elusive, but the conflict in China was then in its fifth year, and despite government propaganda and control of information, the war was extremely unpopular among the Japanese people. From the time of the Meiji Restoration various pan-Asian ideas had commanded much support in Japan, while at the Paris peace conference in 1919 the allied powers, in setting out the Covenant of the League of Nations, denied Japan recognition of the principle of racial equality. Thus after the outbreak of Japan's 'special undeclared war,' Japan embraced a contradictory policy, one that demanded acknowledgement of the principle of racial equality but at the same time involved the prosecution of a war of conquest against another Asian nation. A war against the United States did not present the same moral dilemma for the Japanese, indeed quite the contrary: the attack on Pearl Harbor induced a sense of liberation and relief. From the time of the attack Japan was absolved of blame for the China war: responsibility for that conflict was vested in a China that was a willing tool of western colonialism. Apart from the period between 1945 and 1951, when Japan was under American military occupation and not enunciating such views was *de rigueur*, this Japanese perception of the Pearl Harbor attack has remained largely unchanged. To draw a parallel with a more recent war, the Japanese attack on the US Pacific Fleet at Pearl Harbor was not unlike the Egyptian crossing of the Suez Canal in the war of October 1973. The very fact of the attack paid for past humiliation, and it represented a challenge to a more powerful aggressor that subsequent defeat could neither diminish nor demean. Pearl Harbor was a great military victory but it changed fundamentally and forever the moral balance to Japan's advantage.

Such views largely survived national defeat. The attack on Pearl Harbor provoked no sense of guilt, only criticism that it did not neutralise American naval strength long enough and hence permitted the enemy to recover rapidly. In this context, criticism of the attack came chiefly from former naval officers who took part in the Pacific war. Typical of such criticism, and perhaps the best articulated, emanated from Captain Mayuzumi Haruo. Mayuzumi was among the most respected gunnery officers of the Imperial Navy, and was a survivor of the battle of Leyte Gulf. He had also been commanding officer of the heavy cruiser *Tone*. His criticism was basically shaped by inter-war strategic planning and reflected the fact that the Imperial Navy's standards of night-fighting, gunnery and torpedo operations had reached remarkable heights. Mayuzumi's view was that it would have been wiser for the Imperial Navy to have remained with the defensive strategy that had prevailed for most of the inter-war period, one that envisaged intercepting an advancing US fleet in the designated battle zone in the western Pacific. Once the US fleet was drawn into a Tsushima-type engagement, Mayuzumi argued, its annihilation would have been almost certain.

Interestingly, a similar criticism of the attack came from another distinguished naval officer whose strategic inclinations were very different from those of Mayuzumi. Admiral Inoue Shigeyoshi is now remembered as Yamamoto's right-hand man in preventing Japan's alliance with Germany in the late 1930s. His political creed apart, Inoue differed very considerably from Yamamoto. While Yamamoto built up carrier forces and pursued an aggressively offensive strategy against the United States, Inoue emphasised the importance of shore-based, long-ranged aircraft as the core of Japanese naval strength. By converting the Marshalls (and Marianas) into a chain of impregnable fortresses complete with air groups, Inoue insisted in January 1941 that Japan, even if she could not win, would most certainly not lose a war with the United States. For Inoue the attack on Pearl Harbor was not merely a waste of resources but an act of folly: he was not of the persuasion that war with the United States was inevitable. Not only ex-Imperial Navy veterans but also some contemporary scholars such as Professor Hata Ikuhiko, the foremost authority on Japanese military history, have entertained similar views, that there were alternatives to an attack on Pearl Harbor and a war with the United States.

A recent study of Japanese perceptions of Perry's visit to Japan in 1853* has revealed an intriguing and little-known aspect of the Pearl Harbor attack. At the time of his first meeting with Japanese officials, Commodore Matthew S. Perry attached a white flag to President Buchanan's letter to the Tokugawa Shogun, indicating that the Japanese should seek peace by presenting the white flag if negotiations went wrong and the two countries found themselves at war. This was the first time that the Japanese learnt about the meaning of the white flag in the western conduct of war. With the establishment of formal diplomatic relations between the two countries, the two Governments deliberately suppressed the record of this episode. But the facts were known to a small number of individuals who formed the political and intellectual elite within Japan at that time, and these included members of the Yamamoto clan into which Takano Isoroku was inducted, and whose family name he adopted after his parents died. Thus the future commander of the Combined Fleet inherited that part of the clan memory which harboured strong anti-American sentiment as a result of this event. According to Miwa, Yamamoto executed the attack on Pearl Harbor in order to establish a 'balance of vengeance' between the two countries, to make good the humiliation of the Japanese nation by Perry's gunboat diplomacy in 1853. It was likely that in 1941 the majority of the Japanese, even if they were unaware of the detail of events in 1853, more or less shared Yamamoto's sentiments.

Be that as it may, the national mythologies of the United States and Japan still insist on very different interpretations of the attack on Pearl Harbor. For the Americans, it remains 'The Day of Infamy', for the Japanese 'The Greatest Single Victory that Disproved White Supremacy'. The perception gap between the two countries has continued for a lifetime, and no doubt will continue into the future, but agreement between the two countries exists in the fact that the Pearl Harbor attack was the single event which gave momentum to both the Americans and Japanese to fully and whole-heartedly commit themselves to the war which was initiated on this day. Whether the war was one that was in the interest of either or both countries is another matter, suffice to note the author's use of the Clausewitzian dictum: wars rarely proceed or end as their authors intend. One would note that in December 1941 neither the Japanese nor the Americans could have anticipated that within four years Japan would be a country under American occupation. This, indeed, was a fact of life that followed inexorably from the attack on Pearl Harbor, and it may be the one point on which there can be general agreement.

*Miwa Kimitada, *Hidden White Flag of Perry*: A Psycho-historical study of US-Japan Relations, Tokyo, Sophia University Press, 1999.

PEARL HARBOR AND THE AMERICAN ODYSSEY

W. SPENCER JOHNSON

The Pacific war was fought by American military forces with a ferocity that was largely absent from their conduct of operations in the European theatre of operations. In part this stemmed from a racist disdain for the Japanese and a difference in cultural approach to the conduct of war, but in part, it stemmed from the attack on Pearl Harbor: the exhortation 'Remember Pearl Harbor' was not a mere slogan, manipulated by those in power to move the American people and its military forces once again to war, a mere updated version of the incidents that had justified America's previous wars, the *Lusitania* (the liner sunk in May 1915 and used as justification for America's entry into the First World War in April 1917), Fort Sumter and John Brown (at the outset of the American civil war), and Lexington and Concord (and the War of Independence). For Americans of the WWII generation 'Remember Pearl Harbor' had genuine and obvious meaning, and its relevance was in no way demeaned by the onset of the Cold War. The emergence of deterrence as the basis of national defence carried with it implications in terms of preparation and readiness that were unprecedented, and which rendered Pearl Harbor ever more pertinent as example of the perils and pit-falls that were likely to beset the unready. A slogan of 'No More Pearl Harbors' enervated the Cold War years and persists today in the American approach to security affairs In this period, too, Pearl Harbor absolved the United States of guilt or blame for the attacks on Hiroshima and Nagasaki with which the Pacific war ended.

These were times of massive certainties, not least in terms of the United States and the American people being assured of the loyal support and endorsement of all who upheld Western values of God and country. The reality of American power throughout these decades, and the subsequent national triumph in the post-war confrontation that left the United States as the world's only superpower, has confirmed that element of certainty and national confidence. Throughout this period, Pearl Harbor has retained its place in American national consciousness, not least because of its physical location and the preservation of the battleship *Arizona* as memorial to the Day of Infamy, but also with the recent addition of the battleship *Missouri*, moored next to the *Arizona*, on whose deck the instrument of Japanese surrender was signed four years later, evidence of America's new power and place in the world. For Americans, WWII begins and ends in Pearl Harbor.

Nonetheless, American perceptions of the Pacific war itself have changed and for various reasons. The onset of the Cold War, and the confrontation with the Soviet Union, saw the United States and Japan share common concerns and shoulder common efforts to hold at bay a threat to both. Japan also emerged as the United States' major trading partner. The reconstitution of the Japanese armed services gradually took place to the extent that, in terms of destroyers and surface units, the Japanese Maritime Self-Defence Force (JMSDF) today has more and more modern and sophisticated units than can be found in the British and French navies combined. With American naval units given access to Japanese home ports, and the Japanese military able to double US forward deployed naval and air strength overnight, Japan has arguably become the United States's most important ally in Northeast Asia, while her significance in eastern Asia and the western Pacific, where the three major powers [the United States, Russia and China] in the world meet, is self-evident. These matters have made for change over time in the American relationship with Japan. Japan's deeply felt post-WWII abhorrence of war and the post-war American-influenced Japanese constitution, have combined to define Japanese restraint on the international stage: Japan has not involved herself in any military activity beyond the home islands, not even under UN auspices. The United States remains in many ways the guarantor of Japan's good faith and restraint in a part of the world where memories of Japanese military occupation are never far from the surface. There is obvious irony in such developments, and always in such cases some public bemusement: Americans did not fight the Second World War to such ends, but then peace, invariably, is more difficult to wage than war. In the intervening years since Pearl Harbor was bombed, American society itself has undergone profound changes, much of it led by the very generation that came of age during WWII. The old industries have been largely replaced, as have many of the worst aspects of racial discrimination and denigration, and Japanese Americans today most certainly are not subjected to the kind of treatment that they were forced to endure before and during the Second World War. There remains a certain wariness with regard to Japan, largely on account of economic policies and trading practices, but in real terms what divides the United States and Japan are largely nickel-and-dime matters and these do not even begin to equate to those that divided the two countries in the 1930s and early 1940s.

But Pearl Harbor, indeed the Second World War in general, retains a very special place in American thinking. This is partly because the Second World War was the first moving-picture war and therefore one that is presented, seemingly endlessly, on both the big screen and on television. It also possesses a profile in terms of national achievement that the Korean and Vietnamese conflicts lacked. As Studs Terkel termed it, WWII was the "last good war". But there is also the fact that the Second World War saw the emergence of the United States as the world's greatest power, and therefore the importance of the Pearl Harbor attack is both obvious and at the same time elusive. The Japanese attack set in motion the process of America's transformation, but its real importance lies in America's capacity to reverse the consequences of the attack that was designed, and very nearly succeeded, to render American power in the Pacific impotent. In a sense we do not grasp the larger meaning of Pearl Harbor for America and the world. Great Powers are not powers that win every battle. or for whom the issue is never in doubt. Great Powers are those that can absorb defeat, and then go on to win either that or the next war. Paradoxically, Pearl Harbor was proof of national greatness because the United States, inside the space of four years, was able to move forward to historically unprecedented victories in Europe and the western Pacific. Herein lies the basis of national faith, the touchstone of a national confidence that sometimes is perceived as impatient and insistant on doing things the American way. All great powers, and the United States is no exception, have their mythologies, their *credo*. For the American nation there are few battlefields for the Pacific war: the islands of the western Pacific are, for the most part, small, distant, and rarely visited accept by aging veterans who fought and lost their comrades of a lifetime there. Naval battles are demarcated in terms of latitude, longitude, and time. Their only marker is a procession of waves, each like the other. Pearl Harbor, therefore, occupies a unique place in American history and national identity, as the place that can gather together all the battlefields of the Pacific war and the defeat that was the first faltering step in the American wartime odyssey, across the Pacific, to Tokyo Bay and its national emergence as the greatest single power on earth.

APPENDICES AND OPERATIVE DETAILS

The Aircraft Establishment of the First Carrier Striking Force

Arguably one of the most irritating aspects of the Japanese attack on the US Pacific Fleet at its base at Pearl Harbor on 7 December 1941 lies in history's inability, over six decades, to definitively state the number of aircraft available and used for this operation. To give but one example of this problem, one only has to consult Gordon W. Prange's *At Dawn We Slept, The Untold Story of Pearl Harbor* to understand this problem. On pp. 391 and 392 Prange sets out the air establishment of every carrier, making a total of 378 aircraft. On p. 375, however, Prange states that the number of aircraft committed to the two strikes was 355, and on p. 376 that 54 aircraft were retained for combat air patrol – a total of 409 aircraft.

According to the Japanese official history, it would seem that in planning for this operation the First Carrier Striking Force was to sail with a total of 432 aircraft. This total consisted of the *Akagi* and *Kaga* each contributing 27 Kates, eighteen Vals and eighteen Zekes; the *Soryu* and *Hiryu* each having eighteen-strong formations of all three types of aircraft, and the *Zuikaku* and *Shokaku* each having 27 Kates, 27 Vals and eighteen Zekes. Each and every sub-formation, however, was to have a reserve element of three units: thus the *Akagi* and *Kaga* in fact had 27 and three Kates, eighteen and three Vals and eighteen and three Zekes,

and carried over 63 plus nine aircraft. The overall totals by aircraft would have been 144 plus eighteen Kates for a total of 162 Kates, 126 plus eighteen Vals for a total of 144 dive-bombers, and 108 plus eighteen Zekes for a total of 126 fighters: the overall totals would be 378 plus 54, giving a grand total of 432 aircraft.

Figures to support this argument are shown in Table 1.

The total overall, and certain of the individual totals, present genuine problems of understanding, because they seemingly cannot be reconciled with the standard reference work on Japanese warships, A.J. Watts and B.G. Gordon's *The Imperial Japanese Navy*. Published in 1971, this book gives the maximum operational, spare and total capacity of the units of the First Carrier Striking Force as 392, 101 and 493 respectively. The last of these figures is confirmed by Hansgoerg Jentschura, Dieter Jung and Peter Mickel in *Warships of the Imperial Japanese Navy, 1869–1945*, though this source does not make any distinction between operational and spare aircraft. This distinction is admitted in other sources, but is misleading in the sense that the spare capacity of Japanese carriers did not refer to crated or prefabricated aircraft which could be assembled and brought into service while the carrier

TABLE 1 AIRCRAFT WITH THE CARRIERS OF THE FIRST CARRIER STRIKING FORCE

Carrier	The total number of aircraft afforded by pre-operational planning, (Operational plus Reserve)				A.J. Watts and B.G. Gordon, *The Imperial Japanese Navy* Operational and spare	Jentschura, Jung and Mickel, *Warships of the Imperial Japanese Navy, 1869–1945*	The total number of aircraft embarked in the carriers: source, *Hawai sakusen... p. 235.*			
	Type 97 B5N2 Kates	Type 99 D3A1 Vals	Type 00 A6M2 Zekes	Total			Type 97 B5N2 Kates	Type 99 D3A1 Vals	Type 00 A6M2 Zekes	Total
Akagi	27 + 3	18 + 3	18 + 3	63 + 9 = 72	66 + 25	91	27	18	21	66
Kaga	27 + 3	18 + 3	18 + 3	63 + 9 = 72	72 + 18	90	27	27	21	75
Hiryu	18 + 3	18 + 3	18 + 3	54 + 9 = 63	57 + 16	73	18	18	21	57
Soryu	18 + 3	18 + 3	18 + 3	54 + 9 = 63	53 + 18	71	18	18	21	57
Shokaku	27 + 3	27 + 3	18 + 3	72 + 9 = 81	72 + 12	84	27	27	18	72
Zuikaku	27 + 3	27 + 3	18 + 3	72 + 9 = 81	72 + 12	84	27	27	18	72
Sub-total	144 + 18	126 + 18	108 + 18	378 + 54 =	392 + 101					
Total	162	144	126	432	493	493	144	135	120	399

The numbers in the planning columns are the number of operational aircraft and the reserve that were to be given to individual carriers. The totals given in the Watts & Gordon column refer to operational aircraft and spares. The numbers given in the final columns relate only to operational aircraft.

was engaged in operations. Reserve capacity in Japanese carriers referred to the space which would have been occupied by fully assembled units. The reserve dimension referred to aircraft and aircrew committed to the carrier in addition to standard sub-formations. Thus the total number of aircraft that could be carried was not 392, however tempting that figure may seem to be as the *ne plus ultra*: the final line in the sand was 493.

What numbers were embarked for the operation, as distinct from the numbers that planning dictated should be embarked, is given in the official Japanese history as 399, a figure that would seem to be too low. This total numbered 144 Kates, 135 Vals and 120 Zekes and consisted of the *Akagi*'s contribution of 27 Kates, eighteen Vals and 21 Zekes for a total of 66 aircraft, the *Kaga*'s 27 Kates, 27 Vals and 21 Zekes for a total of 75 aircraft; both the *Soryu* and *Hiryu* had eighteen Kates, eighteen Vals and 21 Zekes for totals of 57 aircraft each; and both the *Zuikaku* and *Shokaku* embarked 27 Kates, 27 Vals and eighteen Zekes for totals of 72 aircraft each.

As noted elsewhere, Japanese planning allowed for 189 aircraft in the first attack wave whereas 183 actually took part in the operation, and for 171 aircraft in the second attack wave whereas 167 actually took part in the operation. Overall, therefore, planning allowed for two attacks with a total of 360 aircraft: on the day, the two attack forces numbered 350 aircraft. In addition, according to the Japanese National Defence Agency's official history of the Pacific war, *Hawai sakusen*, pp. 239–240, the Japanese flew combat air patrol in four different phases. Initially, between 0600 and 0900 combat air patrol consisted of three Zekes drawn from the *Hiryu* and *Soryu* and twelve from the *Shokaku* and *Zuikaku*: between 1000 and 1115 it consisted of 23 Zekes, five from the *Akagi* and *Kaga*, six from the *Soryu* and *Hiryu* and twelve from the *Zuikaku* and *Shokaku*: between 1115 and 1300, and as a mirror image of the second phase, it consisted of three Zekes drawn from the *Soryu* and *Hiryu* and twelve from the *Zuikaku* and *Shokaku*: between 1300 and 1730 it consisted of first eighteen and then nine Zekes drawn evenly from the three constituent carrier divisions.

The various totals within these various combat air patrol numbers can be accommodated within the total number of aircraft which may be assumed to have been embarked, specifically the total of 21 Zekes – the eighteen plus three formula – allegedly embarked in each of the *Akagi*, *Kaga*, *Soryu* and the *Hiryu*. Unfortunately, there is also one reference, again cited in *Hawai sakusen* and on the same pages as the previous reference, to the *Zuikaku* and *Shokaku* each committing three Vals to anti-submarine patrols around the carrier force at the time when the first combat air patrol was launched. It is unclear whether these aircraft represented three aircraft over and above the strike forces' allocation or whether, possibly, the number really meant a divisional contribution from the first strike numbers, which declined from 189 to 183 with three Vals in the 'absent' column. Whichever way numbers are counted, calculations on the basis of formations seem always likely to be beset by problems of ambiguity and incompleteness.

Similar problems attend any attempt to calculate the size of formations from the other direction. It is known, for example, that once all the returning aircraft from the two attack waves were recovered, the carrier force had 265 aircraft available for operations. The First Carrier Striking Force also had a minimum of 111 aircraft that had been damaged, but this is a figure which takes no account of the number of aircraft from the *Hiryu* that had been damaged other than one Kate. Her sister ship, the *Soryu*, reported that she had three Kates from the first wave, thirteen Vals from the second, and two Zekes from the first and four Zekes from the second out of service, a total of five aircraft from the first and seventeen from the second wave damaged and not immediately available for operations. But a return from the Second Carrier Division indicating three Kates, 23 Vals and twenty Zekes damaged is obviously erroneous: even on incomplete return the *Hiryu* and *Soryu* recorded four Kates damaged, and if twenty Zekes were damaged while the *Soryu* had six fighters damaged, then every one of the fourteen fighters from the *Hiryu* must have incurred damage, including the one recorded as having been lost. There is nothing in the returns of all the other carriers to suggest that every single fighter from one of their number might have incurred battle damage.

Nonetheless, and accepting the figure of 111 not available, one can surmise that with 29 aircraft having been lost in the course of the two attacks, the number of aircraft available for further operations from the total of 350 aircraft in the two attack formations must have been 210, i.e. 350 less 29 less 111. This would suggest that the total number of aircraft retained by the carriers during the offensive phase must have been 55, i.e. the total of 265 which were available less the 210 which were available from the two attack formations. The result – 55 aircraft – is desperately close to what certain sources suggest was the number of aircraft retained by the carriers for combat air patrol and reserve duties. If the total of 55 is added to the number of aircraft which took part in the raid, we have an aggregate total of 405 aircraft.

Moreover, there remain two problems. First, lurking over any suggested figure is the return of one Kate plus made by the *Hiryu* in the aircraft damaged column. If the number of damaged aircraft was anything like what might have been expected, then probably the total number of aircraft embarked would have been somewhere between 425 and 435. Second, there is the question of the number of aircraft which were either written off or damaged to some degree during the recovery phase. No real answer exists, in part because the question never seems to have been put, but given the heavy sea conditions which prevailed, and the fact that these worsened during the day, it seems likely that a number of Japanese aircraft, particularly those damaged over Pearl Harbor, must have been written off. Prange noted that 'several' badly damaged aircraft were ditched after they had landed back on their carriers, but only one history – the first volume of the US Army Air Force's official history of the Second World War – has ever given any figures for these categories of Japanese aircraft: twenty written off and another 30 damaged. This source cites as its sources three interrogations conducted as part of the US strategic bombing survey: the problem herein is that two of the interrogations here cited do not carry any figures and the record of the third interrogation does not appear to have survived.

With no other figures available for this somewhat esoteric subject, one has to assume that these figures, if accurate, must have been accommodated within the totals of 29 aircraft that were lost and the 111 (plus) known to have incurred some form of damage during operations. If, however, the number written off in the course of landing operations was indeed twenty and came on top of the other figures, and if the total of 111 (plus) came on top of a full and proper record of the

TABLE 2 AIRCRAFT WITH THE CARRIERS OF THE FIRST CARRIER STRIKING FORCE (2)

CARRIER	TYPE 97 B5N2 KATES	TYPE 99 D3A1 VALS	TYPE 00 A6M2 ZEKES	TOTAL	SOURCE
Akagi	27	18	18 + 3	63 + 3 = 66	*Kishu Hawai Sakusen*, pp. 104–105. figure is given for 7 December 1941.
Kaga	27	27	21	75	*Nippon no Kubo*, p. 67. Figure is given for 7 December 1941.
Soryu	18 + 3	18 + 3	18 + 3	54 + 9 = 63	Figure is based simply on the establishment of the slightly larger *Hiryu* and therefore is almost certainly wrong.
Hiryu	18 + 3	18 + 3	18 + 3	54 + 9 = 63	*Nippon no Kubo*, p. 84. Figure is given for December 1941.
Zuikaku	27	27	18	72	*Nippon no Kubo*, p. 72. Figure is given for 7 December 1941.
Shokaku	27	27	18	72	*Nippon no Kubo*, p. 72. Figure is given for 7 December 1941.
	144 + 6	135 + 6	111 + 9	390 + 21	
Total	150	141	120	411	

One would assume that the number of Zekes with the *Kaga* was eighteen plus three rather than 21 and that all totals would be adjusted accordingly, i.e. the *Kaga*'s first total would read 72 + 3, the Zeke total for the formation would read 108 + 12, and the first figures in the overall total would read 387 + 24.

Hiryu's air group, then the total number of aircraft embarked in the six carriers may have been as high as 440 to 445. These totals, being greater than the total that Japanese planning allowed for, would seem to be too high, and perhaps a more realistic figure, based on acceptance of the figure of 111, would be about 425. Perhaps the most realistic figure, however, is based upon the calculation of 411 aircraft for the whole formation since this total, with twenty written off, would bring the total number of aircraft with the carriers to 431, i.e. just one aircraft short of the total number which the Japanese planned should be involved in this operation and which Kusaka, in his memoirs, states to have been the number embarked. The neatness of these calculations is countered, however, by the known totals for four, possibly five, of the carriers and the fact that the missing total could not possibly provide enough aircraft to bring the overall total of the formation to 431 or 432.

Nonetheless, there are two Japanese sources which provide two sets of figures which would accommodate the known component totals within their individual and collective totals but for the total of 55 aircraft left over when the various deductions are made from certain figures: in one of these two sets of figures there would be an error of one solitary aircraft. Moreover, certain of the individual ship totals are known to be relevant to the Hawaiian operation. These figures, with their sources, are shown in Table 2.

It should be noted that the problem of determining the establishment of the First Carrier Striking Force lies in the fact there is no definitive statement of the strength of the air groups of the *Soryu* and *Hiryu*. While the *Hiryu* may be assumed to have embarked 63 aircraft, it is not possible to state the establishment of the *Soryu*'s air group. In these circumstances, there is little real alternative but to accept a figure comparable to the *Hiryu* and known to be compatible with relevant sub-totals. With the *Akagi* allocated 66 aircraft, this would mean that the six carriers of the First Carrier Striking Force are deemed to have embarked a total of 411 aircraft. This is a total assumed to have

been embarked and it is a total that would not be able to accommodate within itself the twenty aircraft allegedly written off during the recovery phase. The 30 aircraft which were damaged could be accommodated within a total of 111 (plus) deemed to have been damaged during the attack.

This total of 411 therefore has been adopted in this work, and the explanation offered in these pages hopefully will convince the reader that this total represents a considered and reasoned judgement, though it may well be wrong. The 411 total cannot be given, however, without an acknowledgement that there is one source which does provide some reason for thinking that the Japanese carriers did indeed embark 432 aircraft for this operation – and these pages in the interests of objectivity must acknowledge this fact. The source is the Kusaka memoir, pp. 192–198, which state that when the First Carrier Striking Force was raised on 10 April 1941 it had a total of five carriers with 228 aircraft.

Figures to support this argument are shown in Tables 3 and 4.

The *Kasuga Maru*, which was commissioned into service in September 1941, was the future *Taiyo*. Why she, as an escort carrier, should have been with the carrier force is not exactly clear, but apparently she had a nominal establishment of nine fighters, with two reserve units, and fourteen torpedo bombers, with two reserve units, for a total of 27 aircraft. It seems however the Imperial Navy did not have enough aircraft to equip all its carriers, and therefore the *Kasuga Maru*'s assigned aircraft were distributed amongst the groups of the carriers of the First, Second and Fifth Carrier Divisions.

The outbreak of war saw the *Ryujo* committed to operations in southeast Asia and not the central Pacific. Her removal from the lists, therefore, would have reduced the overall carrier establishment to 432 aircraft and, what is more, would have reduced the numbers of Kates and Vals to exactly the totals set out in the planning brief. On such

TABLE 3

FIRST AIR FLEET: 10 APRIL 1941	KATES	VALS	ZEKES	CLAUDES	TOTAL
Akagi	9 + 3	18 + 6	18 + 6	none	45 + 15 = 60
Kaga	18 + 6	27 + 9	18 + 6	none	63 + 21 = 84
Soryu	18 + 6	18 + 6	12 + 4	none	48 + 6 = 54
Hiryu	18 + 6	18 + 6	12 + 4	none	48 + 6 = 54
Ryujo	18 + 6	none	none	9 + 3	27 + 9 = 36
Total	81 + 27	81 + 27	60 + 20	9 + 3	231 + 57 = 288

According to same source, by 1 October 1941 the First Carrier Striking Force had no fewer than eight carriers with a total of 474 aircraft, and its rapid expansion had been made possible by drawing on personnel from the Third and Fourth Carrier Divisions and the Eleventh Air Fleet. By this one assumes that Kusaka meant the *Hosho*, *Zuiho* and shore-based establishments, though it may also include the *Ryujo*, with less experienced aircrew taking the place of those 'moved up' into the three senior divisions. The figures given are as follows:

TABLE 4

FIRST AIR FLEET: 10 OCTOBER 1941	KATES	VALS	ZEKES	CLAUDES	TOTAL
Akagi	27 + 3	18 + 3	18 + 3	none	63 + 9 = 72
Kaga	27 + 3	18 + 3	18 + 3	none	63 + 9 = 72
Soryu	18 + 3	18 + 3	18 + 3	none	54 + 9 = 63
Hiryu	18 + 3	18 + 3	18 + 3	none	54 + 9 = 63
Ryujo	18 + 3	none	none	18 + 3	36 + 6 = 42
Kasuga Maru	none	none	none	none	none
Zuikaku	27 + 3	27 + 3	18 + 3	none	72 + 9 = 81
Shokaku	27 + 3	27 + 3	18 + 3	none	72 + 9 = 81
Total	162 + 21	126 + 18	108 + 18	18 + 3	414 + 60 = 474
The Pearl Harbor operation, according to planning data and the Kusaka memoir	144 + 18	126 + 18	108 + 18	none	378 + 54 = 432
	162	144	126	none	432

numbers, of course, the 'missing' 20 aircraft could be accommodated, and interestingly one of the latest publications, *Kishu Hawai sakusen* (Surprise Attack: Hawaii Operation), p. 21, gives the total embarked in the carriers as either 426 or 432. The latter figure conforms exactly to the planning figures, with the variation of six attributed to alternative totals of 66 and 72 aircraft being with the *Akagi*.

In any event, even if the number of aircraft in the formation cannot be stated with any certainty, the number of seaplanes embarked in the battleships and cruisers of the screen would seem to present fewer problems. The battleships *Hiei* and *Kirishima* both embarked three Type 95 E8N2 Daves, the cruisers *Chikuma* and *Tone* two Daves and two Type 00 E13A1 Jakes each, and the *Abukumo* embarked one solitary Type 94 E7K2 Alf. Overall, therefore, the battleships and cruisers of the First Carrier Striking Force deployed one Alf, ten Daves and four Jakes, a total of fifteen seaplanes – to serve alongside the 411, or some such number, of aircraft with the carriers.

Formations, Aircraft and Targets

TABLE 5 THE CARRIER AIR GROUPS AND THE TWO-ATTACK FORMATIONS, WITH TARGETS THAT WERE ATTACKED

FORMATION AND HOME BASE	CARRIER	AIRCRAFT, NUMBERS AND WEAPONRY	FORMATION COMMANDER	PLAN	ON THE DAY	TARGET(S) ATTACKED
Overall Commander	Akagi	Kate	Cdr. Fuchida Mitsuo			
Deputy Commander	Kaga	Kate	Cdr. Hashiguchi Takashi			
FIRST ATTACK FORCE						
1st Group	Akagi	Kate	Cdr. Fuchida Mitsuo			
1st Attack Unit	Akagi	Kates x 15	Cdr. Fuchida Mitsuo	5	5	Maryland
(Kagoshima):		800-kg AP bomb	Lt. Iwasaki Goro	5	5	Tennessee, West Virginia
			Lt. Furukawa Izumi	5	5	Tennessee, West Virginia
2nd Attack Unit	Kaga	Kates x 15	Cdr. Hashiguchi Takashi	5	5	Tennessee, West Virginia
(Kagoshima):		800-kg AP bomb	Lt. Maki Hideo	5	5	Arizona, Vestal
			Lt. Mikami Yoshitaka	5	4	Tennessee, West Virginia
3rd Attack Unit	Soryu	Kates x 10	Lt. Abe Heijiro	5	5	Tennessee, West Virginia
(Demizu):		800-kg AP bomb	Lt. Yamamoto Sadao	5	5	Nevada
4th Attack Unit	Hiryu	Kates x 10	LCdr. Kusumi Tadashi	5	5	Arizona
(Demizu):		800-kg AP bomb	S/Lt. Hashimoto Toshio	5	5	California
Kates armed with the Type 5 800-kilogram AP bomb:				50	49	
1st Torpedo Attack Unit	Akagi	Kates x 12	LCdr. Murata Shigeharu	3	3	West Virginia
(Kagoshima):		Mk 91 Torpedo	Lt. Goto Jinichi 2 i/c	3	3	Oklahoma
			Lt. Negishi Asao	6	6	California, Oklahoma, West Virginia
2nd Torpedo Attack Unit	Kaga	Kates x 12	Lt. Kitajima Ichiryo	6	6	Oklahoma, West Virginia
(Kagoshima):		Mk 91 Torpedo	Lt. Suzuki Mimori	6	6	Nevada, Oklahoma, West Virginia
3rd Torpedo Attack Unit	Soryu	Kates x 8	Lt. Nagai Tsuyoshi	4	4	Helena, California, Utah
(Demizu):		Mk 91 Torpedo	Lt. Nakajima Tatsumi	2	2	Utah
				2	2	Raleigh
4th Torpedo Attack Unit	Hiryu	Kates x 8	Lt. Matsumura Heita	2	2	West Virginia
(Demizu):		Mk 91 Torpedo		2	2	Oklahoma
			Lt. Sumino Hiroharu	4	4	Helena
Kates armed with the Mk 91 Torpedo:				40	40	
2nd Group	Shokaku	Val	LCdr. Takahashi Kakuchui			
15th Attack Unit	Shokaku	Vals x 27	LCdr. Takahashi Kakuchui	9	9	Ford Island
(Oita):		250-kg GP bomb	Lt. Yamaguchi Masao	9	8	Hickam Field
			Lt. Fujita Hisayoshi	9	9	Hickam Field
16th Attack Unit	Zuikaku	Vals x 27	Lt. Sakamoto Arika	9	9	Wheeler Field
(Oita):		250-kg GP bomb	Lt. Ema Tomatsu	9	}16	Wheeler Field
			Lt. Hayashi	9		Wheeler Field
Vals armed with the Type 99 250-kilogram GP bomb:				54	51	
3rd Group	Akagi	Zeke	LCdr. Itaya Shigeru			
1st Fighter Combat Unit:	Kaga	Zekes x 9	Lt. Shiga Yoshio	9	9	Hickam Field and Ewa
2nd Fighter Combat Unit:	Akagi	Zekes x 9	LCdr. Itaya Shigeru	9	9	Hickam Field and Ewa
3rd Fighter Combat Unit:	Soryu	Zekes x 9	Lt. Suganami Masaharu	9	8	Wheeler Field and Ewa
4th Fighter Combat Unit:	Hiryu	Zekes x 6	Lt. Okajima Kiyokuma	6	6	Wheeler Field and Ewa
5th Fighter Combat Unit: (Omura then Oita):	Shokaku	Zekes x 6	Lt. Kaneko Tadashi	6	5	Kaneohe Bay and Bellows Field
6th Fighter Combat Unit: (Omura then Oita):	Zuikaku	Zekes x 6	Lt. Sato Masxao	6	6	Kaneohe Bay and Bellows Field
Zeke fighters:				45	43	

TABLE 5 (continued)

SECOND ATTACK FORCE

1st Group	Zuikaku	Kate	LCdr. Shimazaki Shigekazu			
5th Attack Unit (Usa):	Shokaku	Kates x 27				
		2 x 250-kg GP bombs	Lt. Ichihara Tatsuo	9	9	Ford Island (?)
		1 x 250-kg GP bomb	Lt. Hagiwara Tsutomu	9	9	Ford Island (?)
		and 6 x 60-kg bombs	Lt. Ikuin Yoshiaki	9	9	Hickam Field
6th Attack Unit (Usa):	Zuikaku	Kates x 27				
		2 x 250-kg GP bombs	LCdr. Shimazaki Shigekazu	9	9	Kanoehe Bay
		2 x 250-kg GP bombs	Lt. Iwami Takemi	9	9	Kanoehe Bay
		1 x 250-kg GP bomb and 6 x 60-kg bombs	Lt. Tsubota Yoshiaki	9	9	Ford Island
Kates, variously armed:				54	54	
2nd Group	Soryu	Val	LCdr. Egusa Takeshige			
11th Attack Unit	Akagi	Vals x 18	Lt. Chihaya Takehiko	9	9	Shaw, Neosho
(Miyataka):		250-kg bomb	Lt. Abe Zenji	9	9	Maryland
12th Attack Unit	Kaga	Vals x 27	Lt. Makino Saburo	9	8	Nevada
(Miyataka):		250-kg bomb	Lt. Ogawa Shoichi	9	9	Maryland, Nevada, West Virginia
			Lt. Ibuki Shoichi	9	9	Nevada
13th Attack Unit	Soryu	Vals x 18	LCdr. Egusa Takeshige	9	9	California, Dobbin, naval yard
(Kasanohara):		250-kg bomb	Lt. Ikeda Masatake	9	8	California, Raleigh, naval yard
14th Attack Unit	Hiryu	Vals x 18	Lt. Kobayashi Michio	9	8	Maryland, Helm, naval yard
(Kasanohara):		250-kg bomb	Lt. Nakagawa Shun	9	9	California, Maryland, West Virginia, naval yard
Vals armed with Type 99 250-kg bomb:				81	78	
3rd Group	Akagi	Zeke	Lt. Shindo Saburo			
1st Fighter Combat Unit:	Akagi	Zekes x 9	Lt. Shindo Saburo	9	9	Hickam Field
2nd Fighter Combat Unit:	Kaga	Zekes x 9	Lt. Nikaido Yasushi	9	9	Ford Island (?)
3rd Fighter Combat Unit:	Soryu	Zekes x 9	Lt. Iida Fusata	9	9	Kanoehe Bay
4th Fighter Combat Unit:	Hiryu	Zekes x 9	Lt. Nono Sumio	9	8	Kanoehe Bay and Bellows Field
Zekes:				36	35	

TABLE 6 AIRCRAFT WITH THE CARRIERS OF THE FIRST CARRIER STRIKING FORCE AND THEIR EMPLOYMENT IN THE ATTACK OF 7 DECEMBER 1941

Carrier	FIRST ATTACK FORCE								SECOND ATTACK FORCE						Size of air group in plan	Size of air group as executed
	Planned				As executed				Planned			As executed				
	B5N2 Kates	B5N2 Kates	D3A1 Vals	A6M2 Zekes	B5N2 Kates	B5N2 Kates	D3A1 Vals	A6M2 Zekes	B5N2 Kates	D3A1 Vals	A6M2 Zekes	B5N2 Kates	D3A1 Vals	A6M2 Zekes		
Akagi	15	12	—	9	15	12	—	9	—	18	9	—	18	9	63	63
Kaga	15	12	—	9	14	12	—	9	—	27	9	—	26	9	72	70
Soryu	10	8	—	9	10	8	—	8	—	18	9	—	17	9	54	52
Hiryu	10	8	—	6	10	8	—	6	—	18	9	—	17	8	51	49
Shokaku	—	—	27	6	—	—	26	5	27	—	—	27	—	—	60	58
Zuikaku	—	—	27	6	—	—	25	6	27	—	—	27	—	—	60	58
	50	40	54	45	49	40	51	43	54	81	36	54	78	35		
		90	54	45		89	51	43								
TOTALS	189				183				171			167			360	350

NB In the First Attack Force listing, the first B5N2 Kate column gives level-altitude bombers, the second column torpedo-bombers

First Carrier Striking Force

FIRST CARRIER STRIKING FORCE AND FIRST CARRIER DIVISION

Commander:
VICE ADMIRAL NAGUMO CHUICHI.

Chief of Staff:
REAR ADMIRAL KUSAKA RYUNOSUKE.

Senior Staff Officer:
CDR. OISHI TAMOTSU.

Air Officer:
CDR. GENDA MINORU.

THE *AKAGI*:
CAPTAIN HASEGAWA KIICHI.

Air Group commander:
CDR. MASUDA SHOGO AT KAGOSHIMA.

Laid down as battlecruiser in 1920 and completed as carrier in 1927. Rebuilding: laid down 24 October 1935: completed 31 August 1938. 855 x 103 x 29 = 36,500 tons (standard).

Air Group: 27 B5N2 Kates, eighteen D3A1 Vals and eighteen A6M2 Zekes. Maximum capacity 66 operational and 25 reserve aircraft. Armament: Ten 7.9-in, twelve 4.7-in, 28 x 25-mm AA guns. Armour: 11-in belt.

Machinery: Nineteen boilers, four shaft turbines and 123,300 shp. Maximum speed: 31.25 knots. Fuel: 5,775 tons oil. Range: 8,200 n.m. at 16 knots.

Scuttled 5 June 1942 in 30.30 North 179.08 West in the battle off Midway Islands after being crippled by US carrier aircraft the previous day.

THE *KAGA*:
CAPTAIN OKADA JISAKU.

Air Group commander:
CDR. SATA NAOHIRO AT TOMITAKA.

Laid down as battleship in 1920 and completed as carrier in 1928. Rebuilding: laid down 25 June 1934 and completed 25 June 1935.

812 x 107 x 31 = 38,200 tons (standard).

Air Group: 27 B5N2 Kates, 27 D3A1 Vals and 21 A6M2 Zekes. Maximum capacity 72 operational & eighteen reserve aircraft. Armament: Ten 7.9-in, sixteen 5-in, 22 x 25-mm AA guns. Armour: 10-in belt.

Machinery: Eight boilers, four shaft turbines and 127,400 shp. Maximum speed: 28.3 knots. Fuel: 8,208 tons oil. Range: 10,330 n.m. at 16 knots.

Sunk 4 June 1942 in 30.20 North 179.17 West in the battle off Midway Islands by US carrier aircraft.

SECOND CARRIER DIVISION

Commander:
REAR ADMIRAL YAMAGUCHI TAMON.

Senior Staff Officer:
CDR. ITO SEIROKU.

Air Officer:
LCDR. SUZUKI EIJIRO.

THE *SORYU*:
CAPTAIN YANAGIMOTO RYUSAKU.

Air Group commander:
CDR. KUSUMOTO IKUTO AT KASANOHARA.

One of class of two fleet carriers. Laid down 20 November 1936: completed 5 July 1939. 747 x 70 x 25 = 15,900 tons (standard), 18,800 tons (full).

Air Group: 27 B5N2 Kates, eighteen D3A1 Vals, eighteen A6M2 Zekes: maximum capacity 53 operational & eighteen reserve aircraft. Armament: Twelve 5-in DP, 28 x 25-mm AA guns.

Machinery: Eight boilers, four shaft turbines and 152,000 shp. Maximum speed: 34.5 knots. Fuel: 3,670 tons oil. Range: 7,750 n.m. at 18 knots.

Sunk 4 June 1942 in 30.28 North 179.13 West in the battle off Midway Islands by US carrier aircraft.

THE *HIRYU*:
CAPTAIN KAKU TOMEO.

Air Group commander:
CDR. AMAGAI TAKAHISA AT IZUMI.

One of class of two fleet carriers. Laid down 8 July 1936: completed 5 July 1939. 746 x 73 x 26 = 17,300 tons (standard), 20,250 tons (full).

Air Group: 27 B5N2 Kates, eighteen D3A1 Vals, eighteen A6M2 Zekes: maximum capacity 57 operational & sixteen reserve aircraft. Armament: Twelve 5-in DP, 31 x 25-mm AA guns.

Machinery: Eight boilers, four shaft turbines and 152,000 shp. Maximum speed: 34.5 knots. Fuel: 4,400 tons oil. Range: 10,330 n.m. at 18 knots.

Scuttled 5 June 1942 in 31.38 North 178.51 West in the battle off Midway Islands after being crippled by US carrier aircraft the previous day.

FIFTH CARRIER DIVISION

Commander:
REAR ADMIRAL HARA CHUICHI.

Senior Staff Officer:
CDR. OHASHI KYOZO.

Air Officer:
LCDR. MIENO TAKESHI.

THE *ZUIKAKU*:
CAPTAIN YOKOKAWA ICHIBEI.

Air Group commander:
CDR. SHIMODA HISAO.

One of class of two fleet carriers. Laid down 25 May 1938: completed 25 September 1941. 845 x 85 x 29 = 25,675 tons (standard), 36,601 tons (full).

Air Group: 27 B5N2 Kates, 27 D3A1 Vals, eighteen A6M2 Zekes and space for twelve reserve aircraft. Armament: Sixteen 5-in DP, 36 x 25-mm AA guns. Armour: 8.5-in belt, 6.7-in deck (maximum).

Machinery: Eight boilers, four shaft turbines and 160,000 shp. Maximum speed: 34.25 knots. Range: 9,700 n.m. at 18 knots.

Sunk 25 October 1944 in 19.20 North 125.15 East off Cape Engano by US carrier aircraft.

THE *SHOKAKU*:
CAPTAIN JOJIMA TAKATSUGU.

Air Group commander:
CDR. WADA TETSUJIRO.

One of class of two fleet carriers. Laid down 12 December 1937: completed 8 August 1941.

Sunk 19 June 1944 in 11.50 North 137.57 East during the battle of the Philippine Sea by the US submarine *Cavalla*, operating from Pearl Harbor.

SUPPORT FORCE AND THIRD BATTLESHIP DIVISION

Commander:
VICE ADMIRAL MIKAWA GUNICHI.

Senior Staff Officer:
COMMANDER ARITA YUZO.

THE BATTLESHIP *HIEI*:
CAPTAIN NISHIDA MASUO.

Kongo-class battlecruiser when originally built, 1911–1914. Rebuilt at the Kure naval yard. Begun .. November 1936: completed 31 January 1940. 728 x 101 x 32 = 32,156 tons (standard), 36,601 tons (full).

Armament: Eight 14-in, fourteen 6-in, eight 5-in AA, twenty 25-mm AA guns, three aircraft. Armour: 8-in belt, 11-in turret, 4.75-in deck.

Machinery: Eight boilers, four shaft turbines and 136,000 shp. Weight: 2,929 tons. Maximum speed: 29.7 knots. Fuel: 6,330 tons oil. Range: 10,000 n.m. at 18 knots.

Sunk 13 November 1942 in 9.00 South 159.00 East in the first Battle of Guadalcanal as a result of damage inflicted by US warships, carrier and land-based aircraft.

THE BATTLESHIP *KIRISHIMA*:
CAPTAIN YAMAGUCHI JIHEI.

Kongo-class battlecruiser when originally built, 1912–1915. Rebuilt at the Sasebo naval yard. Begun .. June 1934: completed 8 June 1936. 728 x 101 x 31 = 32,156 tons (standard), 36,601 tons (full).

Armament: Eight 14-in, fourteen 6-in, eight 5-in AA, twenty 25-mm AA guns, three aircraft. Armour: 8-in belt, 11-in turret, 10-in barbette, 4.75-in deck. Weight of armour: 10,732 tons.

Machinery: Eight boilers, four shaft turbines and 136,000 shp. Maximum speed: 30.5 knots. Fuel: 6,330 tons oil. Range: 10,000 n.m. at 18 knots.

Sunk 14 November 1942 in 9.05 South 159.42 East in the second Battle of Guadalcanal by the US battleship *Washington*.

EIGHTH CRUISER DIVISION

THE *CHIKUMA*:
CAPTAIN KOMURA KEIZO.

One of two *Tone*-class heavy cruisers. Laid down 1 October 1935: completed 20 May 1939. 662 x 61 x 21 = 11,215 tons (standard), 15,200 tons (full).

Armament: Eight 8-in, Eight 5-in DP, twelve x 25-mm AA guns, twelve x 24-in torpedo tubes, five aircraft, two catapults. Armour: 5.7-in belt (maximum), 3-in turret, 2.2-in deck.

Machinery: 8 boilers, four shaft turbines and 152,200 shp. Maximum speed: 35.2 knots. Fuel: 2,950 tons oil. Range: 10,000 n.m. at 18 knots.

Scuttled 25 October 1944 in 11.22 North 126.16 East, off Samar, after having been damaged by US carrier aircraft.

THE *TONE*:
CAPTAIN OKADA TARUEJI.

Nameship of class of two heavy cruisers. Laid down 1 December 1934: completed 20 November 1938.

Sunk 24 July 1945 in 34.14 North 132.27 East off Kure, in the Inland Sea, by US carrier aircraft.

FIRST DESTROYER SQUADRON

Commander:
REAR ADMIRAL OMORI SENTARO.

Senior Staff Officer:
CDR. ARICHIKA ROKUJI.

THE *ABUKUMA*:
CAPTAIN MURAYAMA SEITOKU.

One of six *Nagara*-class light cruisers. Laid down 8 December 1921: completed 26 May 1925. 535 x 48 x 16 = 5,610 tons (standard).

Armament: Seven 5.5-in, two 5-in DP guns, eight 24-in torpedo tubes, one aircraft.

Armour: 2.5-in belt (maximum), 1.25-in deck.

Machinery: 12 boilers, four shaft turbines and 90,000 shp. Maximum speed: 36 knots. Fuel: 1,500 tons oil. Range: 9,000 n.m. at 10 knots, 7,000 n.m. at 12 knots, or 5,700 n.m. at 14 knots.

Sunk 26 October 1944 in 9.20 North 122.30 East, southeast of Negros, Philippines, by US land-based aircraft after being rendered *hors de combat* by US warship the previous day.

THE *AKIGUMO*:
CDR. ARIMOTO TERUMICHI.

One of twelve *Yugumo*- or Improved *Kagero*-class destroyers, 1939 programme. Laid down 20 July 1940: completed 27 September 1941. 391 x 36 x 12 = 2,077 tons (standard), 2,520 tons (full).

Armament: Six 5-in (75 degree) DP, four 25-mm AA guns, eight 24-in torpedo tubes, 36 depth charges.

Machinery: Three boilers, two shaft turbines and 52,000 shp. Maximum speed: 35 knots. Fuel: 600 tons oil. Range: 5,800 n.m. at 12 knots, 5,700 n.m. at 14 knots or 5,000 n.m. at 18 knots.

Sunk 11 April 1944 in 6.43 North 122.23 East, southwest of Mindanao, by the US submarine *Redfin*, operating from Fremantle.

SEVENTEENTH DESTROYER DIVISION

THE *HAMAKAZE*:
CDR. ORITA TSUNEO.

One of twelve *Kagero*-class destroyers, 1937 programme. Laid down 20 November 1939: completed 30 June 1941. 389 x 35 x 12 = 2,033 tons (standard), 2,490 tons (full).

Armament: Six 5-in DP, four 25-mm AA guns, eight 24-in torpedo tubes, sixteen depth charges.

Machinery: Three boilers, two shaft turbines and 52,000 shp. Maximum speed: 35 knots. Fuel: 600 tons oil. Range as per Akigumo.

Sunk 7 April 1945 in 30.47 North 128.08 East, southwest of Kyushu, by US carrier aircraft.

THE *ISOKAZE*:
CDR. TOYOSHIMA SHUNICHI.

One of twelve *Kagero*-class destroyers, 1937 programme. Laid down 25 November 1938: completed 30 November 1940.

Scuttled 7 April 1945 in 30.46 North 128.29 East, south-west of Kyushu, after being badly damaged by US carrier aircraft.

THE *TANIKAZE*:
CDR. KATSUMI MOTOI.

One of three *Kagero*-class destroyers, 1939 programme. Laid down 18 October 1939: completed 25 April 1941.

Sunk 9 June 1944 in 5.42 North 120.41 East, off Tawi Tawi, Philippines, by the US submarine *Harder*, operating from Fremantle.

THE *URAKAZE*:
CDR. SHIRAISHI NAGAYOSHI.

One of twelve *Kagero*-class destroyers, 1937 programme. Laid down 11 April 19397: completed 15 December 1940.

Sunk 21 November 1944 in 26.09 North 121.23E, off north-west Formosa, by the US submarine *Sealion*, operating from Pearl Harbor.

EIGHTEENTH DESTROYER DIVISION

THE DESTROYER *ARARE*:
CDR. OGATA TOMIE.

One of ten *Asashio*-class destroyers, 1934 programme. Laid down 5 March 1937: completed 15 April 1939. 388 x 34 x 12 = 1,961 tons (standard), 2,370 tons (full).

Armament: Six 5-in DP, four 25-mm AA guns, eight 24-in torpedo tubes.

Machinery: Three boilers, two shaft turbines and 50,000 shp.

Maximum speed: 35 knots. Fuel: 600 tons oil. Range as per *Akigumo*.

Sunk 5 July 1942 in 52.00 North 177.40 East, off Kiska in the Aleutians, by the US submarine *Growler*, operating from Pearl Harbor.

THE *KAGERO*:
CDR. YOKOI MINORU.

Nameship of class of twelve destroyers, 1937 programme. Laid down 30 August 1937: completed 20 December 1939.

Sunk 8 May 1943 in 8.08 South 156.55 East, south-west of Rendova, in the Solomons, by mine and land-based aircraft.

THE *KASUMI*:
CDR. TOMURA KIYOSHI.

One of ten *Asashio*-class destroyers, 1934 programme. Laid down 1 December 1936: completed 28 June 1939.

Scuttled 7 April 1945 in 31.00 North 128.00 East, south-west of Kyushu, after being badly damaged by US carrier aircraft.

THE *SHIRANUHI*:
CDR. AKAZAWA SHIZUO.

One of twelve *Kagero*-class destroyers, 1937 programme. Laid down 30 August 1937: completed 20 December 1939.

Sunk 27 October 1944 in 12.00 North 122.30 East, off Panay in the Philippines, by US carrier aircraft.

SUPPLY GROUP NO. 1

THE OILER *KYOKUTO MARU*:
CAPTAIN OTO MASANAO.

502 x 65 x 37 = 10,051 tons. Built in 1934. 19 knots.

Sunk 21 September 1944 in 14.30 North 120.45 East, in Manila Bay, Luzon, by US carrier aircraft.

THE OILER *KENYO MARU*:
CAPTAIN KANEMASU YOSHIO.

10,024 tons. Built in 1939. 19.5 knots.

Sunk 14 January 1944 in 5.22 North 141.27 East, south-west of Eauripik, by the US submarine *Guardfish*, operating from Brisbane.

THE OILER *KOKUYU MARU*:
CAPTAIN HIDAI TORAJI.

Kokuyo Maru: 500 x 65 x 37 = 10,027. Built in 1938. 19.5 knots.

Sunk 30 July 1943 in 6.03 North 119.54 East, off north-east Borneo, by US submarine *Bonefish*, operating from Fremantle.

THE OILER *SHINKOKU MARU*:
CAPTAIN ITO TOKUTAKA.

10,020 tons. Built in 1940. 19 knots.

Sunk 17 February 1944 in 7.00 North 151.00 East, in the Truk anchorage, Carolines, by US carrier aircraft.

SUPPLY GROUP NO. 2

THE OILER *TOHO MARU*:
CAPTAIN NIIMI KAZUTAKA.

500 x 65 x 37 = 9,997 tons. Built in 1936. 19 knots.

Sunk 29 March 1943 in 00.00 118.18 East, in northern Makassar Strait, by the US submarine *Gudgeon*, operating from Fremantle.

THE OILER *NIPPON MARU*:
CAPTAIN UEDA KONOSKAE.

499 x 65 x 37 = 9,974 tons. Built in 1936. 19 knots.

Sunk 14 January 1944 in 5.02 North 140.43 East, south-west of Eauripik in the central Pacific, by the US submarine *Scamp*, operating from Brisbane.

THE OILER *TOEI MARU*:
CAPTAIN KUSAKAWA KIYOSHI.

502 x 65 x 37 = 10,022 tons. Built in 1938. 16 knots.

Sunk 18 January 1943 in 6.21 North 150.23 East, south-west of Truk, by the US submarine *Silversides*, operating from Brisbane.

Submarine Formations

PATROL FORMATION:
CAPTAIN IMAIZUMI KIJIRO.

With First Carrier Striking Force

The I.19.
CDR. NARAHARA SHOGO.

Type B.1 scout-submarine. Completed 28 April 1941.
351 x 31 x 17 = 2,198 tons (standard), 2,589 tons (full),
3,654 tons (maximum submerged). Armament: six 21-in.
torpedo tubes, seventeen torpedoes. One 5.5-in,
two 25-mm AA guns. One seaplane.

Two-shaft diesels, 12,400 bhp: maximum speed
23.6 knots. Maximum range 14,000 n.m. at 16 knots.
Two electric motors, 2,000 ehp: maximum speed 8 knots.
Maximum range 96 n.m. at 3 knots. Sunk 25 November
1943 in 3.10 North 171.55 East, west of Makin, by
US destroyer *Radford*.

The I.21.
CDR. MATSUMURA KANJI.

Type B.1 scout-submarine. Completed 15 July 1941.
Missing from late November 1943 off Tarawa, in the
Gilberts: cause of loss unknown.

The I.23.
CDR. SHIBATA GENICHI.

Type B.1 scout-submarine. Completed 27 September
1941. Missing from mid-February 1942 south of Oahu:
cause of loss unknown.

FIRST SUBMARINE GROUP:
REAR ADMIRAL TSUTOME SATO.
The I.9:
CDR. FUJII AKIYOSHI.

Type A.1 headquarters/command-submarine. Completed
13 February 1941. 367 x 31 x 18 = 2,434 tons (standard),
2,919 tons (full), 4,149 tons (maximum submerged).
Armament: six 21-in. torpedo tubes, eighteen torpedoes.
One 5-in, two 25-mm AA guns. One seaplane.

Two-shaft diesels, 4,700 bhp: maximum speed 17.7 knots.
Maximum range 22,000 n.m. at 16 knots. Two electric
motors, 1,200 ehp: maximum speed 6.2 knots. Maximum
range 75 n.m. at 3 knots. Missing from 15 June 1944:
probably sunk 13 June 1944 in 52.08 North 177.38 East,
off Kiska in the Aleutians, by US destroyer *Frazier*.

The I.15.
CDR. ISHIKAWA NOBUO.

Type B.1 scout-submarine. Completed 30 September
1940. Missing from 3 November 1942: possibly sunk
2 November 1942 in 10.53 South 161.50 East, north
of San Cristobal, by US destroyer *McCella*.

The I.17.
CDR. NISHINO KOZO.

Type B.1 scout-submarine. Completed 24 January 1941.
Sunk 19 August 1943 in 23.26 South 166.50 East,
south-east of Noumea, New Caledonia, by New Zealand
corvette *Tui* and US land-based aircraft.

The I.25.
CDR. TAYAMI MEIJI.

Type B.1 scout-submarine. Completed 15 October 1941.
Missing from 20 September 1943: cause of loss unknown.

SECOND SUBMARINE GROUP:
REAR ADMIRAL YAMAZAKI SHIGEAKI.

The I.1.
CAPTAIN: LT.CDR. SAKAMOTO EICHI.

Type J.1 cruiser-submarine. Completed 10 March 1926.
319 x 30 x 18 = 1,970 tons (standard), 2,135 tons (full),
2,791 tons (maximum submerged).
Armament: six 21-in. torpedo tubes, twenty torpedoes.
Two 5.5-in, one).3-in AA guns.

Two-shaft diesels, 6,000 bhp: maximum speed 18 knots.
Maximum range 24,400 n.m. at 10 knots. 545 tons oil.
Two electric motors, 2,600 ehp: maximum speed 8 knots.
Maximum range 60 n.m. at 3 knots. Sunk 29 January 1943
in 9.13 South 159.40 East, in Kamimbo Bay, Solomon
Islands, by New Zealand corvettes *Kiwi* and *Moa*.

The I.2.
CDR. INOIDA HIROSHI.

Type J.l cruiser-submarine. Completed 24 July 1926.
Sunk 7 April 1944 in 2.17 South 149.14E off New Hanover
by US destroyer *Saufley*.

The I.3.
CDR. TONOSUKA KINZO.

Type J.l cruiser-submarine. Completed 30 November
1926. Sunk 10 December 1942 in 9.12 South 159.42 East,
off Kamimbo Bay, Solomon Islands, by US warship PT-59.

The I.4.
CDR. NAKAGAWA HAJIME.

Type J.1 cruiser-submarine. Completed 30 November
1926. Missing from 21 December 1942: possibly sunk
25 December 1942 in 8.32 South 148.17 East,
off Kumuni Point in Eastern New Guinea, by US warship.
Richard Frank *Guadalcanal*, p. 500, has her being sunk
20 November 1942 by the submarine *Seadragon*.

The I.5.
CDR. SHICHIJI TSUNEO.

Type IM scout-submarine. Completed 31 July 1932.
309 x 30 x 18 = 2,080 tons (standard), 2,243 tons (full),
2,921 tons (maximum submerged). Armament: six 21-in.
torpedo tubes, twenty torpedoes. Two 5.5-in, one 12-mm
and one 0.3-in AA guns. One seaplane.

Two-shaft diesels, 6,000 bhp: maximum speed 18 knots.
Maximum range 24,000 n.m. at 10 knots. 548 tons oil.
Two electric motors, 2,600 ehp: maximum speed 8 knots.
Maximum range 60 n.m. at 3 knots. Missing from 19 July
1944: possibly sunk 19 July 1944 in 13.01 North 151.58
East, east of Guam, by US destroyer escort *Wyman*.

The I.6.
CDR. INABA MICHIMUNE.

Type 2 cruiser-submarine. Completed 15 May 1935.
323 x 30 x 18 = 1,900 tons (standard), 2,243 tons (full),
2,061 tons (maximum submerged).
Armament: six 21-in. torpedo tubes, seventeen
torpedoes. One 5-in, one 13-mm AA guns.

Two-shaft diesels, 8,000 bhp: maximum speed 20 knots.
Maximum range 20,000 n.m. at 10 knots. 580 tons oil.
Two electric motors, 2,600 ehp: maximum speed 7.5
knots. Maximum range 60 n.m. at 3 knots. Missing from
30 June 1944 in Saipan area: cause of loss unknown.

The I.7.
CDR. KOIZUMI KI'ICHI.

Type 3 scout-submarine. Completed 31 March 1937.
355 x 30 x 17 = 2,231 tons (standard), 2,525 tons (full),
3,538 tons (maximum submerged).

Armament: six 21-in. torpedo tubes, twenty torpedoes.
Two 5.5-in, two 13-mm AA guns. One seaplane.

Two-shaft diesels, 11,200 bhp: maximum speed 23 knots.
Maximum range 14,000 n.m. at 16 knots. 800 tons oil.
Two electric motors, 2,800 ehp: maximum speed 8 knots.
Maximum range 60 n.m. at 3 knots.

Ran aground in 51.49 North 177.20 East following

damage in action with US destroyer *Monaghan* off Kiska, in the Aleutians, 22 June 1943: the wreck was destroyed 5 July 1943 by US land-based aircraft.

THIRD SUBMARINE GROUP:
REAR ADMIRAL MIWA SHIGEYOSHI.

The I. 8.
CDR. EMI TETSUSHIRO.

Type 3 scout-submarine. Completed 5 December 1938. Sunk 31 March 1945 in 25.29 North 128.35 East, south-east of Okinawa, by US destroyers *Morrison* and *Stockton*.

The I. 68.
CDR. NAKAMURA OTOJI.

Type 6A submarine. Completed 31 July 1934. 336 x 27 x 15 = 1,400 tons (standard), 1,785 tons (full), 2,440 tons (maximum submerged). Armament: six 21-in. torpedo tubes, fourteen torpedoes. One 4-in, one 13-mm AA guns.

Two-shaft diesels, 9,000 bhp: maximum speed 23 knots. Maximum range 14,000 n.m. at 10 knots. Two electric motors, 1,800 ehp: maximum speed 8.2 knots. Maximum range 65 n.m. at 3 knots. Sunk 27 July 1943 in 02.05 South 149.01 East, north of New Hanover, by the US submarine *Scamp*, operating from Brisbane.

The I. 69.
CDR. WATANABE KATSUJI.

Type 6A submarine. Completed 31 July 1934. Sunk 4 April 1944 in Truk in course of air raid by US land-based aircraft.

The I. 70.
CDR. SANO TAKASHI.

Type 6A submarine. Completed 31 July 1934. Sunk 10 December 1941 in 23.45 North 155.35 West, off Pearl Harbor, by carrier aircraft.

The I. 71.
CDR. KAWASAKI MUTSUO.

Type 6A submarine. Completed 31 July 1934. Sunk 1 February 1944 in 5.37 South 154.14 East, off Buka in the upper Solomons, by US destroyers *Guest* and *Hudson*.

The I. 72.
CDR. TOGAMI ICHIRO.

Type 6A submarine. Completed 31 July 1934. Sunk 10 November 1942 in 10.13 South 161.09 East, off Guadalcanal in the Solomons, by US destroyer *Southard*.

The I. 73.
CDR. ISOBE AKIRA.

Type 6A submarine. Completed 31 July 1934. Sunk 27 January 1942 in 28.24 North 178.35 East, west of Midway, by US submarine *Gudgeon*, operating from Pearl Harbor.

The I. 74.
CDR. IKEZAWA MASAYUKI.

Type 6B submarine. Completed 15 August 1938. 337 x 27 x 15 = 1,420 tons (standard), 1,785 tons (full), 2,440 tons (maximum submerged). Armament: six 21-in. torpedo tubes, fourteen torpedoes. One 5-in, two 13-mm AA guns.

Two-shaft diesels, 9,000 bhp: maximum speed 23 knots. Maximum range 14,000 n.m. at 10 knots. 350 tons oil. Two electric motors, 1,800 ehp: maximum speed 8 knots. Maximum range 65 n.m. at 3 knots. Missing from early April 1944 in the Carolines: cause of loss unknown.

The I. 75.
CDR. INOUE CHIKANORI.

Type 6B submarine. Completed 18 December 1938. Missing from 30 January 1944: cause of loss given alternatively as US warship on 1 February 1944 or two American warships in 06.48 North 168.08 East, off Jaluit in the Marshalls, on 4 February 1944.

Other Submarines
(midget submarine carriers)

The I. 16.
CDR. YAMADA KAORU.

Type C.1 cruiser-submarine. Completed 30 March 1940. 351 x 30 x 18 = 2,184 tons (standard), 2,554 tons (full), 3,561 tons (maximum submerged). Armament: eight 21-in. torpedo tubes, twenty torpedoes. One 5.5in, two 25-mm AA guns.

Two-shaft diesels, 12,400 bhp: maximum speed 23.6 knots. Maximum range 14,000 n.m. at 10 knots. Two electric motors, 2,000 ehp: maximum speed 8 knots. Maximum range 60 n.m. at 3 knots. Sunk 19 May 1944 in 5.10 South 158.17 East, north of the Solomons, by US destroyer escort *England*.

The I. 18.
CDR. OTANI KIYONORI.

Type C.1 cruiser-submarine. Completed 31 January 1941. Sunk 11 February 1943 in 14.15 South 151.59 East, south of San Cristobal, by US destroyer *Fletcher*.

The I. 20.
CDR. YASUDA TAKASHI.

Type C.1 cruiser-submarine. Completed 26 September 1940. Missing from 30 August 1943: possibly sunk 3 September 1943 in 13.10 South 165.28 East, north-east of Espiritu Santo, by US destroyer *Ellett*: alternatively listed as marine casualty 10 October 1943.

The I. 22.
CDR. AGATA KIYO:

CAPTAIN SASAKI HANKU, CO midget submarines embarked.

Type C.1 cruiser-submarine. Completed 10 March 1941. Missing from 5 October 1942 in the Solomons.

The I. 24.
CDR. HANABASA HIROSHI.

Type C.1 cruiser-submarine. Completed 31 October 1941. Probably sunk 10 June 1943 in 53.16 North 174.24 East, north-east of Attu in the Aleutians, by US warship *PC 487*.

Other Submarines
(distant reconnaissance)

The I. 10.
CDR. KAYAHARA YASUCHIKA.

Type A.1 headquarters/command-submarine. Conducted reconnaissance of Suva on 29 November and Pago Pago on 4 December. Missing from 28 June 1944: possibly sunk 4 July 1944 in 15.26 North 147.48 East, off Saipan, by the US destroyer *David W. Taylor* and destroyer escort *Riddle*.

The I. 26.
CDR. YOKOTA MINORU.

Type B.1 scout-submarine. Completed 24 January 1941. Conducted reconnaissance of Kiska on 25 November, Dutch Harbor on 27–28 November with her seaplane, and of Adak and Kodiak on 30 November. Thereafter sank the *Cynthia Olsen* on 7 December 1941: disputed whether this was before or after the attack on Pearl Harbor. Missing from 25 October 1944: possibly sunk 28 October 1944 in 10.56 North 127.13 East, north-east of Surigao, by the US destroyers *Gridley* and *Helm*.

Intelligence and the wider Pearl Harbor controversy

Perhaps the most persistent problem concerning the Japanese planning for and conduct of the attack on Pearl Harbor concerns American intelligence or, more accurately, the treatment afforded American intelligence by various investigations, hearings and apparently historical works on the subject. The least that can be said is that in the immediate post-war situation, indeed even before victory over Japan was an accomplished fact, there were a series of moves – primarily by a deliberately and bitterly partisan Republican Party in an attempt to discredit Franklin D. Roosevelt, president, administration and memory – which gave rise to a number of conspiracy theories. These, frankly, have been afforded infinitely more attention than they deserved. Specifically, these charges have been that Roosevelt, personally, and Washington, generally, knew that the attack on Pearl Harbor was coming but that the commanding military and naval officers in Hawaii were not properly warned; that the British knew that an attack on Pearl Harbor was planned but made no attempt to warn the Americans because it was in Britain's national interest to ensure American entry into the war, not necessarily that she avoided attack; and that the Soviet Union also knew but, like the British and for similar reasons, her representatives managed to avoid mentioning this knowledge in conversation with their American opposite numbers.

In addition to these three main theses, there were repeated claims by the commanders on Oahu, Admiral Husband E. Kimmel, commander-in-chief US Pacific Fleet, and Lieutenant-General Walter C. Short, overall commander of the army and army air force formations in the islands, that they were deliberately denied vital information which prevented their being alerted against a surprise attack, this information supposedly being available in Washington. Kimmel and Short protested their innocence until their deaths, since which time various individuals have continued to demand that both men be reinstated with full rank in order to provide some form of posthumous vindication.

It has been a wholly unedifying spectacle whereby commissions and publications over six decades have sought scapegoats and to expose alleged conspiracies. One can only note that so many of the American arguments have been underpinned by the assumption that the United States leadership should have known what was happening, and one can only suspect that this assumption, and indeed much of the bitterness toward the Japanese, stemmed from contemporary attitudes which, not to put too fine a point on it, held the Japanese to be lying, perfidious, little yellow bastards whose intentions should have been seen by a manifestly superior white race. But quite why the Americans should have been able to discern Japanese intent is unclear – not least because the Japanese were making every effort to ensure that their intention remained concealed from their intended victim. One can also note that in the last days before war, and after Japanese staffs in various parts of the world received instructions to destroy codes, ciphers and machines, the Americans closed appreciably on Japanese

intent. They remained, however, just that critical fraction of time adrift of this intent, and in the last two days the Americans were clearly distracted by the knowledge that the Japanese were in the process of moving against southern Siam and northern Malaya. The events in the Gulf of Siam clearly had a very important role in drawing American attention to south-east Asia and at the expense of the central Pacific, though whether this American attention might ever have focussed upon Oahu had it not been for the Gulf of Siam must be considered very dubious indeed.

In one very obvious sense, final responsibility for the gross mismanagement which afflicted the timely and accurate dissemination of information gained through signals intelligence lay with Roosevelt in his capacity as president. However, it is difficult to pin blame upon Roosevelt other, perhaps, than with respect to his not insisting that advance warning of the message which was to be delivered on Sunday 7 December 1941 to Hull, the Secretary of State, and which the president received late on the previous evening, was not immediately passed to certain key individuals. Roosevelt's own reaction on reading the message that was that it foreshadowed war, but even if Roosevelt was culpable in not arranging for its immediate distribution, it is impossible to convict him of knowing first, that war was to come next day, second, that war was to begin at Pearl Harbor and, third, that he failed to do anything about it. But, of course, that is not the sum of the charge against Roosevelt: the charge is that Roosevelt deliberately betrayed his office by leaving an unprepared fleet in the path of a Japanese attack. Yet there is no indication whatsoever that Roosevelt, while correctly grasping that Japan was intent on war, anticipated Japanese actions in terms of going to war with an attack on the US Pacific Fleet at Pearl Harbor on 7 December 1941, and in this respect Roosevelt was not alone. Part of the American problem was one of imagination, that the individuals within the American intelligence community simply could not imagine a Japanese attack upon the United States, and could not imagine a Japanese attack on the main American base in the Pacific – a Japanese attack which would have been the equivalent of a British carrier force sailing from Scapa Flow to a position off the Panama Canal in order to strike at any American carriers and battleships known to be gathered there. In retrospect, and with the hindsight which always provides full understanding, perhaps these individuals should have known, although American failure in such circumstances was hardly unique. One only has to consider the German failure to discern the Allied intention to land in Normandy in 1944 to realise that the American failure in 1941, if such it was, was in good company. But the German failure in 1944 was within a theatre of war whereas the American failure in 1941 was not local, within a theatre, but trans-oceanic: indeed such a characteristic – the separation of targets by entire oceans – was unknown in war before 1941 and hence, in no small measure, the American inability to anticipate the Japanese move against Pearl Harbor. The Japanese moves in south-east Asia were local and could be foreseen precisely because they were local and conformed to patterns of operations which were known. Nothing could have prepared the American political and military leadership for a strike on Oahu.

An eminent source has written that

'the ... cause ... for the disaster at Pearl Harbor was an unworkable system of military intelligence, including the fact that the Navy withheld from the Army vital intelligence information that called for Army action,' and that '... the intelligence-gathering process of the time was not up to the job. The system for handling communications intelligence was neither operationally efficient nor accurate in its analytical predictions. And while the two services might have paid lip service to the concept of mutual co-operation ... their good intentions were nothing more than that.'

The assertion that weakness existed in the intelligence-gathering process is not entirely convincing, since it seems far more credible that the real weaknesses existed in the analysis and dissemination phases of the intelligence cycle. In short, what is suggested here is what Clausewitz so accurately identified as friction, but what is really at issue is that, just as there is a difference between errors of judgement and dereliction of duties – and this seldom seems to be appreciated by those who have pronounced on this subject – so there is a difference between systemic faults and those errors which fall within the realm of individual responsibility.

The lack of any single central agency, capable of ensuring timely dissemination of material to all interested parties, lay at the heart of the American intelligence failure regarding the Japanese attack on Pearl Harbor. There were various individual failures in terms of contributing factors, and perhaps one of the most important, and least recognised, was the distraction of Naval Intelligence attention on account of the antics of Rear Admiral Richmond K. Turner, head of the War Plans Department. In common with virtually all naval officers, Turner was of the opinion that being a naval officer made him an expert in all matters. In reality he knew nothing about intelligence, and his assault on the Naval Intelligence Department and Rear Admiral Theodore S. Wilkinson in what was clearly Turner's idea of a turf war clearly had an effect in that it distracted both the Department and Wilkinson in the days immediately before the outbreak of war. Moreover, it has been suggested that it was Turner who stopped decrypts and other material being passed to the commanders in Hawaii, and apparently it was Turner who ordered the destruction of material in order that the role of the code-breakers could not be investigated by any of the subsequent Pearl Harbor inquiries.

But if the basic cause of American failure was system, there is no escaping the fact that there is little evidence to support the assertions of Kimmel and Short that they were deliberately denied vital information which prevented their being alerted against a surprise attack. Indeed, the evidence would seem to point the other way – that they were properly warned and that really there was very little, and nothing of real importance, which they were denied in the way of information by the authorities in Washington: put another way, they were denied some material but they were supplied with enough to have been properly alerted to the dangers facing their commands. Furthermore, it is possible to consider that the evidence of manifest failure on the part of both commanders is overwhelming, most obviously in the instance of Short. His failure to act upon the two messages sent by Marshall on

7 February and 5 March 1941, his unilateral alteration of standard operating procedures regarding states of alert without informing Washington of these changes, his failure to ensure radar coverage and his inattention to ensuring adequate reconnaissance by aircraft from Oahu and proper co-ordination with the Navy would all seem overwhelming. Short's own admission that, on his way to take up an appointment which he clearly did not want, he chose to read a novel rather than his brief was both revealing and damning, although it proves neither error of judgement nor dereliction of duty in his post. Kimmel, perhaps to a lesser extent than Short, was also responsible for errors of commission and omission, not least in not ensuring that Short was kept fully informed, but his claims of not being in receipt of proper warning likewise cannot be sustained. Both individuals had received the 'war warning' message of 27 November and were aware that Japanese embassies and consulates had or were in the process of destroying codes, ciphers and signals machines on and after 3 December.

One is tempted to suggest that in very large measure the difficulties which have surrounded attempts to get at the truth of the American intelligence failure at Pearl Harbor have been the product of the deliberate lies told by certain individuals to protect themselves and their careers. In a number of cases, these lies have been justified in terms of national security interests, specifically the need to keep secret the fact that American intelligence was reading some of the most secret and sensitive of Japanese signals. The trouble here, of course, is the distinction between reason and rationalisation, and compounding the problem is the fact that the one individual at the heart of so many of the lies was army chief of staff, General George C. Marshall.

The problem with Marshall is that he long ago entered the pantheon of American heroes that allows no questioning or doubt, an individual beyond reproach. But in terms of the inquiries that were set in train in the immediate aftermath of the attack and then at various stages until the end of the war, Marshall was at the heart of various efforts to ensure that certain witnesses perjured themselves and he personally deliberately lied to every board of enquiry. What is clear is that while he played the national security card to justify his actions, his was the final responsibility for the defence of the Hawaiian Islands. If Short was manifestly negligent in discharging his duties, not least in failing to act upon warnings which were issued by Marshall's own office, then Marshall bore final responsibility for such a situation: as it was, Marshall was in possession of an inspection report which was highly critical of Short's command – 'a perpetual happy hour' – and deliberately chose not to do anything about it. Moreover, if the view is taken that the restricted distribution of Magic intelligence material to only Stimson, Gerow, Miles, Bratton, Knox, Turner, Ingersoll, Watts and, belatedly, Roosevelt and Hull was perhaps ill-advised, then responsibility therein lies in part with Marshall since it was he and Admiral Harold R. Stark, the Chief of Naval Operations, who together took the decision to thus restrict distribution, and even at one stage to deny Roosevelt access. In addition, it was Marshall and Stark who denied the Hawaiian code-breakers the right to work on intercepted Purple signals. As it turned out, Stark was relieved of his post after Pearl Harbor, but Marshall was retained, even though Stark carried less responsibility in terms of the defence of the Hawaiian Islands and for what had happened on 7 December 1941 than did Marshall. In so many ways the trail of evidence always seems to come back to Marshall's door, as does the trail of lies and evasion of responsibility.

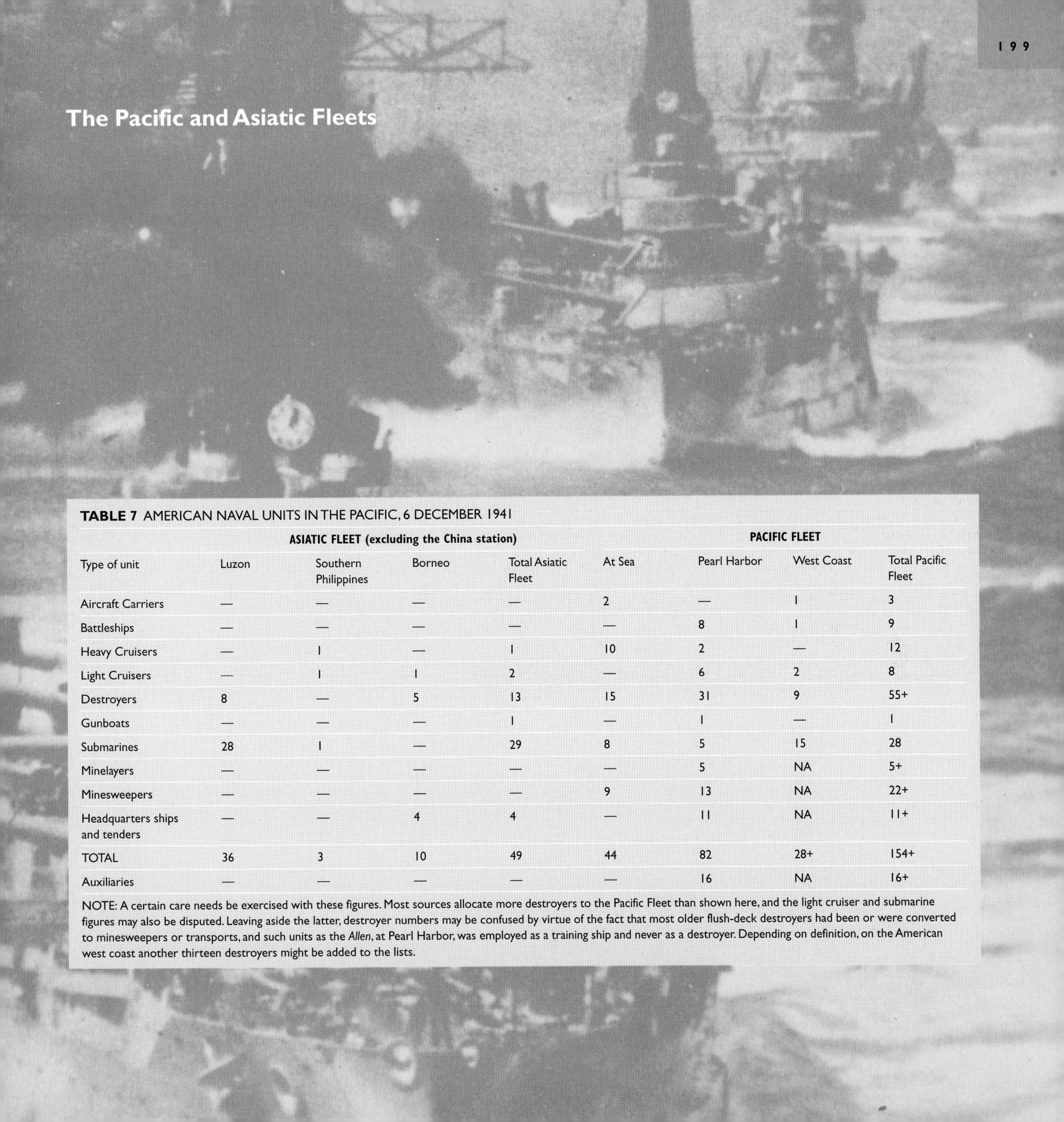

The Pacific and Asiatic Fleets

TABLE 7 AMERICAN NAVAL UNITS IN THE PACIFIC, 6 DECEMBER 1941

| Type of unit | ASIATIC FLEET (excluding the China station) | | | | PACIFIC FLEET | | | |
	Luzon	Southern Philippines	Borneo	Total Asiatic Fleet	At Sea	Pearl Harbor	West Coast	Total Pacific Fleet
Aircraft Carriers	—	—	—	—	2	—	1	3
Battleships	—	—	—	—	—	8	1	9
Heavy Cruisers	—	1	—	1	10	2	—	12
Light Cruisers	—	1	1	2	—	6	2	8
Destroyers	8	—	5	13	15	31	9	55+
Gunboats	—	—	—	1	—	1	—	1
Submarines	28	1	—	29	8	5	15	28
Minelayers	—	—	—	—	—	5	NA	5+
Minesweepers	—	—	—	—	9	13	NA	22+
Headquarters ships and tenders	—	—	4	4	—	11	NA	11+
TOTAL	36	3	10	49	44	82	28+	154+
Auxiliaries	—	—	—	—	—	16	NA	16+

NOTE: A certain care needs be exercised with these figures. Most sources allocate more destroyers to the Pacific Fleet than shown here, and the light cruiser and submarine figures may also be disputed. Leaving aside the latter, destroyer numbers may be confused by virtue of the fact that most older flush-deck destroyers had been or were converted to minesweepers or transports, and such units as the *Allen*, at Pearl Harbor, was employed as a training ship and never as a destroyer. Depending on definition, on the American west coast another thirteen destroyers might be added to the lists.

Intelligence, Diplomacy and the Declaration of War

Apart from the events at Pearl Harbor, perhaps the most celebrated episode of 7 December 1941 has proved to have been the meeting between Secretary of State Cordell Hull and Ambassadors Nomura Kichisaburo and Kurusu Saburo. Whatever status this episode has commanded is largely the result of the combination of three sets of circumstances: the fact that the Japanese Embassy was instructed to deliver a memorandum to the State Department at 1.00 p.m. on 7 December 1941 EST, this being the only occasion in living memory when a Japanese representative had been instructed to deliver a paper to the American government at a specified time; the fact that Nomura was late in delivering the message; and the fact that the most senior members of the Roosevelt administration and the armed services were aware of the contents of the memorandum, and that Roosevelt, when reading all but the last part of the memorandum after it was sent to Washington on 6 December, noted that it meant war.

In no small measure the memorandum that Nomura was to present, the (in)famous fourteen-part message, has attracted critical consideration because its prior reading by American signals intelligence really provided the last opportunity to have undertaken some action that might have spared the US Pacific Fleet at least some of what it was to suffer. The warning that was issued by Washington, sent by Marshall, was to the Philippines, Hawaii, Panama and west coast commands, and informed them that:

'Japanese are presenting at one pm eastern standard time today what amounts to an ultimatum also they are under orders to destroy their code machine immediately. Just what significance the hour set may have we do not know but be on alert accordingly. Inform naval authorities of this communication.'

The signal to Hawaii was delayed by transmission problems and had to be sent by Western Union to San Francisco for transmission by RCA to Honolulu. It was sent to Western Union at 0647 Hawaii time but arrived in Hawaii as the Japanese attack was in progress.

Considerable historical attention has been devoted to a most wearisome matter, the allegation that the lateness of the delivery of the memorandum was deliberate. Conversely, very little historical attention has been devoted to the contents of this memorandum. There is a general assumption that the memorandum was a declaration of war, an assumption that stems in part from the representation of this episode in the film *TORA! TORA! TORA!*. In the relevant scene, Yamamoto paces the quarterdeck of his flagship and bemoans the fact that late delivery of the memorandum will ensure Japan being exposed to the full force of righteous American anger. But this representation is vacuous. If Yamamoto really believed that delivering a declaration of war twenty minutes before Japanese aircraft hit Battleship Row was going to deflect the worst of American anger, then this shows just how little he understood the American temper. And that same temper was never going to pass over the simple fact, stated by President Roosevelt

in his address to Congress on the following day, 'that the distance of Hawaii from Japan makes it obvious that the attack was deliberately planned many days or even weeks ago. During the intervening time the Japanese government has deliberately sought to deceive the United States by false statements and expressions of hope for continued peace'.

It is one of the odd features of this memorandum that the passing of the years has robbed it of context and virulence: to read it today leaves one with little impression of the seriousness and immediacy of the crisis in which Japan found herself in her dealings with the United States. There is a certain sharpness, the occasional comment and, inevitably, the reference to various events in a biased or mendacious manner, but for the most part the memorandum reads as a strange mixture of wearied disappointment, exasperation and special pleading. It appears restrained and was not a declaration of war. Moreover, it was not an ultimatum and did not represent the severing of diplomatic relations between the two countries. Technically, it did not end the round of discussions that had been going on for some weeks, although it was clear that Tokyo attributed the failure to secure an agreement to Washington's bad faith during the talks and that it 'regrets to have to notify hereby the American government that in view of the attitude of the American government it cannot but consider that it is impossible to reach an agreement through further negotiations'. Seemingly this would have left the way open for renewed negotiations if there was a major shift of American policy, although the real point, of course, was that negotiations of all description had been overtaken by events. The fact that Nomura was late in delivering this memorandum, as a result largely of the inadequacy of the Japanese Embassy's cable and typing sections on a Sunday morning, was neither here nor there. American records timed the delivery of the document at 2.20 p.m: Nomura, who had asked at 1.00 p.m. for a meeting and then missed his appointment at 1.45, had previously been admitted to the presence of Secretary Hull at 2.05 (all times EST).

What is no less interesting is what was happening in Tokyo. At 7.00 a.m. on 8 December, Tokyo time, which was 5 p.m. 7 December EST and 11.30 a.m. in Hawaii, United States Ambassador Joseph C. Grew received a telephone call from the Foreign Ministry requesting his attendance. Within 'half an hour' Grew was received by Foreign Minister Togo Shigenori, who opened proceedings with reference to a message, dated 6 December, from Roosevelt to the Emperor. With Grew stating that he had requested an audience with the Emperor, he was given the memorandum that Nomura had submitted to Hull and told that Japan had decided to end the talks in Washington. Grew's attitude was very casual, the Ambassador reasoning that talks had been abandoned before only to resume. The meeting was brought to a close by Togo thanking Grew for his efforts for peace.

At no stage of proceedings was there any reference to an ultima-

Unknowingly already at war: Special
Envoy Kurusu Saburo with Admiral
Nomura Kichisaburo, Japanese
ambassador to the United States, with
one assistant, in the State Department
on 7 December 1941. Few ambassadors
have been so misused by their national
authorities as was Nomura in autumn
1941. His personal sincerity, and his
attempts to find a solution to Japan's
problems in dealing with the United
States, were all but certainly doomed
to failure, but were very deliberately
used by the authorities in Tokyo to
cloak intentions. Kurusu was sent to
steady Nomura but did not know of
the plan to attack Pearl Harbor.

tum, the severing of diplomatic relations or a declaration of war, and it was only after he returned to his Embassy did Grew hear, from newsboys in the street, of a special edition newspaper, in fact a single-sheet special edition which, once secured, announced to Grew that Imperial General Headquarters – not the government and most certainly not the Foreign Ministry – at 6.00 a.m. (4.00 p.m. 7 December EST/10.30 a.m. 7 December Hawaii) had proclaimed that a state of war existed between Japan and the United States and Britain. The American naval attaché in Tokyo was thereupon sent to the Naval Ministry, where he was afforded a friendly reception by Rear Admiral Nakamura Katsuhei, and ascertained that this information was correct.

The full text of the proclamation by Imperial General Headquarters was as follows:

We, by the grace of Heaven, Emperor of Japan, seated on the throne of a line unbroken for ages eternal, enjoin upon ye, our loyal and brave subjects:

We hereby declare war on the United States of America and the British Empire.

Men and officers of our Army and Navy shall do their utmost in prosecuting the war, our public servants of various departments shall perform faithfully and diligently their appointed tasks and all other subjects of ours shall pursue their respective duties: the entire nation with united will shall mobilise their total strength so that nothing will miscarry in the attainment of our war aims.

To insure the stability of East Asia and to contribute to world peace is the far-sighted policy which was formulated by our great, illustrious imperial grandsire and by our great imperial sire succeeding him and which we lay constantly to heart. To cultivate friendship among the nations and to enjoy prosperity in common with all nations has always been the guiding principle of our Empire's foreign policy.

It has been truly unavoidable and far from our wishes that our Empire has now been brought to cross swords with America and Britain. More than four years have passed since China, failing to comprehend the true intentions of our Empire and recklessly courting trouble, disturbed the peace of East Asia. Although there has been re-established a national government of China with which Japan has effected neighbourly intercourse and co-operation, the regime which has survived at Chungking, replying upon American and British protection, still continues its fratricidal opposition.

Eager for the realisation of their inordinate ambition to dominate the Orient, both America and Britain, in giving support to the Chungking regime, have aggravated the disturbances in East Asia. Moreover, these two powers, inducing other countries to follow suit, increased military preparations on all sides of our Empire to challenge us. They have obstructed by every means our peaceful commerce, and finally have resorted to the direct severance of economic relations, menacing gravely the existence of our Empire.

Patiently have we waited and long have we endured in the hope that our Government might retrieve the situation in peace.

But our adversaries, showing not the least spirit of conciliation, have unduly delayed a settlement, and in the meantime they have intensified economic and political pressure to compel thereby our Empire to submission.

This trend of affairs would, if left unchecked, not only nullify our Empire's efforts of many years for the sake of stabilisation of East Asia, but also endanger the very existence of our nation. The situation being such as it is, our Empire, for its existence and self-defence, has no other recourse but to appeal to arms and to crush every obstacle in its path.

Hallowed spirits of our imperial ancestors guarding us from above, we rely upon the loyalty and courage of our subjects in our confident expectation that the task bequeathed by our forefathers will be carried forward and that sources of evil will be speedily eradicated and enduring peace immutably established in East Asia, preserving thereby the glory of our Empire.

Interestingly, the following day President Franklin D. Roosevelt in his address to Congress, which officially was timed at 12.30 pm 8 December 1941 EST, did not ask for a declaration of war on Japan and clearly stated that the memorandum which had been delivered by Nomura the previous day had not been a declaration of war. What Roosevelt said, in part, was:

Yesterday, December 7, 1941 – a date which will live in infamy – the United States of America was suddenly and deliberately attacked by naval and air forces of the Empire of Japan.

The United States was at peace with that Nation and, at the solicitation of Japan, was still in conversation with its Government and its Emperor looking toward the maintenance of peace in the Pacific. Indeed, one hour after Japanese air squadrons had commenced bombing in Oahu, the Japanese Ambassador to the United States and his colleague delivered to the Secretary of State a formal reply to a recent American message. While this reply stated that it seemed useless to continue the existing diplomatic negotiations, it contained no threat or hint of war or armed attack ....

I ask that the Congress declare that since the unprovoked and dastardly attack by Japan on Sunday, December seventh, a state of war has existed between the United States and the Japanese Empire.

The Congress, in passing Public Law 328 at 4.10 p.m. 8 December 1941 EST, acknowledged that a state of war existed and provided formal recognition of that fact, stating:

Whereas the Imperial Government of Japan has committed unprovoked acts of war against the Government and the people of the United States of America: therefore be it Resolved by the Senate and House of Representatives of the United States of America in Congress assembled, That the state of war between the United States and the Imperial Government of Japan which has thus been thrust upon the United States is hereby formally declared; and the President is hereby authorized and directed to employ the entire naval and military forces of the United States and the resources of the Government to carry on war against the Imperial Government of Japan; and to bring the conflict to a successful termination, all of the resources of the country are hereby pledged by the Congress of the United States.

The resolution was passed in the Senate by a vote of 82 to none. An identical resolution had been passed by the House by 388 votes to one. The dissenting voter claimed that reports from Pearl Harbor had not been confirmed and was likely to be British disinformation: this individual failed to secure re-election in 1942.

Employment and Losses

TABLE 8 AIRCRAFT WITH THE CARRIERS OF THE 1st CARRIER STRIKING FORCE AND THEIR EMPLOYMENT IN THE ATTACK OF 7 DECEMBER 1941

	AIRCRAFT EMBARKED			TOTAL	FIRST ATTACK FORMATION				SECOND ATTACK FORMATION			RETAINED		
	Type 97 B5N2 Kates	Type 99 D3A1 Vals	Type 00 A6M2 Zekes		Type 97 B5N2 Kates	Type 97 B5N2 Kates	Type 99 D3A1 Vals	Type 00 A6M2 Zekes	Type 97 B5N2 Kates	Type 99 D3A1 Vals	Type 00 A6M2 Zekes	B5N2 Kates	D3A1 Vals	A6M2 Zekes
Akagi	27	18	21	66	15	12	—	9	—	18	9	—	—	3
Kaga	27	27	21	75	15	12	—	9	—	27	9	—	—	3
Soryu	18 + 3	18 + 3	18 + 3	63	10	8	—	9	—	18	9	3	3	3
Hiryu	18 + 3	18 + 3	18 + 3	63	10	8	—	6	—	18	9	3	3	6
Zuikaku	27	27	18	72	—	—	27	6	27	—	—	—	—	12
Shokaku	27	27	18	72	—	—	27	6	27	—	—	—	—	12
					50	40								
	144 + 6	135 + 6	114 + 6	393 + 18	90		54	45	54	81	36	6	6	39
	150	141	120	411			189			171			51	

TABLE 9 THE CARRIER AIR GROUPS AND THE LOSSES INCURRED BY JAPANESE CARRIER AIRCRAFT IN THE ATTACK ON PEARL HARBOR

	FIRST ATTACK FORMATION				SECOND ATTACK FORMATION			AIRCRAFT LOST AND DAMAGED	
	B5N2 Kates	B5N2 Kates	D3A1 Vals	A6M2 Zekes	B5N2 Kates	D3A1 Vals	A6M2 Zekes	Lost	Damaged
Akagi	15 0 3	12 0 4	NA	9 1 3	NA	18 4 12	9 0 1	0 4 1	7 12 4
Kaga	14 0 2	12 5 5	NA	9 2 2	NA	26 6 16	9 2 3	5 6 4	7 16 5
Soryu	10 0 2	8 0 1	NA	8 0 2	NA	17 2 13	9 3 4	0 2 3	3 13 6
Hiryu	10 0 1+	8 0 NRA	NA	6 0 NRA	NA	17 2 NRA	8 1 NRA	0 2 1	1 –NRA–
Zuikaku	NA	NA	25 1	6 0	27 0 14	NA	NA	0 1 0	16 17 4
Shokaku	NA	NA	26 0 (17)	5 0 (4)	27 0 2	NA	NA	0 0 0	
Totals by type and wave	49 0 8+	40 5 10			54 0 16	78 14 41+	35 6 8+	5 15 9	34 58 19
	89 5 18+		51 1 17	43 3 17		167 20 65+		29	111+
		183 9 46+							
2nd wave	54 0 16		78 14 41	35 6 8					
By Type	143 5 34+		129 15 58	78 9 19					
OVERALL		350 29 111+							

NRA = no record available.   NA = not applicable.

In the first attack formation lists the first column represents Kates in the level-altitude bombing role, the second column the torpedo-bombers. The totals given in the attacking formations represent the number in that strike, those lost and those damaged. The totals given under lost and damaged, and thus by carrier, represent Kates, Vals and Zekes in that order. The overall totals, for the formation, must be understated.

In the preparation of this book acknowledgement must be made in four groups. First there is my debt to friends, specifically to Patrick Burke, Tony Clayton, Michael Coles, Nigel de Lee, Christopher Duffy, Paul Harris, John and Tine Olsen, Raymond Sibbald, and Jack and Gee Sweetman, who continued to demonstrate the real meaning of concern at a time of very considerable upheaval and uncertainty. To them I add the students and staff at Greenwich Maritime Institute who helped to provide focus and commitment in these same difficult times.

Second, in the writing of this book my primary debt of gratitude must be to Angus MacKinnon and Steven Weingartner, who were very closely associated with it from the outset and whose contributions thereafter took a thousand forms, all difficult to define but collectively vital to the enterprise. I greatly regret that, for reasons beyond their control, both had parted company from the formation before it finally reached harbour. No less important were Tohmatsu Haruo and Spencer Johnson, whose contributions to the book were far greater than their respective chapters. Without Haruo's efforts in the libraries and archives of Tokyo the book would not have been worth a quarter of what value it presently commands: without the perspectives given by both he and Spencer most of the remaining value would have disappeared.

Third, in the production of this book I express my appreciation for the unstinting efforts of Harry Green and Bob Travis; Malcolm Swanson; George Sharp, Jamie Tanner, Richard Carr and Richard Lucas; Barry Holmes, Veneta Bullen and Elaine Willis. In addition, I thank Jennie Wraight and Ian MacKenzie for all their efforts at the Admiralty Library, and for their willing co-operation in the face of any number of unreasonable requests on my part. I also sincerely thank Dr Bernard D. Cole for his willing, prompt and thorough checking of sources in Washington, and Kobayashi Go for his various contributions when in London to the final product. Collectively, to all involved in the preparation of this work, I thank you for your efforts and acknowledge that without them it could never have been completed. But whatever errors lie within its pages are my responsibility alone.

Fourth, I acknowledge debt to family, specifically to Pauline and to my sister Vivien: as always I trust they will think the effort that went into this book was justified by the result. In addition, and as always in my books, I acknowledge my debt to Everton, Sherry and Kondor and trust that they are at peace, and to Jamie, Lancaster and Miska, and to Suki and Junior, whose insistence on being properly exercised helped bring a certain balance to proceedings.

H. P. WILLMOTT
February 2001

ACKNOWLEDGEMENTS

INDEX

PHOTO CREDITS

Corbis Images: 4; 80–81; 104–105; 112l; 112c; 114–115; 120tl; 129; 135; 140c; 150tr; 200–201.

Hulton Archive: 2–3; 88; 96tl; 106–107; 108–109; 112c; 112–113; 113tr; 116–117; 118– 119; 122–123; 126; 128; 140–141.

Imperial War Museum: 26–27; 28; 30–31; 32; 34; 35; 37; 38–39; 40–41; 42b; 46–48; 50–53; 58–59

National Archives: 28

Peter Newarks Pictures: 12–13; 44; 45; 60; 74–75; 142tc; 154–156; 16–161; 168–169

Popperfoto: 16–17; 18

Rex Features/Time Life Picture Syndication: 152–153

Topham Picture Point: 19

TRH Pictures: 6;15; 22; 24–25; 42t; 62b; 63t; 68–69; 71tr; 72–73; 84b; 85b; 96—99; 106bl; 120–121; 124–125;130–132; 138–139; 144–145; 146–49; 158–159; 162–163b; 166–167; 173c

Robert Hunt Library: 36; 62–63; 70–71; 72tl; 81cr